RUMOURS OF WARS:
CIVIL CONFLICT IN
NINETEENTH-CENTURY LATIN AMERICA

Rumours of Wars:

Civil Conflict in Nineteenth-Century Latin America

Edited by

Rebecca Earle

Institute of Latin American Studies
31 Tavistock Square, London WC1H 9HA
http://www.sas.ac.uk/ilas/publicat.htm

Nineteenth-Century Latin America Series

The Institute's Nineteenth-Century Latin America series results from the annual workshop on nineteenth-century Latin American history held at the Institute, and is aimed at encouraging the study of various aspects of what has largely been a neglected period in the modern historiography of the region. The General Editor of this series is Eduardo Posada-Carbó, Senior Lecturer in History at the Institute of Latin American Studies.

Publications in the Series

No. 1 *Wars, Parties and Nationalism: Essays on the Politics and Society of Nineteenth-Century Latin America*
Eduardo Posada-Carbó (ed.) – 1995 (out of print).

No. 2 *In Search of a New Order: Essays on the Politics and Society of Nineteenth-Century Latin America*
Eduardo Posada-Carbó (ed.) – 1998

No. 3 *Independence and Revolution in Spanish America: Perspectives and Problems*
Anthony McFarlane and Eduardo Posada-Carbó (eds.) – 1999

No. 4 *Judicial Institutions in Nineteenth-Century Latin America*
Eduardo Zimmermann (ed.) – 1999

No. 5 *The Politics of Religion in an Age of Revival*
Austen Ivereigh (ed.) – 2000

No. 6 *Rumours of Wars: Civil Conflict in Nineteenth-Century Latin America*
Rebecca Earle (ed.) – 2000

> **Institute of Latin American Studies**
> School of Advanced Study
> University of London

British Library Cataloguing-in-Publication Data
  A catalogue record for this book is available
  from the British Library

ISBN 1 900039 33 8

  Institute of Latin American Studies
  University of London, 2000

Printed and bound by Short Run Press Limited Exeter

And you will hear of wars and rumours of wars

Matthew 24:6

CONTENTS

Acknowledgements

This volume began its life as the fifth nineteenth-century history work-shop organised at the University of London's Institute of Latin American Studies in 1997. The workshop was attended by the contributors to this volume and by some three dozen others, many of whom participated in that day's instalment of the lively discussions that have come to characterise the Institute's workshops. Samuel Valenzuela presented a critique of Maurice Zeitlin's *Civil Wars in Chile*,[1] David Brading and Christopher Abel chaired the day's sessions and Enrique Florescano, John Lynch, Malcolm Deas and Alan Knight offered incisive commentary on individual papers. The involvement of these individuals, together with the other participants and the Institute of Latin American Studies's administrative staff, combined to make a successful and interesting conference, and I would like to acknowledge their contribution in the conception of this book.

This book also benefited from the assistance of several talented translators. David Passingham provided an efficient translation of Carlos Malamud's chapter and Fiona Mackintosh ably rendered into English the chapter by Elena Plaza. Colin Jones further assisted with the translation of the chapter by Marie-Danielle Demélas-Bohy. I greatly appreciate their help and also the support of the British Academy which made their work financially feasible.

Without doubt, however, the greatest thanks should go to Eduardo Posada-Carbó, creator of the nineteenth-century history workshop, tireless proponent of nineteenth-century history, erudite scholar and *buen tipo*. I am very grateful to Eduardo for having invited me to edit this book and I would like to offer him my most cordial thanks.

Rebecca Earle
Leamington Spa
September 1999

---

[1] Maurice Zeitlin, *The Civil Wars in Chile (or the bourgeois revolutions that never were)* (Princeton, 1984).

List of Tables and Appendices

Notes on Contributors

John Charles Chasteen is Associate Professor in the Department of History at the University of North Carolina in Chapel Hill. His published research focuses on the nineteenth-century cultural history of Latin America, spanning a wide variety of topics, from political culture (*Heroes on Horseback: A Life and Times of the Last Gaucho Caudillos* and 'Fighting Words: the Discourse of Insurgency in Latin American History', *Latin American Research Review*, vol. 28) to, more recently, the history of social dance ('The Prehistory of Samba': Carnival Dancing in Rio de Janeiro, 1840–1917', *Journal of Latin American Studies*, vol. 28).

Marie-Danielle Demélas-Bohy is professor of history at the Institut des Hautes Études de l'Amérique Latine (Université de Paris III). Her research concerns Andean history and the history of nineteenth- and twentieth-century Spain and focuses on issues such as social Darwinism, positivism, elections, political instability, Francoism and the Wars of Independence. She is currently exploring the process of disamortisation in Latin America and Spain, the idea of the city as a lineage and the genesis of nineteenth century guerrilla warfare in Bolivia. She is the author of *L'invention politique. Bolivie, Équateur, Pérou au XIXe siècle* and *Jérusalem et Babylone. Religion et politique en Amérique du Sud. Le cas équatorien.*

Rebecca Earle is a Lecturer in the School of Comparative American Studies at the University of Warwick. Her research concerns the social and political history of late colonial and early national Colombia. She is the author of *Spain and the Independence of Colombia* and the editor of *Epistolary Selves. Letters and Letter-Writers, 1600–1945*. She is currently investigating the impact of political independence on gender and racial ideologies in early nineteenth-century Spanish America, looking in particular at the use of Indians as political symbols.

Darío A. Euraque was born in Honduras and received his doctorate in Latin American History and Latin American Studies at the University of Wisconsin at Madison. He is the director of the International Studies Program at Trinity College, where he also teaches history. His current research explores Honduran cultural history in the nineteenth and twentieth centuries and particularly the representations of race and ethnicity in elite discourses on historiography, social movements and national identity. He is the author of *Estado, poder, nacionalidad y raza en la historia de Honduras: Ensayos* and *Reinterpreting the 'Banana Republic': Region and State in Honduras, 1870–1972*, which has been published in Spanish as *El capitalismo de San Pedro Sula y la historia política de Honduras (1870–1972)*.

Will Fowler lectures in Latin American and Spanish history and literature at the University of St Andrews in Scotland. As well as having edited
four volumes on Latin American political history, he is the author of
Mexico in the Age of Proposals, 1821–1853 and *Tornel and Santa Anna:
The Writer and the Caudillo, Mexico, 1795–1853*. He is currently writing a biography of Santa Anna.

Carlos Malamud was born in Buenos Aires and received his doctorate in
history from the Universidad Complutense de Madrid. He teaches history at the Universidad Nacional de Educación a Distancia in Spain and
is sub-director of the Instituto Universitario Ortega y Gasset. He has
published on the economic history of colonial Spanish America and his
current research concerns the political history of Argentina in the late
nineteenth and early twentieth centuries. He is the author of *Cádiz y
Saint Malo en el comercio colonial peruano (1698–1725)* and *Partidos
políticos y elecciones en la Argentina: la Liga del Sur (1908–1916)* and
the editor of *Mejorando la ciudadanía: las reformas electorales en
España y América Latina (1880–1930)*.

Elena Plaza received her doctorate in history from the Universidad
Católica Andrés Bello in Caracas, after also having trained as a sociolo-
gist and political scientist. She teaches at the Escuela de Estudios Políticos y Administrativos at the Universidad Central de Venezuela. She has
published widely on the development of positivism and social Darwinism
in nineteenth-century Europe.

Frank Safford is Gerald and Marjorie Fitzgerald Professor of Economic
History at Northwestern University. His primary research has dealt with
aspects of the economic, political and social history of nineteenth-
century Colombia. However, he has also ventured to write broader
comparative and synthetic work on the political and economic history of
nineteenth-century Spanish America as a whole, most notably in the
Cambridge History of Latin America. He has recently completed a history of Colombia with Marco Palacios.

Introduction

Rebecca Earle

> The liberals were determined to go to war. Since Aureliano at that time had very confused notions about the difference between conservatives and liberals, his father-in-law gave him some schematic lessons. The liberals, he said, were Freemasons, bad people, wanting to hang priests, to institute civil marriage and divorce, to recognise the rights of illegitimate children as equal to those of legitimate ones, and to cut up the country into a federal system that would take power away from the supreme authority. The conservatives, on the other hand, who had received their power directly from God, proposed the establishment of public order and family morality. They were the defenders of the faith of Christ, of the principle of authority, and were not prepared to permit the country to be broken into autonomous entities.
>
> (Gabriel García Márquez, *One Hundred Years of Solitude*)[1]

Civil war has become emblematic of nineteenth-century Latin America. The interminable conflicts between liberals and conservatives, between federalists and centralists, have come to characterise the century both in works of history and fiction. In *One Hundred Years of Solitude* Gabriel García Márquez portrayed the civil wars of his native Colombia far more sombrely than the light-hearted parody of conservative views quoted above might suggest. The 32 failed uprisings of Colonel Aureliano Buendía mirror the inevitable decline into incest of the Buendía family, itself representative of the traditional aristocracy of the Colombian coast. In García Márquez's narrative, futility and degeneration taint both civil war and the local elite. As William Rowe has observed, 'the failure of Colombia's civil wars to bring any radical change is placed on the same level as the impossibility of undoing Oedipal fatality: the tragic code prevails, spelling out a script beneath history which history fulfils'.[2] The

---

[1] Gabriel García Márquez, *Cien años de soledad* (1967). I quote from the English translation of Gregory Rabassa: Gabriel García Márquez, *One Hundred Years of Solitude* (London, 1970), pp. 84–5.

[2] William Rowe, 'Gabriel García Márquez', in John King (ed.), *Modern Latin American Fiction: a Survey* (Cambridge, 1987) p. 198. The theme of incest is further discussed in Edwin Williamson, 'Magical Realism and the Theme of Incest in One Hundred Years of Solitude', in Bernard McGuirk and Richard Cardwell (eds.), *Gabriel García Márquez: New Readings* (Cambridge, 1987); and Michael Palencia-Roth, *Myth and the Modern Novel: García Márquez, Mann and Joyce* (New York, 1987). Analyses of *One Hundred Years of Solitude* as a work of historical commentary have offered differing interpretations of the civil war episodes. Scholars have identified Colonel Aureliano Buendía variously as the Argentine arch-barbarian Facundo, see María A. Salgado, '"Civilización y Barbarie" o "Imaginación y Barbarie"?', in Francisco E. Porrata (ed.), *Explicación de cien años de soledad* (San José, 1976), and as the Colombian General Rafael Uribe Uribe — see the extended analysis in Lucila Inés Mena, *La función de la historia en cien años de soledad* (Barcelona, 1979)). Such works, while usefully stressing that the novel is based in part on historical precedents and thus not the pure product of its author's magical imagination, fail to stress the extent to which the work is an interpretation of history, rather than a sim-

certainty with which the novel's liberals launched their first uprising transforms as the work progresses into a meaningless struggle with a Conservative Party scarcely distinguishable from its adversary. The ideological vigour of the first revolts degenerates into a tragic obsession:

> One night [Colonel Aureliano Buendía] asked Colonel Gerineldo Márquez:
>
> 'Tell me something, old friend: why are we fighting?'
>
> 'What other reason could there be?' Colonel Gerinaldo Márquez answered. 'For the great Liberal Party.'
>
> 'You're lucky because you know why', he answered. 'As far as I'm concerned, I've come to realise only just now that I'm fighting because of pride.'[3]

The terminus of Liberal revolt (and the Buendía family) is, ultimately, incest:

> 'Can a person marry his own aunt?' he asked, startled.
>
> 'He not only can do that,' a soldier answered him, 'but we're fighting this war against the priests so that a person can marry his own mother.'[4]

The tragedy of Colombia's civil wars thus parallels the tragedy of the Buendía family. The use of nineteenth-century civil war as a vehicle for exploring the decline of a particular family or indeed nation recurs in the literature of twentieth-century Latin America. Ernesto Sábato's *On Heroes and Tombs* juxtaposes the catastrophic 1841 march of the *anti-rosista* General Lavalle with the tortured relationships of the novel's twentieth-century characters. In this work, as in *One Hundred Years of Solitude*, the nineteenth century's civil wars are presented as fundamentally purposeless. Celedonio Olmos, a lieutenant in General Lavalle's decimated forces, muses at the novel's close on the meaning of their revolt:

> Eight hundred leagues of defeats. He understands nothing now ... He doesn't understand anything anymore. And everything was so clear two years ago: Freedom or Death. But now ... Twenty-five years of battles, of victories, and defeat. But at least in those days they knew what they were fighting for: they wanted to free the continent, they were doing battle for the Great Fatherland. But now ... So much blood has run in the rivers of America, they have seen so many desperate afternoons, they have heard so many battle cries ring out between brothers.[5]

---

ple reflection of fixed historical events. For an examination of the historical accuracy of the banana massacre section, see Eduardo Posada-Carbó. 'Fiction as History: The *bananeras* and Gabriel Garcia Márquez's *One Hundred Years of Solitude*', Journal of Latin American Studies, vol. 30, no. 2 (1998).

[3] Márquez, *One Hundred Years of Solitude*, p. 116.

[4] Márquez, *ibid.*, p. 127; and Rowe, 'Gabriel García Márquez', p. 198.

[5] Ernesto Sábato, *Sobre héroes y tumbas* (1961). I quote from the English translation by Helen R. Lane: Ernesto Sábato, *On Heroes and Tombs* (London, 1990) pp. 454, 457. For varied interpretations of the novelistic purpose of the Lavalle episodes see David William Foster, *Currents in the Contemporary Argentine Novel: Arlt, Mallea, Sábato and Cortázar* (Columbia, 1975); Carlos Catama, *Genio y figura de Ernesto Sábato* (Buenos Aires, 1987);

Through such novelistic reinterpretation Latin America's nineteenth-century civil wars have been imbued with immense poetic meaning, with the ability to distil the promise and tragedy of the whole course of the continent's modern history. Underlying many of these fictions is the view that civil war, begun in an idealistic spirit of ideological division, soon degenerated into a meaningless struggle. This fundamentally pessimistic assessment of civil war has been shared by many historians, who have likewise described the continent's civil conflicts as the result of nothing more than the blind obedience of individual soldiers to a charismatic leader. As the Argentine historian Juan Alvarez commented acerbically in his own study of civil war:

> Because method has been lacking in research, Argentina's past appears [in many historical accounts] as a confusing accumulation of moments of violence and disorder, and it is generally believed that thousands of men fought and died on our battlefields simply because of the affection they felt towards a particular leader.[6]

Civil war has thus been accorded an ambiguous place in Latin American historiography. On the one hand, the conflicts of the nineteenth century are permitted to represent the tragedy of modern Latin America, and are widely recognised as moments of immense and continuing importance. Yet at the same time these wars appear stripped of meaning, devoid of political content: this, indeed, is what allows them so effectively to represent the tragic dimensions of the continent's history. In such accounts the nineteenth century emerges fundamentally as a period of epic chaos.

This volume joins the growing body of historiography that rejects, or at least questions, this interpretation. The varied essays that make up this volume subject the hypothesis that nineteenth-century civil wars were essentially purposeless tragedies to a prolonged examination. Their authors suggest, first, that civil wars did not always represent catastrophic ruptures of existing political norms. Elections, *pronunciamientos* and revolt should perhaps be seen as part of the normal, if problematic, functioning of nineteenth-century politics. They should thus be viewed within the context of the existing political frameworks. Second, a number of contributors argue that civil conflicts were not necessarily devoid of ideological content, and that their participants were not necessarily ignorant of these aims. Together, the eight chapters survey the existing historiography of civil war, examine the relationship between such phenomena as elections, freedom of the press and rebellions, explore the persistence of rebellion in certain revolutionary 'sites of origin' and offer new interpretations of a number of civil wars.

The volume begins with several thematic surveys that reinterpret the significance of nineteenth-century civil war in Argentina, Colombia, Honduras, Mexico and, more broadly, Latin American as a whole. In the first chapter, Frank Safford presents a critique of a number of com-

---

and Gerald Martin, *Journeys through the Labyrinth: Latin American Fiction in the Twentieth Century* (London, 1989), p. 115.

[6] Juan Alvarez (1914), quoted by Carlos Malamud in chapter 2.

monly offered interpretations of nineteenth-century civil war. His account emphasises the 'variety and multiplicity of the region's internal
wars' and the need for more research into the local features of civil war.
Attempts to catalogue civil wars according to cause are, Safford argues,
usually futile, as single wars are often either multi-causal or display
shifting causalities as they progress. In chapter two Carlos Malamud
surveys civil conflict in nineteenth-century Argentina. He devotes particular attention to measuring the personal and monetary costs of revolt
to its participants, both of which are found to be low. Like other contributors, he gives sustained attention to the relationship between elections and revolt; the relative impunity which rebellions enjoyed
encouraged politicians to view revolt simply as a continuation of politics,
in classic Clausewitzian fashion.

In chapter three Will Fowler offers a bold reinterpretation of Mexican
history, insisting that early nineteenth-century Mexico was not characterised
by civil war and chaos. His chapter is accompanied by a remarkable appendix
listing the hundreds of revolts, *pronunciamientos* and uprisings that occurred
in Mexico between 1821 and 1857. This appendix notwithstanding, Fowler
insists that these acts rarely resulted in significant loss of life, usually enjoyed
little civilian participation and only infrequently led to political change at the
national level. On average, a major civil conflict occurred only every three
years, rather than being the weekly occurrence suggested by the appendix. In
common with other contributors, Fowler notes that *pronunciamientos*, the
typical signal of an impending revolt, ought in fact to be viewed as attempts to
forestall violent conflict. The *pronunciamiento* was often intended to focus
the minds of the opposing parties, thereby facilitating negotiation. Fowler
thus argues that civil war, narrowly defined to exclude indigenous rebellion
and other forms of popular mobilisation, was an infrequent but politically
meaningful occurrence.

There follows Darío Euraque's study of civil conflict in nineteenth-
century Honduras. Arguing that the collapse of the Central American
Federation in 1842 did not result in increased anarchy, Euraque main-
tains that the level of political violence remained largely stable for a century after Independence. Like Malamud, he regards the electoral system
itself as a powerful contributor to civil conflict. Euraque also analyses two
major studies of nineteenth-century Central America in order to assess
their interpretations of the causes of war.[7] Euraque's study suggests that,
while Honduran civil wars were not necessarily political in origin, they
were not devoid of content. Euraque points to the importance of regional
and economic factors in creating a climate conducive to revolt.

The subsequent contributions offer more detailed studies of specific
civil wars. In chapter five John Charles Chasteen examines the Brazilian

---

[7] Lowell Gudmundson and Héctor Lindo-Fuentes, *Central America, 1821–1871: Liberalism before Liberal Reform* (Tuscaloosa, 1995); and R.G. Williams, *States and Social Evolution: Coffee and the Rise of National Governments in Central America* (Chapel Hill, 1994).

liberal revolts of the 1830s–40s from the perspective of the anti-Portuguese nativism that pervaded revolutionary discourse. Opposition to the Portuguese, as a sentiment that crossed class and racial lines, paved the way for a firmer sense of national identity. Chasteen thus sees these liberal revolts as a means of exploring both popular attitudes and the roots of nationalism. Chasteen also gives prolonged attention to the role of the press in spreading political beliefs. This concern with the dissemination of political sentiment is continued in chapter six, in which I examine Colombia's 1839–41 War of the Supremes. Here too the importance of the periodical press as a source of both information and opinion is given prominence. In a conflict typically described as originating in the political ambitions of a handful of men, I suggest signs of popular involvement, stressing that regionalism and the defence of the Catholic church were genuinely popular causes.

Elena Plaza's account in chapter seven of the 1859–63 Federal War in Venezuela concerns itself less with the popular dimensions of the conflict than with the meaning of revolutionary slogans for its political participants. Plaza explores the significance of the term 'federation' to the liberal and conservative politicians caught up in the war, concluding that although the meaning of the term was not fixed, it came to encapsulate the very essence of the war for many liberal guerrillas. Finally, in chapter eight Marie-Danielle Demélas-Bohy examines the Bolivian civil war of 1898–99. Demélas-Bohy, along with the authors of a number of other chapters, shares an anxiety about the desirability of seeking the 'origins' of civil war. She writes instead of the 'sites of origin' ('*lieux d'origine*'), in a reference to the work of French historians on sites of memory, or '*lieux de memoire*', and she also explores the idea that the origins of a revolt are to be found in its recurrent practices. Demélas-Bohy locates a certain Bolivian region that has served as a site of origin for a series of revolts spanning at least a hundred-year period and in addition examines the *pronunciamiento* as an originary rhetorical practice. Together, the eight contributors to this volume offer new possibilities for the interpretation of nineteenth-century civil war.

CHAPTER 1

Reflections on the Internal Wars in Nineteenth-Century Latin America

Frank Safford

The task of providing a general essay on the 'origins of civil wars' in Latin America seemed, when it was first presented to me, quite daunting. And it still does. How to say something useful, or even accurate, about such a multiform phenomenon? The chapter that follows begins with a brief summary of frequently-adventured explanations of political disorder in nineteenth-century Spanish America, listed without much further comment. The next section offers a typology of various sorts of internal conflicts, categorised by their dominant themes and/or forms, with some elaborative commentary. A subsequent section then suggests a problem with categorising civil wars by dominant themes: in many internal wars a lot of different issues were in play. There follows a brief discussion of interesting approaches to internal conflict (some of them relatively new) that bring out the interconnections between elite politics and the participation of popular classes, rural and urban. Finally, there is a commentary on the role of geography in variously structuring internal wars in Latin America and a note on changes in the forms of war over time. Frequently, general points are illustrated with reference to examples in various parts of Latin America, with some more detailed treatment, not surprisingly, of matter taken from the history of Colombia in the nineteenth-century.

Some common hypotheses about political instability in nineteenth-century Latin America

1. Cultural explanations, including both those that emphasise the phenomenon of assertive individualism and individual need to dominate in Hispanic culture (with regard to *caudillismo*) and those that stress the consequences of the legacy of Spanish monarchical rule (with regard to the difficulty of absorbing and integrating republican institutions).

2. The relationship of economic structures to political instability, in some cases stressing conflicting regional economic interests, in other cases bringing out the political consequences of not having substantial integrated markets.

3. Fiscal weakness as a source of instability.

4. Changing power relations among different elite groups as a possible source of instability.

5. The possible roles of conflicting ideologies, conflicting regional economic interests, or conflicting sectoral economic interests.

All of the hypotheses mentioned above are rather general. The effects of cultural tendencies or of an unintegrated economic structure are of a particularly general and long-term character. They may provide important perspectives on political instability in Spanish America, but, at least in some of their formulations, they may not be directly observable in specific events. The other factors are more readily connectable to events, but it is necessary to go beyond general formulations to specific cases. This chapter attempts to approach a little closer to specific situations by sketching a typology of internal wars in nineteenth-century Latin America. As the next paragraph will suggest, however, it is necessary to descend into specifics to illustrate even the more general points being advanced.

At the outset one wonders whether the analysis really ought to be restricted to the *origins* of civil wars. Might it not be more useful to discuss the *origins and development* of civil wars, or perhaps the *process* of civil wars? Internal wars may be initiated for one set of reasons, but, as they proceed, they may take on a substantially different form, with new and different participants, differing motivations, causes or themes and a different dynamic. An obvious case of this sort is one of the wars discussed in chapter six in this volume. The *Guerra de los Supremos* in New Granada in 1839–42 is conventionally described as having its genesis in a popular protest in the then largely indigenous province of Pasto against the shutting of monasteries in that province. However, after the initial religiously-inspired insurrection was defeated, a second rebellion emerged in a nearby region, but with a different purpose and, apparently, a different popular base. The second rebellion, which took public form in January 1840, started in Timbío, in the region of the Patía River basin, an area populated largely by free blacks and slaves. That rebellion began as a defensive response by the caudillo General José María Obando to accusations that he had arranged the murder of Antonio José de Sucre in 1830. Obando's rebellion was subsequently seconded by sympathising caudillos in Antioquia, Santa Marta, Cartagena and Socorro, all of whom proclaimed that they were rebelling in the name of 'Federation', although beyond this vague slogan their aims remained generally unclear. Because the so-called '*Supremos*' and their followers did not say what they meant by Federation or why they wanted it, it is tempting to guess what the underlying, but unarticulated, purpose was. One possibility is that the War of the Supremos represented an assertion of local control by caudillos with provincial bases against a government in the national capital that was held by civilians of an opposing political faction and which did not (as yet) have effective control over the provinces that it putatively governed. The rebellion also may be construed as a partisan effort to reverse through war Obando's defeat in the presidential election of 1836, although in general this aim was not put forward explicitly by the rebellion's leaders. So a war that began as one thing speedily evolved into two or three others.

Even where the issues at stake in a civil war remain consistent throughout, most conflicts, and particularly those that endure for some time and involve fairly broad participation, are unlikely to be about one thing only. Rather, they are likely to involve coalitions of participants of different classes and/or regions, with somewhat differing sets of motivations or concerns. An exemplification of this point will be presented later in this chapter.

In addition to the questions of origins, forms and processes of internal wars, it would also be desirable to examine their social content and social texture. This focus, which is now entering more and more into the literature on nineteenth-century Latin America, is well exemplified in John Chasteen's contribution to this volume.

Toward a typology of internal wars in nineteenth-century Latin America

The following is a sketch of some different types of internal war in nineteenth-century Latin America. These types of conflict are ordered in part chronologically, but also in terms of some characteristic features, in theme and in form.

1.   In most parts of Latin America the struggle usually called the Wars of Independence often involved, particularly in its early stages, internal war within each broad region — wars between city-regions, as in New Granada or Venezuela, and/or wars between socio-racial groups, as in Mexico or Venezuela. Thus some of the earliest civil wars were fought in the context of the struggle for independence.

2.   Immediately after the winning of Independence there were a series of conflicts that reflected the still-indeterminate character of national boundaries, as well as the ambitions of contending factions within each incipient national state. Brian Loveman calls these conflicts 'wars of political consolidation that determined both the boundaries of new states and the composition of national governments'.[1] Such wars were particularly characteristic of the 1820s and '30s, although they also occurred subsequently. Typically they involved conflicts across the boundaries, and often over the boundaries, of two or more incipient states, but at the same time they also expressed factional ambitions within the contending states themselves.

The following are some examples of how these conflicts were at once 'transnational' and 'internal'. In 1829 collaboration in the Cauca Valley with a Peruvian threat to seize much of what is now Ecuador from Gran

---

[1] Brian Loveman, *Por la Patria: Politics and Armed Forces in Latin America* (Wilmington, 1999), p. 28.

Colombia formed part of the internal political tactics of opponents of Bolívar's dictatorship within New Granada. Subsequently, in 1830–31, some leaders, particularly in the regions of Pasto and Popayán, flirted with the idea of incorporation into Ecuador as a response to the emergence of the regime of General Rafael Urdaneta in Bogotá. So an apparently 'international' war in 1829 also had a clear domestic ingredient, and an internal conflict in 1830–31 had a trans-'national' dimension. Similarly, in 1829–30 a series of conspiracies centred in Masonic lodges in Puno, Arequipa and Cuzco are said to have been inspired by the president of Bolivia, Andrés Santa Cruz, who wished to annex southernmost Peru to Bolivia, but the conspiracies also involved locals with regional or Peruvian factional motivations.[2] Chile's war against the Peru-Bolivia Confederation in 1836–39 was supported by Peruvian exiles in Chile, and was thus, in part, an internal as well as an international war. As Fernando López-Alves has made clear, the complex process of political war involving the Banda Oriental and other parts of the Río de la Plata from 1810 to 1851 had both 'internal' and trans-'national' features.[3]

3.   Many of the internal conflicts before the 1860s are described as caudillistic — that is, conflicts conventionally depicted as representing the personal ambitions of individual caudillos. However, conflicts involving caudillos usually involved more than the ambitions of the caudillos themselves. In most cases, caudillos were to some degree supported, advised and/or manipulated by more-or-less educated and literate civilians for their own ends.[4] In addition, some historians have sought to uncover the representation of broader interests behind the actions of both regional and national caudillos. An early example was Miron Burgin's attempt to detect economic interests underlying regional conflicts in the Río de la Plata before 1852.[5] A more recent endeavour in the same vein is Paul Gootenberg's suggestion that some Peruvian caudillos were in effect operating on behalf of regional economic interests.[6] Others have sought to give a more political (rather than economic) contextualisation of caudillo-led conflicts. An interesting recent example is Peter Guardino's *Peasants, Politics, and the Formation of Mexico's National State: Guerrero 1800–1857*, which gives us a better sense of

---

[2]   Dante Herrera Alarcón, *Rebeliones que intentaron desembrar en el sur del Perú* (Lima, 1961).
[3]   Fernando López-Alves, 'Wars and the Formation of Political Parties in Uruguay, 1810–1851', in Eduardo Posada-Carbó (ed.), *Wars, Parties and Nationalism. Essays on the Politics and Society of Nineteenth-Century Latin America* (London, 1995), pp. 5–26.
[4]   Robert L. Gilmore, *Caudillism and Militarism in Venezuela, 1810–1910* (Athens, OH, 1964).
[5]   Miron Burgin, *The Economic Aspects of Argentine Federalism, 1820–1852* (Cambridge, MA, 1946).
[6]   Paul Gootenberg, *Between Silver and Guano: Commercial Policy and the State in Post-Independence Peru* (Princeton, 1989), pp. 69–73.

both the popular forces supporting Juan Alvarez and the possible ideological content of their cause.[7]

4.   After the initial era of national consolidation, many, if not most,
nineteenth-century internal wars were initiated by elements of the political elite in order to circumvent or influence elections, or to reverse their
outcome. During the 1820s Bolívar and many of his supporters feared
that presidential elections in particular would almost invariably lead to
violent conflict. This was one of the chief justifications for Bolívar's proposed life presidency and for subsequent plans among his Colombian
sympathisers to establish a constitutional monarchy after Bolívar's death.
Such fears of the disruptive effects of elections proved to be prescient.
Some conflicts began in anticipation of losing future elections. In other
cases the violence coincided with the election itself, as occurred in the
elections in post-1840 Brazil described by Richard Graham.[8] Many wars
were fought after electoral loss had already occurred, and as such may
be considered another form of election, waged on the ground rather
than through the ballot. Often, however, other issues overlapped and
reinforced the electoral question.

5.   Another phenomenon was the federalist war, which actually falls
into two different categories or possibly is a single category with two distinct aspects. Some federalist wars were fought at least in part to assert
regional autonomy, as occurred in many of the provincial upheavals in
Brazil during the 1830s. But many of these conflicts also reflected internal divisions within each of the insurgent provinces. In Colombia these
two types, or aspects, of federalist war might superficially appear to be
separable. Colombia's civil war of 1859–63 was fought in part over assertions of regional autonomy; however, who would control locally was
at least as much at issue. The federalist constitution of 1862 provided a
decentralised political structure that encouraged many local struggles
for control of state governments. From 1863 to 1876 there were many
coups d'état or little revolutions at the state level that did not lead to
more generalised civil war. However, such small upheavals at the state
level also had important implications for the national government. Since
each state cast a single vote for president, it mattered nationally who
controlled the electoral machinery at the state level. As a consequence,
the national government frequently intervened in conflicts that disturbed the civil order in only a single state. So, while it may be possible
to make a categorical distinction between struggles to assert regional
autonomy from the central government, and fights to determine who
would rule within the region, in fact the two were often intertwined.

---

[7] Peter Guardino, *Peasants, Politics and the Formation of Mexico's National State. Guerrero, 1800–1857* (Stanford, 1996).

[8] Richard Graham, *Patronage and Politics in Nineteenth-Century Brazil* (Stanford, 1990),
especially chapters five and six.

6.   Some internal wars were motivated by the defence or assertion of corporate interests. Defence of the corporate interest of the military was most evident in Mexico, which inherited a very large army from the Independence era. The defence of military interests also made a brief appearance in Venezuela in the 1830s. It also probably had some long-term importance in Brazil. Elsewhere it seems to have been much less important or more-or-less momentary. Chile is supposed to have escaped praetorian military intervention in part through the creation of aristocratically controlled militias as a counterweight to the standing army.

In Colombia it is less clear whether the militia or national guard was created as a counterweight to the professional military. It is true that in the 1830s and early 1840s university-educated civilian politicians resented the occasional disruption of civil order by the ambitions of military officers. For this reason, as well as for reasons of fiscal economy, civilian politicians of the 1830s, whether 'liberal' or 'moderate' (the latter became 'conservatives' after 1848), sought to reduce the size of the army. The reduction of the national army reached an extreme in the early 1850s, precisely when the 'National Guard' was organised. Thus one may view the emergence of a 'National Guard' in Colombia in the 1850s as an attempt to create a counterweight to the standing army. On the other hand, the National Guard, in practice, often served to complement and reinforce the standing army in the defence of the existing government.

In any event, after the 1820s the military acted less overtly as a corporate group in Colombia than it did in Mexico, Peru or Venezuela. In Colombia (known as New Granada before 1863) the military was weaker as a corporate entity; indeed some military officers behaved in ways not clearly distinguishable from upper-class civilians. The relatively stronger role of civilians and the relatively civilian behaviour of some military officers occurred in part because New Granada had the good fortune to lose much of its military hierarchy when most Venezuelan officers, who predominated in Colombia's army of independence, returned to their homeland after the break-up of Gran Colombia in 1830–31. Anthony Maingot has argued further that a number of the remaining New Granadan officers were of more-or-less aristocratic social origins and acted, apparently as a matter of class interest, to resist the praetorian behaviour of professional officers of lesser social status who remained in direct control of the army.[9] Maingot's argument is dramatically exemplified in the war of 1854, in which upper-class conservatives and liberals, both civilian and military, joined to put down a coup, or revolution, led by General José María Melo, a military officer of lesser social origins whose identity and income depended on his army position, and seconded by the artisans of Bogotá and the popular classes in many other places (the Cauca Valley, Cartagena, Santa Marta). In Maingot's interpretation, for

---

[9] Anthony P. Maingot, 'Social Structures, Social Status and Civil-Military Conflict in Urban Colombia, 1810–1858', in Stephan Thernstrom and Richard Sennett (eds.), *Nineteenth-Century Cities: Essays in the New Urban History* (New Haven, 1969), pp. 297–355.

upper-sector military officers, their class identity was more fundamental than their identification with the military as a corporate group. Therefore, like civilians of their class, they did not hesitate to fight and defeat the Melo-led coalition of standing army and popular classes. Maingot does not argue that Colombia's aristocratic generals were convinced constitutionalists. Indeed, in the case of General Tomás Cipriano de Mosquera such an argument would be rather tricky, given his variable and erratic career. However, some of Colombia's nineteenth-century generals do appear to have had a strong commitment to constitutional order, and even quasi-civilian mentality. This seems to be true to a considerable degree of such mid-century generals as Pedro Alcántara Herrán, José Hilario López and Tomás Herrera.

Mexico offers the pre-eminent example of praetorian politics in the first half of the nineteenth century. In Mexico — whether the army was defending its size, its salaries or the *fuero* — its defence often took the form of coups d'état. In Venezuela, the 'Reform' war of 1835, fought partly as an assertion of the high-ranking military's corporate interests, ended in the rapid defeat of those asserting the cause of the *militares*, a defeat that occurred at the hands of Venezuela's most feared *militar*, General José Antonio Páez. In Brazil, according to one recent interpretation, the 'Sabinada' in Bahia (1837–38) began as a protest against a military reorganisation that affected mulatto and *pardo* military units negatively, although the racial dimensions soon overshadowed the initial military motivation.[10] In Brazil the most significant revolution on behalf of military interests, in terms of long-term effects, was probably the overthrow of the empire in 1889, one important motivation of which seems to have been the frustration of military officers over slow promotion through the ranks.[11]

While the assertion of military interests usually took the form of quick strikes, conflicts over Church privileges and powers affected broadly and deeply-felt popular concerns and consequently tended to lead to broader, longer and bloodier wars. Indeed, some of those who raised the banner of the Church did so precisely because it would engage and inflame popular emotions. In an illuminating letter written in 1852 Mariano Ospina Rodríguez, the pre-eminent ideological and tactical leader of Colombian conservatism from 1842 to at least 1861, argued explicitly that conservatives should give primacy to the banner of the Church because it was more likely to mobilise deeply-felt and emotional support than such causes as the defence of property.[12] Of the various bloody nineteenth-century wars in defence of the Church the most well-known is the Mexican War of the Reform. Colombia's civil wars of 1851 and 1876, both in-

---

[10] Hendrik Kraay, '"As Terrifying as Unexpected": The Bahian Sabinada, 1837–1838', *Hispanic American Historical Review*, vol. 72, no. 4 (1992), pp. 501–27.

[11] William S. Dudley, 'Institutional Sources of Officer Discontent in the Brazilian Army, 1870–1889', *Hispanic American Historical Review*, vol. 55, no. 1 (1975), pp. 44–65.

[12] Mariano Ospina Rodríguez to José Eusebio Caro, Medellín, 22 June 1852, in José Eusebio Caro, *Epistolario* (Bogotá, 1953), pp. 348–52.

volving the simultaneous assertion of claims by the Conservative Party and the Catholic Church, were of lesser magnitude and are less well known outside the circle of Colombian historians.

International (extra-Latin American) ideological, political and economic influences on Latin America's nineteenth-century conflicts affected the forms and features of a number of conflicts involving the Catholic Church. The Revolution of 1848 in Paris had a double impact, in both reviving interest in the French Revolution of 1789 (in part through the writings of Alphonse de Lamartine) and in stimulating more intense interest in contemporary socialist and democratic trends in France. These influences clearly had a mobilising effect upon young liberals in mid-century Colombia and Chile and apparently also, though perhaps less obviously, in Mexico and Peru. The egalitarian effusions of these young liberals, and their anti-clericalism, in turn provided reinforcement to a conservative reaction, which likewise found at least part of its focus in issues involving the Catholic Church. The reaction of Latin American conservatives to liberal democratic and anti-clerical enthusiasms found particularly strong external backing in Pope Pius IX's own reaction to liberal and anti-clerical forces in Europe. It is notable that issues involving the Catholic Church found their most intense and violent expression, at least in Mexico and Colombia, under the double impact of the French Revolution of 1848 and (more particularly) the reactionary shift of the Church under Pius IX.

It is thus possible to put forward a chronologically-ordered hypothesis about conflicts over the status of the Catholic Church. In places with relatively active commerce in the immediate post-Independence period, such as Venezuela, Buenos Aires and Uruguay, the process of partial secularisation occurred before the Church had recovered from the losses it suffered (in bishops, priests and money) during the years of struggle for independence and also before it developed the militantly reactionary spirit established by Pius IX at mid-century. Partly for this reason, the gestures toward secularisation that occurred in Venezuela, Buenos Aires and Uruguay before 1835 were attended by relatively little overt conflict and very little violence. From 1850 through the 1860s, a more militant liberalism in Mexico and Colombia came strongly into conflict with an at least equally militant Vatican. Those countries such as Bolivia and Peru in which liberal forces were rather weak for most of the nineteenth century were able to carry out a process of partial secularisation relatively easily toward the end of the nineteenth and in the early twentieth centuries, when the Catholic Church had begun to accommodate itself to a greater degree to the modern world.

7. Still another modality of internal war is the 'caste war', pitting poor people of distinct culture from the elites against an oligarchically controlled government. The classic cases are the Caste War of Yucatán and

the other indigenous rebellions in nineteenth-century Mexico.[13] The possible meanings of Indian peasant rebellions in the Andes have also been explored, somewhat theatrically, in an ongoing debate between Florencia Mallon and Heraclio Bonilla as to whether Indian peasants did or did not have a sense of Peruvian national identity.[14] Recent work, treated below, has explored interactions between elites and peasants or other elements of the popular classes, particularly during periods of violent political conflict. Much of this work suggests that the term 'caste war,' implying a simple conflict between indigenous people and '*gente de razón*', often fails to capture the extent to which peasants were incorporated into the politics of elite-dominated parties.

8.   External economic change had varied effects in providing the context for, if not directly stimulating, internal conflicts. Great Britain's swing toward freer trade in the 1840s, with the end of protection for colonial producers of tropical products, stimulated an immediate response in at least some parts of Latin America. In Colombia this change in British policy was an important element in the decision to commit fully to foreign trade, the immediate expression of which was the lowering of the tariff on finished goods in 1847. This commitment, sustained for decades afterwards by Colombian elites, both liberal and conservative, provoked strident expressions of class conflict — in Bogotá in 1853, in the military-artisans' revolution of 1854 and in subsequent elite attempts to smash or marginalise artisans as a political force.

Still another impact of the external economy was produced by fluctuations in price and demand for Latin American products in the Atlantic market. The decline of coffee prices in the early 1840s lay at the centre of Venezuelan political divisions for the next decade. Charles Bergquist has argued that a sharp drop in the international market of

---

[13] Nelson Reed, *The Caste War of Yucatán* (Stanford, 1964); Moises González Navarro, *Raza y tierra: la guerra de castas y el henequén* (Mexico, 1970); Leticia Reina, *Las rebeliones campesinas en México (1819–1906)* (Mexico, 1980); and Victoria Reifler Bricker, *The Indian Christ, the Indian King: The Historical Substrate of Maya Myth and Ritual* (Austin, 1981). John Tutino, *From Insurrection to Revolution in Mexico: Social Bases of Agrarian Violence, 1750–1940* (Princeton, 1986) provides a broad synthesis. A number of interesting essays on diverse peasant rebellions in Mexico are brought together in Friedrich Katz (ed.), *Riot, Rebellion and Revolution: Rural Social Conflict in Mexico* (Princeton, 1988). These include Tutino on rebellion in Chalco, Evelyn Hu-Dehart on Yaqui rebellions in Sonora, Leticia Reina on the Sierra Gorda rebellion of 1847–50 and Enrique Montalvo Ortega on peasant revolts in Yucatán. Other essays bearing on alliances between elites and peasants are noted below.

[14] See the contributions of Bonilla and Mallon in Steve J. Stern (ed.), *Resistance, Rebellion and Consciousness in the Andean Peasant World: Eighteenth to Twentieth Centuries* (Madison, 1987). This volume also contains an essay by Tristan Platt which emphasises defence of traditional modes as the chief motive for indigenous rebellion in the Chayanta region of Bolivia. See also a more recent treatment of the cultural-political meaning of indigenous rebellion in Mark Thurner, *From Two Republics to One Divided: Contradictions of Postcolonial Nation-making in Andean Peru* (Durham, NC, 1997).

coffee in the 1880s underlay Colombia's civil war of 1885, and Malcolm Deas has further sketched the ways in which depressed demand for coffee and cinchona bark reduced employment and the government's fiscal resources, thus creating conditions propitious for rebellion.[15]

Overall, economic conditions seem more often to have provided the context for civil war than the direct cause. I noted earlier the theses of Miron Burgin and Paul Gootenberg, both of whom found that conflicting regional interests associated with foreign trade lay at the heart of, respectively, Argentine and Peruvian politics in the early post-Independence period. In the case of the Río de la Plata it is possible to find various conflicting interests between Buenos Aires on the one hand and the interior and littoral provinces on the other.[16] But another important economic fact underlying the political divisions of the period was the change in economic structure that occurred when the flow of silver from Bolivia ceased. This forced Buenos Aires to turn to its pastoral economy as a source of foreign exchange, with the result that Buenos Aires lost an active, effective interest in the interior provinces.

In the case of Colombia it is hard to find conflicting regional economic interests of the sort that might induce or influence internal war until the 1870s. It is true that in the 1830s *antioqueños* were angered by various policies emanating from Bogotá, most notably by legal restrictions on the export of gold dust.[17] But there is no evidence that these irritations induced Antioquia to take up arms. Indeed, it might well be argued that in Colombia, and perhaps also to a degree in Argentina, the economic roots of civil war before 1870 lay not in conflicting regional interests but rather in the lack of an integrated national market. The lack of large integrated markets stunted economic opportunity and inclined elites to political enterprise. Thus, in the case of Colombia, the Cauca region, sealed off from national as well as international markets by two mountain ranges, was through most of the nineteenth century a seedbed of civil war, whereas Antioquia, with its active gold mining economy fostering a substantial concentration of wealth in *antioqueño* merchant capitalists, generally shied away from armed conflict.

In Colombia a clear case of regional economic conflict as a source of political division, providing at least a context for war, does not occur until the 1870s. During that decade, the planned Ferrocarril del Norte, which would have benefited only the eastern cordillera, was one ingredient in the formation of a political coalition between the Caribbean coast and the Cauca, a

---

[15] Charles W. Bergquist, *Coffee and Conflict in Colombia, 1886–1910* (Durham, NC, 1978); and Malcolm Deas, 'Ricardo Gaitán Obeso y su campaña en el río Magdalena en Colombia, 1885', in Malcolm Deas, *Del poder y la gramática y otros ensayos sobre historia, política y literatura colombiana* (Santafé de Bogotá, 1993), pp. 124–6.

[16] As both Juan Alvarez and Miron Burgin did: see Juan Alvarez, *Estudio sobre las guerras civiles argentinas* (Buenos Aires, 1941); and Burgin, *Economic Aspects*.

[17] María Teresa Uribe de Hincapié and Jesús María Alvarez, *Poderes y regiones: problemas de la constitución de la nación colombiana, 1810–1850* (Medellín, 1987).

coalition that became increasingly evident in the 1870s and which provided a critical base of political support for the emerging regime of Rafael Núñez.[18] This suggests that conflicting regional interests become more important politically when an economy is sufficiently integrated for the conflict of interests to have palpable effects on various regions.

Generally, with the exception of Charles Bergquist's *Coffee and Conflict in Colombia*, the expansion of foreign trade has been associated with the establishment of greater political order. The usual argument, taking Porfirian Mexico as a paradigmatic case, is that increased foreign trade generated more revenues for national governments, thus facilitating both the co-optation of potential opponents through patronage and the repression of outright rebels by stronger national armies (that is, '*pan o palo*'). Furthermore, national railway networks created by expanded foreign trade both enhanced the national government's repressive power and, by increasing elite engagement with the economy, made its use less necessary. I find this argument generally persuasive. One should note, however, that the classic example of this argument, Mexico in the *porfiriato*, also provides, over the longer term, a notable counterexample. In Porfirian Mexico the substantial economic growth of northern Mexico did not lead to corresponding political power for the region's elites, which was surely one factor in the breakdown of the regime and the subsequent civil war known as the Mexican Revolution. Also, as indicated in Friedrich Katz's gem of an article on rural labour systems in the *porfiriato*, fluctuations in the external economy also helped to set the stage for the explosion in northern Mexico in 1911.[19]

Regional diversity in civil wars: the rebellion of 1851 in New Granada

Up to this point the discussion has differentiated internal wars by the dominant themes that characterised them. This is a bit artificial, as a number, if not most, civil wars turn out, on close examination, to be quite variegated in character. This point could probably be well illustrated by the diverse regional features of New Granada's War of the *Supremos* (particularly in the years 1840–41), if only we knew more about them. We know something about what was in play in the Cauca at this time, but unfortunately not so much about other regions. However, in the case of the conservative rebellion of 1851 in New Granada some of the regional variations are more visible.

The conservative rebellion of 1851, which first manifested itself in April of that year in the Cauca region, is often depicted as an expression of resistance to the complete abolition of slavery, legislation for which was then making its way through the New Granadan Congress. The idea that the rebellion represented an eruption of slave-owner anger at the

[18] This argument is most clearly and strongly asserted in James W. Park, *Rafael Núñez and the Politics of Colombian Regionalism, 1863–1886* (Baton Rouge, 1985).

[19] Friedrich Katz, 'Labor Conditions on Haciendas in Porfirian Mexico: Some Trends and Tendencies', *Hispanic American Historical Review*, vol. 54, no. 1 (1974), pp. 1–47.

imminent law of abolition was a standard view of nineteenth-century liberals which is still repeated in more recent treatments. There is some circumstantial evidence for such an interpretation. Julio and Sergio Arboleda, who were among the leaders of the rebellion in the Cauca, were substantial slave owners, and they and other slave owners in the region complained about the economic consequences the end of slavery would entail for them. However, slavery in the Cauca was already in process of dissolution. General José María Obando, by recruiting slaves to fight for him with the promise of freedom in 1840–41, had sprung many slaves loose from the control of their former owners. Even after Obando was defeated, bands of free or escaped blacks roamed the wooded areas of the region, stealing from haciendas and, at least on one dramatic occasion in April 1843, assaulting them. As a consequence, long before 1851 the institution of slavery in the region was dissolving and slave owners were increasingly demoralised. By 1850 many slave owners already saw the total extinction of slavery in New Granada as imminent and at least some took action to cut their losses. General Tomás Cipriano de Mosquera, for example, anticipated the inevitable by shipping his slaves off to Panama in 1850, where he would hire them out on labour contracts to work on the construction of the isthmian railway.[20]

Julio Arboleda, the most visible leader of the Cauca uprising in 1851, had shipped many of his own slaves to Peru in the 1840s. But by 1850 he was not responding as enterprisingly to the final crisis of slavery. Like many other slave owners, he was embittered by the inadequate compensation that was being provided for liberated slaves. But it is noteworthy that in his public complaints at the time of the rebellion in 1851, Arboleda did not rail at the abolition of slavery. Rather in his 1851 propaganda sheet, *El Misáforo*, he complained that in 1850–51 liberals had armed free blacks and used them as shock troops against conservative property owners: 'Who are those armed men, almost all blacks, who cross and re-cross the streets of Cali? They are the manumitted and liberated men whom the government has armed. They are agents of the government.'[21] In other words, Arboleda was reacting not so much, or not only, to the end of slavery, but rather to the climate of fear that had been created among property-owners in the Cauca by the liberals' mobilisation of the region's popular classes in 1850–51.

In any event, the conservative rebellion of 1851 was not limited to the Cauca. In Antioquia, which rebelled at the beginning of July, after the effective defeat of the conservative movement in the Cauca, slaves made up less than one per cent of the population, and one of the first acts of Antioquia's rebelling conservatives was to abolish slavery in Antioquia — though with immediate cash compensation rather than the

---

[20] Jorge Castellanos, *La abolición de la esclavitud en Popayán, 1832–1852* (Cali, 1980), p. 108.
[21] *Ibid.*, pp. 112–13.

central government's offer of bonds that were likely to be depreciated.[22] Furthermore, General Eusebio Borrero of Cali, who captained the rebellion in Antioquia, voted *for* the abolition of slavery in the New Granadan senate before he left Bogotá to lead the revolution in Antioquia.

In Antioquia the motivations for rebellion were various. Recent anti-clerical measures by the liberal government provoked outrage among many pious *antioqueños*. Among these acts were the expulsion of the Jesuits in 1850 and various laws affecting the Church in 1851. One on 9 May 1851 interfered with discipline in religious communities; another on 14 May ended the juridical privileges of priests (the *fuero eclesiástico*); on 24 May a law providing bases for a new constitution called for freedom of religion; on 27 May another called for local communities to elect their priests (from options provided by their bishop) and made provincial legislatures responsible for the financial support of the Church. It is notable that parish priests in Antioquia played important roles in initiating and sustaining the rebellion — though a few opposed it.[23]

Another motive in Antioquia was the fear of anarchy. Some communities in the southerly reaches of Antioqueño colonisation worried about the spread of violence and rapine northward from the Cauca. General Borrero played on these fears, saying that the liberal government had approved popular attacks on haciendas and their owners in the Cauca and that, unless the revolution triumphed, *antioqueños* could expect their properties to be robbed, their women raped, their religion destroyed.[24]

Still another grievance was the fragmentation of Antioquia province into three smaller provinces. In 1851 the liberal majority in the National Congress had divided Antioquia into three smaller provinces: Antioquia, Medellín and Córdoba (Rionegro). This move, which had been proposed by Rionegro, would free liberals in Rionegro, in the city of Antioquia and in nearby Sopetrán from domination by conservative Medellín. It also would tend to increase the strength of liberalism in greater Antioquia by creating two potentially liberal provinces and one conservative one, where there had formerly been a single large conservative-dominated entity. Medellín, as well as the smaller towns around it, objected bitterly to the fragmentation of the province. Not surprisingly, one of the first acts of the 1851 revolution in Antioquia was to proclaim the reunification of the province in a new 'Federal State of Antioquia'. Significantly, the slogan of the movement in Antioquia — 'Dios y Federación' — drew together two of the *antioqueños'* major preoccupations.[25]

Up to this point the conservative rebellion was, in the Cauca, an upper-class conservative protest against liberal mobilisation of popular classes, with a strong component of racial fear, and in Antioquia, pri-

---

[22] 'Luis Javier Ortiz Mesa, *El federalismo en Antioquia, 1850–1880: aspectos políticos* (Medellín, 1985), p. 22.

[23] *Ibid.*, pp. 26–7.

[24] *Ibid.*, p. 24.

[25] *Ibid.*, pp. 21, 25.

marily a protest against the anti-clericalism of the liberal-controlled national government and against the dilution of conservative control of the region. But the Cauca and Antioquia were not the only regions participating in the rebellion. In fact, initial plans for the rebellion had been made by conservative leaders in Bogotá, for whom it represented primarily an attempt to overthrow the liberal government and replace it with a conservative one. Conservative Party ambitions were the common denominator linking the rebellion in its various regions. Underlying and supporting this partisan motivation were diverse local concerns. In Pasto insurgents proclaimed the expelled Jesuits as their cause; in Mariquita rebels waved the flag of federalism. The most generally shared conservative banners, other than hostility to the liberals, were the defence of the Church and the security of property.

Social textures of internal war: elite recruitment and popular mobilisation

Until relatively recently most work on Latin American politics (including my own) focused almost exclusively upon political elites and more generally the dominant class. We had relatively little information about the linkages or interactions between elite politics and popular forces. The most encouraging recent development in historical research relating to civil wars (and politics in general) in nineteenth-century Latin America is the emergence of a body of work that provides a broader social perspective on internal conflicts. Some of the older work on caudillos sought to provide some social contextualisation. Two examples are Roger Haigh's 'Creation and Control of a Caudillo' and John Lynch's more recent book on Juan Manuel de Rosas and his broader synthesis on caudillos. The focus of both, however, is still primarily upon elites. Another interesting work on Argentina, now looking to the more silent popular classes, is Mark Szuchman's exploration of why urban residents of Buenos Aires might have viewed Rosas favourably (Rosas meant peace and order).[26]

From a perspective of elite initiatives in, and leadership of, civil wars, the issue of the popular role is framed in terms of recruitment. On the subject of popular recruitment, there are several standard notions:

1. *Hacendados* mobilised the peons on their estates, or perhaps even forced them to fight, on behalf of elite political projects. Malcolm Deas questions whether *hacendado* recruitment of their own peons was such a common source of troops, but he nonetheless does point to a few examples.[27]

---

[26] Roger M. Haigh, 'The Creation and Control of a Caudillo', *Hispanic American Historical Review*, vol. 44, no. 4 (1964), pp. 481–90; Roger Haigh, *Martín Güemes: Tyrant or Tool? A Study of the Sources of Power of an Argentine Caudillo* (Fort Worth, 1968); John Lynch, *Argentine Dictator: Juan Manuel de Rosas, 1829–1852* (Oxford, 1981); John Lynch, *Caudillos in Spanish America, 1800–1850* (Oxford, 1992); and Mark Szuchman, *Order, Family and Community in Buenos Aires, 1810–1860* (Stanford, 1988).

[27] Deas, 'Ricardo Gaitán Obeso', note 54 (pp. 171–2).

2.   Caudillos offered the possibility of booty as an incentive for joining the caudillistic horde. This is the model that Eric Wolf and Edward Hansen had in mind in their analysis of *caudillismo* in what appears to be a Venezuelan context.[28] A variant of this theme can be seen in the Cauca region of Colombia in José María Obando, who in 1840–41 offered freedom to slaves, as well as booty from haciendas, for those who would follow him. Deas's analysis of Gaitán Obeso and the civil war of 1885 raises doubts as to the importance of booty as a popular motivator, preferring to emphasise popular political commitments.[29] Yet his account at the same time reveals that Gaitán Obeso seized a considerable quantity of government revenue funds and goods (imported merchandise, cattle, horses), at least a part of which must have been used to hold the loyalty of his volunteers.

The use of booty was an incentive that was particularly appropriate for the mobilisation of rebel armies, which in many cases started with few resources and therefore had to make use of those appropriated from others. Forces defending the party in power also exacted property from those considered to be sympathetic to their opponents. But the party in power generally had to depict itself as the defender of order, which probably put some constraints on outright pillage. Therefore,

3.   Parties in power, if they lacked the fiscal resources to attract popular recruits to an enterprise they were likely to find unappealing, often had to resort to coercion. In the province of Buenos Aires, government forces dragooned *estancia* labour into military service, against the will both of the peons and of their masters.[30] One of the standard notions, at least for nineteenth-century Colombia, is that the cannon fodder deployed by elite military amateurs was largely composed of ignorant peasants pressed into service. This notion finds some confirmation in contemporary watercolours depicting miserable recruits shuffling along under various forms of restraint. General Joaquín Posada Gutiérrez referred to the:

> mayors and their henchmen who organise to hunt men, using the most violent and irritating methods, to fill the quota asked of them with the poor men who do not have a few pesos to give the barbarous recruiter. Thus are formed the chain of wretches, who tied together like criminals, are driven with sticks.

---

[28] Eric R. Wolf and Edward C. Hansen, 'Caudillo Politics: A Structural Analysis', *Comparative Studies in Society and History*, vol. 9, no. 2 (1967), pp. 168–79.

[29] Deas, 'Ricardo Gaitán Obeso', p. 153.

[30] Richard Slatta emphasises the efforts of gauchos to escape recruitment; Tulio Halperín-Donghi has pointed to landowner distaste at the loss of labour. See Richard Slatta, *Gauchos and the Vanishing Frontier* (Lincoln, NE, 1983), chapter 8; and Tulio Halperín Donghi, 'The Buenos Aires Landed Class and the Shape of Argentine Politics (1820–1930)', in Evelyne Huber and Frank Safford (eds.), *Agrarian Structure and Political Power* (Pittsburgh, 1995), pp. 39–66.

Alvaro Tirado Mejía, who quotes Posada Gutiérrez, adds, 'By force they carried off peasants who had to fight for ideas they did not understand and for interests that were not theirs'.[31] Those who were thus dragooned were naturally tempted to desert, a tendency that warring officers sometimes sought to discourage with exemplary executions.

4.   In contrast to the peasants who were dragooned into service were the 'volunteers' who fought for a cause. Volunteers might be of two sorts. In his analysis of the 1885 rebellion led by Gaitán Obeso, Deas refers to volunteers of the popular classes who fought as loyalists to articulated political symbols (with perhaps also a hope of booty). Most nineteenth-century accounts of Colombian civil wars depict 'volunteers' as a more select group, essentially political elites who fought for a cause they considered just as well as for personal glory. In either case, volunteers could be difficult to lead. In Colombia's civil wars of the nineteenth century volunteers felt free to voice their opinions on tactics, and leaders sometimes had to persuade them on such matters. An unnamed source quoted by Deas said that: 'The volunteer in civil wars demands of his chiefs rapid and fortunate manoeuvres. He does not understand the strategic movements of regular armies. He enrolled to fight, and if the combats are delayed, he considers the adventure lost.'[32] The same phenomenon was noted by María Martínez de Nisser in her diary of the civil war of 1840–41 in Antioquia. In this case the volunteers, at least as she depicted them, were motivated by passion for a cause (as well as for individual glory) rather than by lust for booty.[33]

Martínez de Nisser's account, like a number of other narratives of civil wars by the politically-motivated, strongly emphasises the theme of the honour and glory of the volunteers — not least that of herself, as a woman who cut her hair, donned a uniform and joined the forces of Braulio Enao (in part to shame reluctant men into volunteering also). The force that Martínez de Nisser adorned, however, seems to have differed from the stereotypical picture of a mass of unwilling peasant recruits led by a small minority of upper-class political adventurers. Enao's group, as our heroine depicted it, began with little more than a hundred miserable recruits brought to Antioquia from the neighbouring province of Mariquita. But soon men from towns on Antioquia's south-eastern frontier (Sonsón, Aguadas, Abejorral and Salamina) created a volunteer force five times that of the original group of unmotivated Mariquita *enganchados*. (Predictably, the firearms brought by the *mariquiteños* were redistributed to the *antioqueño* volunteers, while the slack 'recruits' were given lances and placed in the rear guard.) In this case, the cause-

---

[31] Alvaro Tirado Mejía, *Aspectos sociales de las guerras civiles en Colombia* (Bogotá, 1976), pp. 37–8.

[32] Deas, 'Ricardo Gaitán Obeso', p. 142.

[33] María Martínez de Nisser, *Diario de los sucesos de la revolución en la Provincia de Antioquia en los años de 1840–1841* (Bogotá [1843] 1983), p. 53.

motivated volunteers extended well beyond the political elite to men who were modest colonist-farmers.

Another of the possibly cause-motivated popular participants in Colombia's civil wars were artisans. In early civil wars they were recruited into units formed on an emergency basis, but by the 1850s they were forming the backbone of what may have been standing organised militias.

The issue of recruitment looks at the question of popular participation in civil wars from an elite perspective, as a matter of the mobilisation and organisation of resources. Recently, however, some scholars have begun to look at popular participation in internal wars more as a matter of mobilisation from below. We now have a growing body of work that seeks to show the linkages between politics as seen from the national capital and politics in the region, and the relationship between regional leaders and organised political actors in rural communities. Work of this sort on Mexico has been particularly interesting. Guy Thomson, Florencia Mallon and Peter Guardino have made important contributions in this genre, each with a somewhat different style of analysis. Guardino, focusing on the state of Guerrero in the first half of the nineteenth century, seeks to show the structural bases of rural support for the state caudillo, Juan Alvarez.[34] One gets the impression from Guardino's account that Alvarez was generally a direct and faithful representative of the concerns of his rural political base. Mallon, by contrast, tends to see more conflict, in perspective and ideology, between urban political elites at the state level and leaders in the villages.[35] In her account of the Sierra Norte de Puebla and the State of Morelos, the story is substantially one of assertions of hegemonic control from the centre and from state leaders, and local resistance to these assertions. Thomson also deals with the Sierra of Puebla, particularly the period from the 1840s to the 1880s.[36] Writing in a less lofty and categorical mode than Mallon, Thomson's approach is a bit more anthropological in its attention to cultural textures. Among various interesting points in Thomson's work, one of the most important is his depiction of the role of the National Guard, created during the emergency of the Mexican War, in integrating peasants, indigenous as well as mestizo, into the political process from the end of the 1840s into the 1880s. All of these works provide us with a much needed sense of the local, particularly rural, dynamic of Mexican politics.

Similarly useful are the works of Paul Vanderwood and (for a different period) William B. Taylor, which have provided suggestive insights

[34] Guardino, *Peasants, Politics*.

[35] Florencia E. Mallon, *Peasant and Nation: The Making of Post-Colonial Mexico and Peru* (Berkeley, 1995).

[36] See particularly Guy P.C. Thomson, 'Popular Aspects of Liberalism in Mexico, 1848–1888', *Bulletin of Latin American Research*, vol. 10 (1991), pp. 265–92; Guy P.C. Thomson, 'Movilización conservadora, insurrección liberal y rebeliones indígenas, 1854–76', in Antonio Annino et al., *America Latina: Dalla Stato Coloniale allo Stato Nazione* (Turin, 1987), vol. II, pp. 592–614; and by the same author, 'Bulwarks of Patriotic Liberalism: the National Guard, Philharmonic Corps and Patriotic Juntas in Mexico, 1847–88', *Journal of Latin American Studies*, vol. 22, no. 1 (1990), pp. 31–68.

into the relationships between banditry and partisan civil war in Mexico.[37] (Bandits in time of civil war become partisan warriors; when the political wars were over, it was back to banditry unless the government provided alternative employment.) Charles Walker has also published an interesting essay on artisans and bandits as sometime collaborators with elites in the political wars of Peru.[38] In this case Walker finds some underclass participants operated both in Lima and rural areas, moving back and forth between the two.

Some work also has been done on the participation of urban popular classes in political conflicts. Silvia Arrom has analysed what we know, and what we probably can't know, given the surviving sources, about one of the more famous events with political consequences that involved the urban underclass: the Parián riot in Mexico City in 1828. Arrom emphasises that, whatever the various motives of the rioters, they were clearly acting within an elite-framed political context.[39]

Virtually all of the various local or regional upheavals that occurred in Brazil between 1831 and 1845 involved cross-class collaboration between elements of the elite and the underclasses. A number of these were essentially urban and tended to be anti-Portuguese in sentiment, as in the disturbances in Rio de Janeiro in March–April 1831 that led to the abdication of Pedro I and in subsequent reflexive upheavals in various provincial cities in the north-east. The much more violent *Cabanagem* in Pará (1833–35), also essentially urban and anti-Portuguese, was led by some local officials but depended heavily on black mass support. A similarly urban, cross-class movement, also leading to violent conflict was the *Sabinada* in Bahia in 1837–38. The war of the *Cabanos* in Pernambuco (1832–35), also cross-class in character, was exceptional both in that the *Cabanos* were pro-Portuguese and the conflict was fought out largely in rural areas.

A significant example of political mobilisation of the popular classes in nineteenth-century Spanish America occurred in New Granada during the 1850s. During the 1840s New Granada's liberals were clearly subordinated to the governing moderates, or *ministeriales*, particularly after the liberal rebellion of 1840–42 was crushed. During the early 1840s the *ministeriales* insured their dominance by exiling liberal leaders and through various other repressive measures. Nonetheless, in 1849 the liberals, despite having an apparent minority of the voters, were able to win the presidency because of divisions among the *ministeriales*, now called conservatives. Liberals were also aided by

---

[37] Paul J. Vanderwood, *Disorder and Progress: Bandits, Police and Mexican Development* (Lincoln, NE, 1981); and William B. Taylor, 'Banditry and Insurrection: Rural Unrest in Central Jalisco, 1790–1815', in Katz (ed.), *Riot, Rebellion and Revolution*, pp. 205–46.

[38] Charles Walker, 'Montoneros, bandoleros, malhechores: criminalidad y política en las primeras décadas republicanas', in Carlos Aguirre and Charles Walker (eds.), *Bandoleros, abigeos y montoneros: criminalidad y violencia en el Perú, siglos XVIII y XIX* (Lima, 1990), pp. 105–6.

[39] Silvia M. Arrom, 'Popular Politics in Mexico City: The Parián Riot, 1828', *Hispanic American Historical Review*, vol. 68, no. 2 (1988), pp. 245–68.

support from the artisans of Bogotá, who were angered by the lowering of customs duties on finished goods by the Mosquera administration in 1847. In November 1847 a Society of Artisans was formed in Bogotá to press for a more protectionist tariff and, according to one of the founders, to work for the return from exile of the star-crossed liberal hero, General José María Obando. In 1848 the Bogotá Artisans' Society endorsed the liberal candidate for the presidency, General José Hilario López. In 1849, if not earlier, the Artisans' Society reformed as the Sociedad Democrática de Artesanos, becoming for the next two years an instrument of the Liberal Party. During 1849 and 1850 *sociedades democráticas* were formed in many towns across the country, for the purpose of mobilising mass support for the liberals. In some areas where conservatives were dominant, as in the Cauca Valley, the *sociedades democráticas* played a critical role in intimidating conservatives and weakening their control. Cali was particularly a locus of violence in 1850–51 because a longstanding local dispute over land between large landowners and small farmers shaped and reinforced partisan antagonisms. Late in 1850 Cali *democráticos* began attacking conservative landholdings and then the persons of the *gente decente*. When conservatives protested these assaults, some liberal officials dismissed their complaints, saying the attacks were simply '*retozos democráticos*' (democratic frolics).

Liberals themselves, however, would soon have cause not to take *democrático* violence so lightly. The *democráticos* had not only provided muscle to liberal political advantage in many communities across the land, but, as members of National Guard units, they had also played an important role in suppressing the conservative rebellion of 1851 in the Cauca and Antioquia, and probably elsewhere as well. However, despite these services rendered by the artisans in Bogotá and others of the popular classes elsewhere, the artisans of Bogotá were unable to persuade the National Congress to raise duties again on finished goods. Upper-sector liberals actually split on this question. Some, mostly of an older generation, like Lorenzo María Lleras of Bogotá and Juan José Nieto of Cartagena, sympathised with the artisans and supported their request for higher duties. Younger 'radical' liberals, along with conservatives, responded to the artisans' entreaties with scorn and preachments about the doctrines of liberal political economy. Beginning in 1851 and increasingly in 1852–53, Bogotá's artisans turned away from the free-trade liberals in disillusionment.[40] By 1853 antagonism between the artisans of Bogotá and young upper-class liberals was such that violent confrontations occurred on the streets of the capital between men wearing *ruanas* and those dressed in frock coats.

---

[40] An important early document on artisan disillusionment with radical liberalism is the 1851 pamphlet by Ambrosio López, a tailor and one of the leaders of the Bogotá artisans, entitled *El desengaño*. López was disillusioned not only by the liberals' failure to restore tariff protection, but also by their expulsion of the Jesuits in 1850 and their legislation affecting the Catholic Church in 1851.

Meanwhile, radical liberals and conservatives had also alienated New Granada's small professional army, which politicians in both parties had steadily reduced in size since the early 1830s. Anti-military rhetoric, attacks on military pensions and threats to decimate the higher ranks of officers created an antagonism in the army toward upper-class politicians that paralleled the anger of Bogotá's artisans.

Radical liberal and conservative alienation of artisans and officers on active duty in the standing army ended on 17 April 1854 in a coup d'état-cum-social revolution headed by General José María Melo, the military commander in the capital, but also strongly supported by Bogotá's artisans. Free-trade liberals and conservatives quickly joined in an upper-class coalition to fight the Melo revolution and to try to regain dominant-class control of the capital.

The coup-revolution of 1854, however, had broad support across the country, from both some older-generation liberals and apparently also a broad array of elements of the popular classes. In Popayán, a *pronunciamiento* in favour of the Melo coup occurred on 8 April 1854, nine days before Melo actually carried out the coup. The Melo coup also had strong support from popular elements in Quilichao and Cali, as well as elsewhere in the Cauca Valley, and the upper-class free-trade liberal-conservative alliance was able to regain control of the Cauca Valley only by force and intimidation. The Melo revolution also had many sympathisers on the Caribbean coast: in Cartagena, where Juan José Nieto was governor, as well as in Santa Marta, Riohacha and Panama. There were also Melista guerrillas in various towns in Socorro province (the heartland of New Granadan liberalism), in Oiba, Barichara, Pinchote, Simacota and several lesser towns. The governor of Vélez Province was also a Melista. In Bucaramanga General Martín Collazos joined the Melo revolution because he objected to the hostility to the military expressed by many politicians in Bogotá. There was even some scattered support in Antioquia, particularly in the mining town of Supía and in Rionegro.

Some of the support for the Melo revolution is understandable. In addition to some of the older generation of liberals, Melo had the allegiance of a number of professional military officers, particularly in the middle ranks. It is also clear why Melo was backed by the artisans of Bogotá. Much less clear are the reasons why popular classes elsewhere backed the coup-revolution. There are several likely possibilities: (1) Artisans outside Bogotá, for example in Cartagena, were also affected by the refusal of radical liberals and conservatives to restore protection of finished goods. (2) Many in the popular classes, even though not artisans, resented exploitation by, and the arrogance of, local upper-class liberals and conservatives. (Letters of Salvador Camacho Roldán describing the difficulties the anti-Melo coalition faced in regaining control of the Cauca Valley make clear the extent of popular class hostility there to upper-class leaders of both parties.) (3) The democratic societies, fostered by the liberals, provided a means of organising, articulating and acting on popular-class antagonisms, as well as popular-class issue concerns. The latter, for the most part, still remain unknown to us.

Several recent studies have helped to illuminate the ideas and attitudes of the artisans of Bogotá.[41] However, we still don't know much about popular class sentiments outside Bogotá. One of the most informative treatments of the 1854 coup-revolution as it extended across the nation is a contemporary account, Venancio Ortíz's *Historia de la revolución del 17 de abril de 1854*, published in 1855, just after the defeat of Melo and the artisans. Ortiz provides information suggesting the extent of support for the coup-revolution in the provinces. Unfortunately, he generally does not explain why there was support in the various places where it emerged. If we are going to understand what was in play in the war of 1854, one of the clearest examples of undisguised class conflict in nineteenth-century Spanish America, we will need further explorations of the local sociopolitical dynamics in the Cauca Valley (other than Cali, where José Escorcia has provide a distinguished analysis),[42] on the Caribbean coast and in Socorro province.

Geography and varying forms of internal war

The effect of geography in giving distinctive forms to internal conflict in the various regions of Latin America is perhaps obvious, but worth noting. In Mexico the centrality of the valley of Mexico and Mexico City has made them the ultimate prize, though Veracruz was also important during civil war as a source of customs revenues. In Colombia, as in Mexico, the seizure of the coastal customs houses was often a primary concern of those rebelling against the national government. Seizure of revenue sources was an immediate aim of rebels in 1840–41 (salt and tobacco revenues in the interior, customs duties on the coast). Deas's account of the failed revolution of 1885 makes it clear that rebels understood the importance of controlling the Magdalena River and the Caribbean coast, as both offered readily sizeable resources, public (customs revenues) as well as private (imported goods, cattle, horses).[43] In contrast, the conservative rebellion of 1851 and the military-artisan revolution of 1854 both failed to seize control of the Magdalena River and the Caribbean coast, although both would probably have succumbed for other reasons even if their leaders had gained control of these resources.

In other respects Colombia's geographic structure created a rather different framework for civil war than in Mexico. Although the national

---

[41] See in particular David Sowell, *The Early Colombian Labor Movement: Artisans and Politics in Bogotá, 1832–1919* (Philadelphia, 1992). See also Carmen Escobar Rodríguez, *La revolución liberal y la protesta del artesanado* (Bogotá, 1990)

[42] José Escorcia, *Sociedad y economía en el Valle del Cauca*, vol. 3: *Desarrollo político, social y económico, 1800–1854* (Bogotá, 1983).

[43] Deas, 'Ricardo Gaitán Obeso'.

capital may have been the chief goal, civil wars in Colombia reflected the fragmentation of the country's terrain by its two principal cordilleras (the central and eastern) and by the distance of the Caribbean coast from the Andean population centres. In the case of Colombia, furthermore, seizure of the national capital did not necessarily mean that victory had been won. In the case of Venezuela, Robert P. Matthews has suggested the political importance (in the nineteenth century) of the fact that the Venezuelan llanos impinge so closely on the central valleys.[44] This meant that the llanos had a much greater impact in Venezuelan civil wars (and thus in Venezuelan politics) than was the case in Colombia, where the llanos are separated physically from the capital and other highland population centres. There were also some standard geographical patterns in internal conflicts in Peru and Chile. In Peru the perennial contest was between the south (Cuzco and Arequipa) and the centre-north. In Chile the northern mining region and the south were the marginal areas, in the former case of growing importance, challenging the dominant centre. Brazil's far-flung expanse, and lack of territorial connection across large parts of that expanse, surely helped to keep its nineteenth-century conflicts more regionally specific. Undoubtedly similar meditations upon the connection between geographic structure and the structure of internal conflict might be made with regard to other countries. But topography was hardly the only factor shaping the forms of civil war. Change over time — in institutions and technologies — altered the face of internal war. In Mexico in the decades before 1850, units of its national army provided the bases of support for many early coups d'état. After mid-century, partly because of the destruction of the national army by the Mexican War, the War of the Reforma and the French interventions, and because of the development of provincial National Guard units which played important roles in the two latter conflicts, military power became more fragmented and regionalised, not to be recovered by central authority until well into the Porfirian regime. Thus, whereas politically effective use of military force tended to occur more at the centre from the 1820s to the 1840s, from the 1850s into the 1870s effective military challenges tended to come from more distant regions, particularly, of course, from Oaxaca.

A comparison of the civil war in Antioquia 1840–41 as depicted by María Martínez de Nisser and the radical rebellion of 1885 as described by Malcolm Deas reveals much about how the conditions of war had changed over a period of more than 40 years. In 1840–41 in the rugged terrain of Antioquia the whole process moved at a languorous pace. No one in Martínez de Nisser's hometown of Sonsón had much of an idea of what was going on in other parts of Antioquia, not to speak of other parts of the republic. In the slow-moving drama of Antioquia in 1840–41, individual spies

---

[44] Robert Paul Matthews, *Violencia rural en Venezuela, 1840–1858: antecedentes socio-económicos de la Guerra Federal* (Caracas, 1977), p. 61.

moving by horseback were the chief sources of information and there was space for uncommitted men to teeter back and forth between the contending sides, and time for tentative negotiations. Firearms were scarce, and at the battle of Salamina the victorious side had only two packets of powder for each muzzle-loaded weapon. Many were armed only with lances. By contrast, the campaign of Ricardo Gaitán Obeso, in the quite different geographical context of the Magdalena Valley, moved with relative rapidity. Beginning with eight or ten men, he quickly recruited about 200, and soon as many as 2,500. With the telegraph now in place, information travelled instantaneously and troops were transported more rapidly on steamboats along the Magdalena. In an era of expanded foreign trade, larger financial resources were much more readily seized. And although Gaitán Obeso, like other civil warriors before him, had more men than arms, the latter could be obtained more readily by sending agents with seized funds to New York. Civil war was showing some signs of 'progress'.

By way of conclusion

This overview of internal conflicts in nineteenth-century Latin America highlights some possible categories of analysis. It makes some sweeping generalisations with which some readers may well disagree. It suggests that economic factors may well provide a context for conflict and that differing geographic structures and changing technologies inevitably shape their forms. In the end, however, it emphasises variety and multiplicity in the region's internal wars. By emphasising the varying types of dominant themes in civil wars, the typology erected at the start of this chapter tends to give an oversimplified view of these conflicts, which generally had locally varying motives and purposes. More than generalisation, we need above all more exploration of the local features of the societies that underlay politics and civil conflict.

CHAPTER 2

The Origins of Revolution
in Nineteenth-Century Argentina*

Carlos Malamud

Why ... do oppositional movements in the Argentine Republic adopt this
purely negative attitude? Why do they find themselves reduced to this
opposition which tends to overthrow authorities by violent means, using
inflamed propaganda, and why do they abandon all legal avenues for
changing authority structures via the peaceful exercise of citizens' rights?[1]

Between 1810 and 1905 Argentina was plagued by revolution. It began
with the famous May Revolution, the beginning of the process of Independence, and ended with the last great Radical Party riot, prior to the
electoral triumph of Hipólito Yrigoyen in 1916. The tumultuous years
which saw the formation of the first national governments were to be
marked by numerous confrontations. The conflict between the River Plate
colonies and the former Spanish metropolis was but one example of this.
Although at times it constituted the most significant confrontation, it was
never the only one. The process that gave rise to the formation of modern
Argentina, after confrontations between various national projects, was accompanied by the violent secession of Paraguay, Upper Perú (later Bolivia) and the Banda Oriental (later Uruguay) under Artigas. The clashes
between *criollos* and *peninsulares* (or between patriots and monarchists)
were followed by confrontation between federalists and unitarians, in
which the role to be played by Buenos Aires in the nation under construction was subject to constant redefinition. Whilst the figure of
Facundo defines this process in a mythical way,[2] one must turn to other
caudillos, such as Felipe Varela or *Chacho* Peñaloza, in order to understand more clearly the clashes between 'civilisation and barbarism', which
in many places was settled by the intervention of the national army.

On the other hand, from the second half of the nineteenth century
until the first decade of the twentieth, it became common to associate
elections with electoral fraud, violence and coercion, a combination that
became glaringly apparent for many contemporary observers from 1874
onwards. That year, after losing the presidential elections, Bartolomé

* Translated by David Passingham. I am grateful for the comments of Eduardo Posada-
Carbó, Malcolm Deas and Darío Roldán. This chapter forms part of research project
PB97-0080 financed by the Spanish Ministerio de Educación y Cultura.
[1] Carlos Pellegrini, 'Discurso del proyecto de levantamiento del estado de sitio', July 1901,
in Carlos Pellegrini, *Discursos y escritos* (Buenos Aires, 1959), p. xx.
[2] See, for example, Noemí Goldman and Ricardo Salvatore (eds.), *Caudillos rioplatenses.
Nuevas miradas a un viejo problema* (Buenos Aires, 1998). The title notwithstanding,
some of the articles, such as those by Maristella Svampa or Jorge Myers, continue to interpret and reinterpret Facundo, leaving little room to further our knowledge of *caudillismo*.

Mitre, head of the Partido Nacionalista, announced shortly before heading a revolt: 'In the name of patriotism the worst outcome from a legal vote is worth more than the best revolution.'[3] The end of the century brought the Radical Party revolutions of 1890 and 1893, which illustrated the changes in revolutionary customs and practices, starting with the repression meted out by those in power.

This rapid overview of nineteenth-century violence in Argentina alerts us to the enormous diversity of causes lying behind the outbreak of uprisings, revolutions and *pronunciamientos*,[4] concentrating particularly on their political motivations, or on factors connected with politics, over and above other elements that might have given rise to such movements. Nevertheless, it is still an open discussion as to how far it is possible to speak of civil wars in Argentina, a subject which is outside the scope of the present chapter and which would involve a highly nuanced analysis. One of the main objectives of this chapter, therefore, will be to try to group all these uprisings and putsches according to commonly shared motivations, leaving until a later date a more systematic account of all the revolutions of the period, which could form part of a far-reaching project that would include the creation of a typology for these events.[5] In order to approach these subjects it is necessary to define certain central questions, which to a great extent will go unanswered but which will create the space for deeper analysis, while at the same time serving as a frame for future work. Amongst other questions, we need to ask how revolutions were conceived (i.e. whether they broke existing legal norms), who their leaders and principal participants were, what the role of the military was, in what space (urban or rural) they took place, how they were put down, the conditions under which the inevitable amnesty was granted and the extent to which their impetus may be viewed as anti-system, as it has so often been.[6] Another of the objectives of this chapter is to probe the relationship that existed between revolutions and electoral processes, comparing our findings

---

[3] Bartolomé Mitre, cited in José María Bustillo, 'Estudio preliminar' in Pellegrini, *Discursos y escritos*, p. xxxix.

[4] In chapter 8 Marie-Danielle Demélas-Bohy cites some interesting reflections by José Ortega y Gasset on military *pronunciamientos*, which were a feature of Restoration Spain.

[5] See chapter 1 by Frank Safford and, for the period of Independence, Brian Hamnett, 'Las rebeliones y revoluciones iberoamericanas en la época de la Independencia. Una tentativa de tipología', in François-Xavier Guerra (ed.), *Revoluciones hispánicas. independencias americanas y liberalismo español* (Madrid, 1995). Enrique Florescano has drawn attention to the dangers of confusing this sort of conflict, whose content was much more political, with others more connected with social movements (Enrique Florescano, personal communication).

[6] This occurred, for example, with the movements of 1890 and 1893, both of which were associated with radicalism, or with the revolts staged by certain caudillos, such as Felipe Varela or *Chacho* Peñaloza. In this regard, it might be useful to reconsider the caudillos' revolts in terms of strictly political factors which took into account not only the conflict with the central government but also the struggle for power within each province.

with the views held by politicians and analysts of the period.[7] Here, it is important not to lose sight of the extent of popular participation in both phenomena. We must ask ourselves to what degree those who mobilised on election day were the same people that defended their political factions with arms in hand, as apparently occurred, for example, in the radical revolutions of 1890 and 1893.[8]

Revolutions in Argentine politics

We have already pointed to the fact that the first Argentine revolution was the May Revolution of 1810, which was the direct cause of the establishment of the first Government Junta, which replaced the colonial administration headed by Viceroy Cisneros. This event occurred in the midst of the proliferation of provincial and local juntas throughout the whole of Spanish America between 1808 and 1810, as a result of the Napoleonic invasion of the Iberian Peninsula. The same logic which made it possible to support the development of Spanish liberalism in Cadiz (a process which accelerated after the introduction of the liberal Constitution of 1812), was behind the removal of the traditional colonial authorities. In short, sovereignty had fallen to the people and they, in the exercise of it, began to take decisions about their future. Of course, not all the juntas that were formed in the colonies reacted in the same way, nor had the same success. In any event, taking advantage of the power vacuum that reigned in Spain, they let loose a series of lethargic forces which frequently ended up in mutual collision.[9]

This period saw the simultaneous outbreak of a variety of conflicts, many of which were ultimately resolved by violent means. Such was the case with the confrontation between the supporters of the colonial authorities and those who opposed them. The Jacobinism of the first revolutionary government was able to nip in the bud some attempts at rebellion against the new order, as occurred with Santiago de Liniers and Martín de Alzaga. Other efforts were less successful, as was the case with the expeditions sent to Asunción del Paraguay and Upper Peru. New centrifugal movements rapidly broke out, behind which lay different national projects, each posing alternatives to the hegemony of Buenos Aires. Though some provinces of the former viceroyalty of Río de la Plata voted to recognise the provisional governing junta, others, such as Montevideo, Paraguay, Charcas, Córdoba

---

[7] The study by Eduardo Posada-Carbó, 'Elections and Civil Wars in Nineteenth Century Colombia: The 1875 Presidential Campaign', *Journal of Latin American Studies*, vol. 26, no. 3 (1994) establishes clearly the relationship between elections and civil war.

[8] For an earlier period, see Hilda Sábato, *La política en las calles. Entre el voto y la movilización. Buenos Aires, 1862–1880* (Buenos Aires, 1998).

[9] The case of Cuzco is extremely interesting. See Victor Peralta, 'Elecciones, constitucionalismo y revolución en el Cusco, 1809–1815', in Carlos Malamud (ed.), *Partidos políticos y elecciones en América Latina y la Península Ibérica, 1830–1930*, vol. 1 (Madrid, 1995).

and Salta, backed the Council of Regency.[10] Regardless, what rapidly came into play with the winning of independence was, in the view of Frank Safford, a process of political consolidation.[11]

José Carlos Chiaramonte has offered a very interesting and innovative theory which explains some of the principal confrontations that took place in Argentina from 1820 onwards and which is linked to the ideas developed by Safford. Chiaramonte begins by considering the various Argentine 'provinces' as independent states which 'will gradually come to be understood as subject to international law'. Within this framework we can situate many of the conflicts that developed between 1820 and 1853, when the constitution that officially gave birth to modern Argentina was approved:

> After Independence the construction of new Latin American states was still an undefined affair and ... therefore, the political nature of what were termed the River Plate *provinces* was ... open to diverse possibilities. One ... to turn themselves into independent states. Another ... to integrate within a larger State that would include them. And within the latter case, [there were] also different options, given that a great part of what we traditionally tend to consider as federalist tendencies consisted of ... *confederate* politics, if not simply a politics of *leagues* or *alliances*: a kind of politics through which the so-called *provinces* acted as independent sovereign states. And what impedes a better analysis of the question being developed is ... the persistent mistake of referring to the caudillos and other political figures of the period as *federalists*.[12]

The last Argentine revolutions of the nineteenth century were those of 1890 and 1893, which, together with the revolution of 1905 form a radical revolutionary trilogy. However, they were not the only ones to occur that century. In the second half of the nineteenth century there were other movements in the provinces and we must look for the way in which electoral processes and revolutionary explosions were connected. When there was not enough mobilising capacity to achieve sufficient votes to win an election, it was possible to resort to armed conflict, but for such an undertaking it was necessary to have enough weapons and money, or, failing that, to count on substantial support from the military, so as to be able to impose by force that which it had not been possible, or it was felt not to be possible, to win through the ballot-box. It was also essential to be convinced that the revolution could modify the political situation or impasse of the moment

---

[10] For a good synthesis of the civil wars in the River Plate area, see Jaime Rodríguez O., *La independencia de la América española* (México, 1996), pp. 149–65. Chapter 2 of Rodríguez's work offers an interesting description of the 'revolution in the Spanish world'. On the same subject see also François-Xavier Guerra, 'Lógicas y ritmos de las revoluciones hispánicas', in Guerra, *Revoluciones hispánicas*.

[11] See chapter 1.

[12] José Carlos Chiaramonte, 'Provincias o estados?: Los orígenes del federalismo rioplatense', in Guerra, *Revoluciones hispánicas*, p. 193. Also see José Carlos Chiaramonte, 'El federalismo argentino en la primera mitad del siglo XIX', in Marcello Carmagnani (ed.), *Federalismos latinoamericanos: México/Brasil/Argentina* (México, 1993). It would be useful to see how far these proposals, which are much easier to verify in the territories that were linked to the Viceroyalty of the River Plate, can be applied to other regions such as New Granada.

and that if the legal framework did not change, then the authorities, using all means at their disposal, would stop the opposition gaining power. The situation became more serious as provincial governors in Argentina did not have the power to dissolve Congress and call early elections, thereby reconstituting the political balance of power.[13]

One reason for the recurrence of revolutions and other similar movements throughout practically the whole of the nineteenth century was that the political and material cost facing rebels was usually not very high. Thus, a central object of this study is the magnitude of repression, which was determined not only by the strength of the rebels, but also by the size of the national army (or militias) and other forces of repression and by the capacity of the authorities to anticipate these rebellions. Despite its weakness, the value of military intelligence was important and on more than one occasion the plans of the revolutionaries were thwarted, or postponed, because the government was aware of the date set for revolt. In this regard, questions such as the following would seem to be of relevance: What did the establishment of a 'state of siege' mean? How many troops were mobilised? How many casualties occurred? What was the extent of the material damage? How many revolutionaries ended up in prison, either on remand or following conviction? How many were obliged to leave the country or go into exile, and, most importantly, for what length of time? How many years usually elapsed before the victors granted an amnesty to the losers, thereby letting things return to normal and grievances be forgotten? How did revolutions affect daily life at a local level?

One of the elements that perhaps favoured the continuity of armed movements of this kind may have been the low cost involved for defeated participants, in terms of both prison sentences and human losses, although on this last point we must consider the number of losses in proportion to the forces that were actually mobilised. For the revolutions of the 1890s we have access only to fractional data that does not allow an overall picture of the magnitude of post-revolutionary repression. In Buenos Aires in July 1890 revolutionary losses totalled 23 dead and 180 wounded. In 1891, there was a revolt by *cívicos* in Córdoba that left 28 dead and 171 wounded. In July 1893, the radical movement formed a revolutionary junta in San Luis, after a confrontation that caused four deaths. That same month, in Santa Fe, the governor resigned after fierce fighting that left more than 100 dead. In Buenos Aires province, the radicals mobilised 8,000 men and formed a provisional government. In September 1893, new revolutions broke out, first in Tucumán and later in Santa Fe.[14] The repression meted out by troops sent from Buenos Aires and Entre Ríos was very harsh, particularly in the provincial capital, Santa Fe, and in Rosario, the two principal revolu-

---

[13] José Nicolás Matienzo, *El régimen republicano-federal* (Buenos Aires [1910] 1994), p. 148.
[14] Natalio Botana, *El orden conservador. La política argentina entre 1880 y 1916* (Buenos Aires, 1977), pp. 169–70.

tionary foci. Official dispatches stated that in the city of Santa Fe there were 100 causalities, both dead and wounded, although according to Red Cross sources there were 50 dead and 150 wounded. At any rate, the number of victims was far higher than in July.[15]

On the subject of repression and despite differences, there is a certain continuity between the uprisings of 1853 and 1880 and later radical revolts. In June 1868, Senator Nicasio Oroño stated that in the previous six years 117 revolutions and uprisings had taken place and that in the 91 battles recorded, the number of dead totalled 4,728.[16] In Santa Fe, for instance, six revolutions broke out between 1852 and 1870 (one in 1852, two in 1856, and one each in 1857, 1859 and 1867), in three of which the governor was removed from office.[17] In Santiago del Estero, two revolutions triumphed in 1851 and 1860, both of them led by Manuel Taboada. In fact, the Taboada family controlled the province between 1851 and 1875, except for a brief interval. In 1860 the governor was ousted with the support of the legislative body, which approved his removal. In Tucumán, where between 1852 and 1867 the Posse family held power, three more revolutions took place: in 1853, 1861 and 1867. The latter actually put an end to the reigning nepotism and arbitrary practices.[18] In 1872, in Entre Ríos, the rebellion of López Jordán was put down with ferocity. That same year there was some dissension in Corrientes, after 'elections whose legitimacy was questionable'. Sarmiento refused to intervene in the province and his attitude favoured the revolutionaries and prolonged the conflict.[19] Once again we see the importance of the executive in national political life, not only because of its great electoral weight or through its federal interventions, but because its decision to lend support or to hold back in a provincial conflict could swing the balance of the outcome in one direction or the other.

Another factor to take into account is the participation of the military in Argentine political life, something that was fairly common during much of the nineteenth century.[20] Among its main supporters each party was able to

---

[15] R. Etchepareborda, *Homenaje al Dr. Lisandro de la Torre. Las revoluciones de 1893 en la provincia de Santa Fe y Lisandro de la Torre* (Buenos Aires, 1959), pp. 10–11. These questions are discussed in detail in Carlos Malamud, 'La restauración del orden: represión y amnistía en las revoluciones argentinas de 1890 y 1893', in Eduardo Posada-Carbó (ed.), *In Search of a New Order: Essays on the Politics and Society of Nineteenth-Century Latin America* (London, 1998).

[16] Nicasio Oroño, cited in Botana, *El orden conservador*, p. 38 (itself cited in Matienzo, *El régimen republicano-federal*, p. 302.) On average there were 52 deaths per battle or 40 per revolution, though if the two or three battles with the highest casualities were left out these averages would be significantly lower. Moreover, it would be necessary to check the validity of the figures offered by Oroño.

[17] Ezequiel Gallo, *La pampa gringa. La colonización agrícola en Santa Fe (1870–1895)* (Buenos Aires, 1984), p. 43.

[18] Matienzo, *El régimen republicano-federal*, pp. 144–6.

[19] Rosendo Fraga, *El General Justo* (Buenos Aires, 1993), p. 22.

[20] Unfortunately there are no good studies of the nineteenth century military, either for Argentina in particular or Latin America in general. We know little about the degree of

count upon military men favourable to their positions, which became a factor of such influence in political negotiations that President Sarmiento drafted a bill to stop the military from interfering in elections, although in the end it was not passed. Moreover, until 1877 it was necessary to have served in the National Guard in order to vote, since, as part of the procedure, one had to present a ballot paper signed by the commander of the local garrison. This gave the officers of the Guard substantial power when it came to organising the voters and controlling the election process.[21]

The presidential elections of 1874 and 1880 are two clear examples of the relation between armed movements and elections, since on both occasions those who were defeated at the polls organised revolutionary uprisings with the objective of reversing the electoral results. In 1874, Nicolás Avellaneda, backed by the Partido Nacional and Adolfo Alsina's Partido Autonomista, defeated Bartolomé Mitre and his Partido Nacionalista in a stormy and extremely controversial election. Among the numerous scandals associated with the election was the fact that the president of Bolivia turned up in San Justo to vote. When the results of Mitre's electoral defeat became known, the newspapers favourable to him began to speak of 'revolution as a means of redress', and the revolutionary harangues became more shrill after Congress recognised the credentials of the deputies elected in the province of Buenos Aires and belonging to the 'electoral committee', amongst whose numbers were Carlos Pellegrini and Bernardo de Irigoyen. Even José C. Paz, director of *La Prensa* and one of the candidates of the defeated 'Club Nacional', recorded in his paper's editorial on 24 September 1874 that he would exchange his pen for the sword.[22] The subsequent rebellion staged by the pro-Mitre movement, which included navy forces, was defeated by the national army under the command of Colonels Roca and Arias.[23]

For Carlos Pellegrini, who would later succeed Juárez Celman as president of the republic, the revolution of 1874 constituted a real watershed, as it introduced a series of practices that directly attacked the foundations of democracy, and in later years he identified that revolution as the cause of all the others. According to Pellegrini, the negative state of affairs that characterised Argentinean politics at the turn of the century:

> springs from the most blameworthy of all the revolutions that have taken place in the republic, that of '74. That revolution came to destroy the political education of this people who had advanced so much under the administration of General Sarmiento. It managed to destroy all the electoral practices that had taken root during that government. And, coming immediately after the most popular, and the most legitimate election in

---

professionalisation, the routes to a career in the militia, the stability of the officers and the troops, the types of contract that existed, the recruiting mechanisms, the number of forces or the technical and material resources.

[21] Sábato, *La política en las calles*, pp. 133–4.

[22] Bustillo, 'Estudio preliminar', pp. xxxiv–xxxvii.

[23] Isidoro Ruíz Moreno, *La Marina revolucionaria, 1874–1963* (Buenos Aires, 1998).

which the whole republic had taken part, in which the real opinions of the majority of the republic had triumphed, that revolution undid all that had been done. It disorganised parliaments, it destroyed parties and made Dr Avellaneda's government initiate its period in office with a now famous victory in the field of arms, or in other words, as a government based on force or which was 'de facto', as it was called in those days.[24]

Instability continued to reign, and in 1877 there were revolutionary attempts in Jujuy, San Juan, Salta and Santa Fe, in 1878 in Catamarca, Corrientes and San Juan and in 1879 in Córdoba. All except Corrientes failed to conquer provincial power or to capture positions for the presidential elections of 1880. That year General Roca, the candidate of the Partido Autonomista Nacional, took over from Carlos Tejedor, the governor of Buenos Aires. After his defeat, Tejedor rebelled against the national government, justifying his action as a defence of the capital status of Buenos Aires within the Republic. On 2 June 1880 the first armed incident took place and hostilities broke out on 17 June 1880. The conflict concluded with the federalisation of the city of Buenos Aires, which was separated off from the province of the same name.

In other cases, there was a combination of a political trial of the governor (or an attempt at one) and sedition, as happened with the governor of Santiago del Estero in 1884. A revolt drove him from government, after which he was officially removed from office through a political trial. Power passed into the hands of the vice-governor, a supporter of Juárez Celman who would be elected president of the republic two years later.[25]

The low price to be paid for taking up arms is also borne out by the fact that only on rare occasions, and for very well justified reasons, were any of the rebel leaders executed. One of these cases occurred in San Juan after the revolution of 16 November 1860, when the rebels murdered Governor Virasoro in his own house in front of his wife. The victorious Liberal Party named Dr Antonio Aberastain as the new governor. On 25 November 1860 the national government gave the order for federal intervention and on 11 January 1861 the national forces prevailed over the revolutionaries in a 'bloody battle' in Rinconada del Pocito and on the following day shot Aberastain. On this occasion, the execution was not only a clear reply to the assassination perpetrated by the rebels, but also constituted a warning to any who might in the future consider embarking on similar adventures, as it established as doctrine that the national government would not recognise provincial governments that emerged as a result of assassination.[26] At the end of September 1874 General Iwanowski was killed whilst resisting arrest by a rebel group loyal to General Arredondo.[27] Nevertheless, in events of this nature it was unusual for members

---

[24] Carlos Pellegrini, 'Discusión (en el Congreso) del proyecto de levantamiento del estado de sitio' (vii/1901), in *Discursos y escritos*, p. 158.
[25] Matienzo, *El régimen republicano-federal*, p. 164. Matienzo speaks of 'a sham political trial'.
[26] *Ibid.*, pp. 172–3, 176.
[27] Ruíz Moreno, *La Marina revolucionaria*, p. 34.

of the army high command to die. In this, and in other similar cases, it was expedient to establish clearly both the rules of the game and its limits, in order to avoid possible misunderstandings.

Electoral fraud and revolution

In the political discourse of the period, electoral fraud tended to be seen as a way for those in positions of power to subvert the political will of the electorate, although its real aim concerned the popular mobilisation that made it possible to attain victory in the elections. In reality, electoral fraud, practised by all sides although denounced only by the losers, was but one step within an extended process of electoral violence. During the elections, confrontation (political, verbal and sometimes physical) characterised the relations between the authorities and the opposition, and also conditioned the behaviour of winners and losers. For this reason it is appropriate to link Latin American revolutions and civil wars with electoral processes.

The losers frequently wished to impose, through the use of arms, the victorious results that were supposedly snatched from them at the polls through electoral fraud or other irregularities. On other occasions, revolution or civil war prevented the holding of elections that were tainted even before they were held by corruption and illegality, and whose results were widely anticipated, or they served to eliminate electoral reforms aimed at changing the rules of the game and stopping certain political options from gaining power. At the same time, revolutions and civil wars that were bound closely to specific elections did not produce solely negative effects; they also reinforced the population's sense of political identity and partisan loyalty, based on fidelity to party colours and the patronage system. For this reason, it is important to consider the extent to which revolutions were the initiative of national opposition leaders, or whether they were forced into armed conflict by pressure from local leaders, who were far more undisciplined and had a much more rudimentary grasp of the information available for taking decisions.[28]

Carlos Pellegrini, in speaking of 'what is called "the right to revolt"', established a clear connection between revolution and electoral fraud:

> I will be told that if I condemn revolution I should condemn electoral fraud as well. I do not need to ask the parties who has the right to cast the first stone, for me to be able to wrench that condemnation from the depths of my soul, and I am only sorry that it is not enough to wipe from our brow that original sin born of the same human frailty. A little penitence is all that is needed to return the rights stolen away through electoral fraud, but all the power and all the penitence of the revolutionaries is insufficient to return to their homes the sons, fathers and husbands sac-

---

[28] This seems to have been the case in nineteenth century Colombia, where provincial leaders took action based almost exclusively on the consolidated interests of their supporters in their own particular region. See Malcolm Deas, 'Pobreza, guerra civil y política: Ricardo Gaitán Obeso y su campaña en el río Magdalena en Colombia, 1885', in Malcolm Deas, *Del poder y la gramática y otros ensayos sobre historia, política y literatura colombianas* (Bogotá, 1993), p. 156.

rificed on the inglorious fields of civil war; it is insufficient to return to the
country either the credit that has been lost, or the treasures of the nation
that were squandered in such a sterile fashion.[29]

Time and again revolution was stirred up as a reaction to electoral fraud
or to authorities clinging violently to power. This situation was encouraged by the constitutional mechanism that established that the final rati-
fication of electoral results was the prerogative of the very bodies whose
membership was being determined by the election. In the words of
Matienzo, 'each house, both at national and provincial level, is the exclusive adjudicator in the election of its own members'. The system became
even more complicated through the partial way in which the national
parliament and the provincial legislatures were renewed. One half of the
National Congress was re-elected every two years whilst each third of the
Senate went through this process every three years. But in Buenos Aires
province, for example, one half of the Chamber of Deputies was re-
elected every two years, while one third of the Senate was renewed on a
yearly basis. This meant that those who arbitrated in the elections were
the old deputies, who were not up for election and who had in their
hands the means to veto acceptance of the new parliamentarians.[30] Elections, therefore, not only constituted an element that legitimised governments elected through the ballot-box, but also sometimes became the
lever that activated the mechanism of revolution, justified because of
electoral fraud. Juan Alvarez said that 'civil war has been used among us
at times as a means of reacting speedily against legislation which either
could not be modified by vote, or where there was not the general will to
do so'.[31] When faced with such powerful grounds for action there were
always volunteers ready to sacrifice themselves on behalf of the nation.
Agustín P. Justo senior wrote:

> I have faith and am ready to lay down my life if the flag of national revo-
> lution is hoisted against power born of electoral fraud and maintained by
> violence, whether that power be national or provincial, for both are ene-
> mies of popular freedom and are the cynical thieves who deprive us of
> our national rights and political guarantees.[32]

The 1821 Constitution of the Province of Buenos Aires recognised universal male suffrage, which was also included in the National Constitution of
1853. After the passing of the first national electoral law in 1857, the principle of not introducing restrictions to the right to vote was maintained,
the only limitation being the establishment of a minimum voting age,

---

[29] Carlos Pellegrini, cited in Bustillo, 'Estudio preliminar', p. xxxviii–xxxix.

[30] Matienzo, *El régimen republicano-federal*, pp. 158–9.

[31] Juan Alvarez, *Las guerras civiles argentinas y el problema de Buenos Aires en la
República* (Buenos Aires, 1936), p. 5. Alvarez even observed that the revolutionaries of
1810 did try to modify 'the royal legislation' and that 'deprived of the right to legislate,
they recurred to force as a means, not as an end'.

[32] Agustín P. Justo senior to Colonel Vera, 21 November 1875, quoted in Fraga, *El
General Justo*, p. 24.

which varied over the subsequent decades.[33] Nevertheless, and in spite of the absence of other restrictions, all presidents acknowledged that electoral fraud or violence prevented the system from reaching complete maturity. According to Pellegrini, throughout the second half of the nineteenth century 'in practice, the exercise of free suffrage for all electors' was unknown. For Alvarez, an important mitigating factor was the population's lack of education, since, according to the census of 1869, only one out of every six theoretical voters could read and write, and in 1904 this was still true of half the electorate. This posed a dangerous dilemma: 'either to hand the government over to political incompetents, or to govern the country in disregard of the majority'. In addition there existed the problem of representing minorities, something that was not resolved until 1902. Until then, minorities who found themselves in disagreement with the government 'had no escape valve other than revolution, finding themselves in a similar situation to the majorities who were repeatedly expelled from the centres of power'.[34]

The legitimacy of governments elected by ballot is a basic theme in the majority of electoral reforms. This discussion is linked to the greater or lesser centrality of elections in the political systems involved, beyond the question of fraudulent practices that might call them into question. The legitimacy of power, closely linked to the question of legality, whether that in force at the time or that considered desirable to introduce, was a central question within the polemic about electoral reform. It is no surprise that, in 1902, dealing with electoral reform in parliament, Joaquín V. González should have remarked: 'there can be no doubt that we are dealing with the single most important question which can arise in the political life of our country. Electoral law is the basis of the existence of the constitution; it is the very life-blood of a republican regime based on popular representation.'[35] González attempted to prevent the explosion of new revolutionary outbreaks, because of their powerful destabilising component. Since the passing of the National Constitution in 1853, there had been three substantial revolutions (1860, 1874 and 1890), and they shook the regime to its foundations. From the revolutionary perspective, they were justified reactions to injustice and the abuse of political power, identified with electoral fraud.[36] If the objective was to stop the revolutionary commotion and global questioning that destabilised the political system, it was necessary to end once and

---

[33] The laws of 1857 and 1859 established a voting age of 21 years. In 1863 it was lowered to 18; in 1873 and 1877 it was further lowered to 17 and in subsequent laws the voting age returned to 18.

[34] Alvarez, *Las guerras civiles*, pp. 138–9.

[35] Joaquín V. González, *Obras Completas*, vol. 6 (Buenos Aires, 1935), p. 87.

[36] The relationship between the revolutions of the second half of the nineteenth century ('national' ones, such as have been described here, or provincial ones) and electoral processes needs further probing. Historians ought to explore the relationship between civil unrest and both elections that had already taken place and those shortly to be held. See Malamud, 'La restauración del orden'.

for all the recurrent uprisings, whatever their political colouring. For González, revolutions were to be avoided at all costs and the means had to be electoral reform. That is why he wondered:

> Has the period of revolutions ended in our country? They may be over for a matter of years, for a period of larger or shorter duration; but ... whilst we do not get the system right and establish an electoral regime that is secure enough to give real expression to the popular will and effective representation to all the movements that fire the people and the different interest groups that are active in Argentinean society, I do not believe there can exist a man of state able to state categorically that the era of revolutions is over.[37]

Federal intervention, justice and amnesty

In Argentina we find two mechanisms at the disposition of the national government that directly affected the political situation: the state of siege and federal intervention. Intervention made it possible to modify the rules of the game and alter the correlation of forces that shaped the majorities and minorities on which the formation of governments and legislatures depended. It was a mechanism contained in Article 6 of the Constitution of 1853/1860,[38] which could affect the three provincial powers, depending on the will of the executive or the National Congress. The possibility of replacing the provincial governor through federal intervention opened the doors to the removal from office of *jueces de paz, comisarios de policía, jefes políticos, intendentes* and holders of other provincial posts, generally at a local level, who were key to the functioning of the electoral 'machine', putting in their place men who could be relied upon and modifying the existing political balance of power.

In the view of Juan Alvarez, federal intervention had produced 'the *simulation* of civil war', a source of 'perpetual discredit' to the federal system.[39] It was thus not unusual for oppositional forces in the provinces to ask for the president's aid to 'depose the governor of the province or

---

[37] González, 'La reforma electoral de 1912', in *Jurisprudencia y política* (Buenos Aires, 1914), libro II, *Obras Completas*, vol. 11, p. 131, cited in Darío Roldán, *Joaquín V. González y el pensamiento político liberal en Argentina* (Buenos Aires, 1993), pp. 48–9. In fact González was not mistaken, since the reform that was passed in 1902 was suspended after the elections of 1904 and in 1905 a new radical putsch took place.

[38] Article 6 of the 1853 Constitution states: 'The federal government intervenes by requisitioning the powers of the provincial legislatures or governments or, without doing so, by entering onto the territory of any of the provinces, with the sole aim of re-establishing public order when there has been a breach of the peace through sedition, or of protecting national security when it is threatened by attack or in danger of outside intervention'. The reform of 1860 modified the text in the following way: 'The federal government intervenes on provincial territory to guarantee the republican form of government, or to repel invasion from outside, and requisitions the powers of the established authorities, with the aim of either upholding them or restoring them, should they have been deposed as a result of sedition or invasion from another province'.

[39] Alvarez, *Las guerras civiles*, p. 50.

subject him to their will', or for certain revolutions to be connected, simultaneously, with the sending of federal forces to intervene, or with the desire that they be sent. In these cases, the direct objective of the revolution might be not so much to remove the provincial government from office (for which end there were not always sufficient forces and weapons available), as to generate a state of affairs that could end up justifying federal intervention. The permanence in office of certain governors affected provincial and national political life. The governors were key figures in the presidential elections, giving their support to certain candidates and guaranteeing their election. Candidates who did not have the backing of certain provinces and had the support of the National Executive, could attempt to replace governors hostile to them with men inclined towards their cause.

In Argentina, governors did not have the power to dissolve the provincial chambers, although on certain occasions the need for dissolution was so pressing that it tended to be brought about by the indirect route of national intervention. The procedure was to attract the attention of the federal government by means of a dispute of some seriousness or by armed revolution. As the most suitable recourse for re-establishing order or so that the *interventor* could more comfortably carry out his task, the government would then dissolve the legislative body.[40]

Eduardo Zimmermann has emphasised the enormous extent of the financial crisis and scarcity of human resources experienced by the Argentine judiciary between 1860 and 1880, and the resulting repercussions when they attempted to enforce the law.[41] He has concentrated on the example of the federal judiciary, whose powers related to 'crimes against the internal security of the nation'. This lack of resources meant not only that there were great difficulties in reaching verdicts, but also that it was equally difficult to apply the sentences and punish the guilty. Thus, the slow pace of justice and the failure to try those accused began to create a climate of impunity and attitudes favourable towards amnesty.[42] To this must be added the fact that prison sentences for those who rose up against the national government were not contemplated in the legislation of the day. Punishment consisted only of enforced exile, the carrying out of military service on the border, or fines.

Aside from the victims, for most revolutionaries the conflict would be settled sooner or later with a broad amnesty. General Mitre and the other military leaders of the revolution of 1874 were readmitted into the

---

[40] Matienzo, *El régimen republicano-federal,* p. 148. An *interventor federal,* or acting governor, could be appointed by the executive with the approval of the congress.

[41] Eduardo Zimmermann, 'El Poder Judicial, la construcción del estado y el federalismo: Argentina, 1860–1880', in Posada-Carbó (ed.), *In Search of a New Order,* pp. 140–5. See also Eduardo Zimmermann (ed.), *Judicial Institutions in Nineteenth-Century Latin America* (London, 1999).

[42] Alvarez shows that 'the repetition of the procedure allows us to understand better why amnesty followed each revolution in our society'. See Alvarez, *Las guerras civiles,* p. 6.

armed forces three years later, within the framework of a wide amnesty decreed by President Avellaneda and his minister Alsina.[43] The argument brandished by Joaquín V. González in relation to this question is forceful, and explains why his opinion of the amnesties was so critical:

> The certainty of amnesty being granted has in many cases provided the main incentive for revolutions in our country. The organisers of mutinies and revolts in the heart of our old army — since political astuteness has availed itself of all these resorts in order to overthrow or set up governments — have been stimulated by their confidence that they will go unpunished, receiving eventual pardon, in the absolute absence of any definitive irreversible punishment for their offence. When all these causes combine to form the public spirit and this situation of listlessness, which is the word that properly describes this organic phenomenon, it is necessary to see what the most effective remedies are for changing this state of morale. The truth is that the people, in the political history of our nation, lacking faith in results from civil action, have become convinced that there is no road for changing established situations other than revolution.[44]

It is obvious that the existing legal and political situation determined where the limits of repression lay and, in particular, what punishment should be meted out to those guilty of the offence of rebellion. As the judiciary managed to consolidate its position and had better and greater resources at its disposal, the nature of the repressive response began to change and the people perceived a hardening in approach. Some of this can be seen in the different approach to the events of 1890 and 1893, even though many of the leaders were the same as on previous occasions.

Juan Alvarez and the 'civil wars'

In 1914 and 1918 Juan Alvarez wrote *Las guerras civiles argentinas* and *El problema de Buenos Aires en la República*. The latter was presented as a continuation of the first work and both titles give us a complete idea of the interpretation that was generally made of the causes which gave rise to the political instability of the nineteenth century, taking shape as it did in a long series of revolutions and civil wars. Discussion of the centralist and federalist models for the country and the dispute around the predominant position of Buenos Aires in Argentina are fundamental to the question, although, after 1880, the date when the city of Buenos Aires became a federality, new explosions were to follow. In the opinion of Alvarez, Buenos Aires had constituted a factor of economic and social imbalance in nineteenth century Argentina, with the senate acting as a counterweight.[45]

---

[43] Ruíz Moreno, *La Marina revolucionaria*, p. 69.

[44] Joaquín V. González, 'La reforma electoral de 1912', in *Jurisprudencia y política*, p. 141.

[45] The Senate, with 'twenty senators from the *interior* and eight from the *litoral* (plus two representing the federal capital once it was established) gave a permanent majority to the interior, capable of stopping any law from being passed with its two thirds of the vote. It was impossible to modify the constitution against the votes of those two thirds and, even less so, under the formula of

This idea was not new. Alberdi himself had expressed similar opinions. For him, there were two causes of the anarchy: on the one hand, the lack of an economically solid central government with sufficient strength to impose its authority on the provincial governors and, on the other hand, the power of Buenos Aires. The latter manifested itself through the port's monopoly of foreign trade and the confiscation by Buenos Aires of the monies collected in customs duties. Despite being a national organism, the Customs Authority was exploited by a single province: 'The Argentine Republic constitutes a singular example of a nation in which three quarters of its inhabitants pay contributions so that they can be enjoyed by the other quarter'.[46]

Alvarez was heavily imbued with positivist ideals and through study of the past was attempting to find the economic elements that could determine when a revolution was going to occur. His intention was to find the correct mechanisms with which to neutralise such occurrences, though he was not unaware of the existence of other motives, such as ideals or the individual factor. At any rate, without intending to give a total explanation of the phenomenon, he focused on the economic causes.[47] Among them, the following stand out: the geographical problem (territory and transportation); regional interests, linked to provincial autonomy; the inadequacy of the government's economic formula, dependent as it was on income from customs; the revolt of the gauchos as a consequence of changes in ranching; protectionism; the loss of value in exports;[48] the value of land; natural disasters;[49] the value of paper money and salaries.[50] In any event, the relationship between economic

---

1853 which gave the senate the exclusive right to initiate reforms. The election of senators lay in the hands of the local legislative bodies'. See Alvarez, *Las guerras civiles*, p. 48.

[46] Alberdi, cited in Jorge Mayer, *Alberdi y su tiempo,* vol. 2, (Buenos Aires, 1963), pp. 811–2.

[47] Alvarez, *Las guerras civiles*, pp. 7–8.

[48] The per capita fall in imports (or their low value) would coincide with moments of revolution. The revolutions of 1874, 1880 and 1890 took place at such conjunctures. The 1893 revolution occurred when a new drop in imports was about to begin, while that of 1905 happened in the middle of the process of recovery of import and export prices. The revolution of 1890 coincided with a bad wheat crop and that of 1893 with poor corn harvests. However, it is difficult to establish a model, since the revolutions of 1890 and 1893 were preceded by a sharp drop in the price of leather, corn and wool (of wheat also in 1893), while in 1905 there was a moment when there were good prices for nearly all articles. See Alvarez, *Las guerras civiles*, plate II (between pp. 106–7), plate III (between pp. 108–9) and p. 109.

[49] According to Alvarez, the influence of drought was very important. There was a drought at the time of the *montonera* guerrillas of 1817, during the anarchy of 1819–20, in the civil war of 1828–31 and in the campaign against Rosas of 1851. In 1859, the year of the battle of Cepeda, four million sheep died in the Province of Buenos Aires, through lack of rain. Something similar occurred in 1861 (Battle of Pavón). In 1873–74, immediately before the civil war, drought caused the deaths of 28% of the cattle in intensive grazing pastures. In 1879–80, which saw the conversion of Buenos Aires into federal territory, thereby offering a definitive solution to the longstanding problem of the city's status, drought caused the total loss of the wheat crop; in 1889, bad wheat crop and disaster for the sheep, drought again in 1890 and 1893. See Alvarez, *Las guerras civiles,* pp. 112–3.

[50] On two occasions, 1828–31 and 1890–93, the 'sharp devaluing of paper money immediately preceded the outbreak of civil war'. See Alvarez, *Las guerras civiles*, pp. 121–3.

cycles and revolutions is something that has not been satisfactorily resolved. While some revolutions occur at moments of crisis, when the
population is restless due to scarcity and the fact that access to resources
is more restricted, with other revolutions the opposite is the case. In a
situation of conjectural upturn in the economy, those who feel they
might be excluded from the resultant benefits may be roused to action,
and may come to view insurrection in a favourable light.[51]

'Civil war emanates from forces that have not been properly stud-
ied.'[52] It is principally for this reason that Alvarez ruled out an analysis
that put excessive emphasis on the role of caudillos:

> Because method has been lacking in research, Argentina's past appears as a
> confusing accumulation of moments of violence and disorder, and it is gener-
> ally believed that thousands of men fought and died on our battlefields simply
> because of the affection they felt towards a particular leader, there being no
> cause prepared to act wholeheartedly in their interest, to defend their rights or
> their usual way of life ... Much of the mistake comes from attributing more im-
> portance to the outer appearance of things than to investigating the causes. It is
> as if one were to mistake the detonator for the explosive substance. On nearly
> all occasions there was a military chief or caudillo who acted as the detonator,
> and those who followed him actively took the cause to the highest logical level:
> the revolution, therefore, appears to be the result of the will of the caudillo ...
> The support for the leader is born from the inability of the masses to reform the
> legislation or the state of things that sparks off the explosion: they obey him, as
> they would obey the orders of the doctor to cure a sickness that they cannot
> work out how to fight by themselves. There is room, without a doubt, for the
> man in charge to make his suggestions, and for the affections of the masses to
> run away with them; but these two elements are not on their own sufficient to
> bring about a chronic state of social warfare.[53]

Another element at play was the excessive influence of the army, and the
need to have enough resources available to pay the salaries of the chiefs of
staff, officers and troops. Of course, the soldiers had to put up with the
worst of this, and Alvarez believed that the conditions under which the latter had to serve and their small numbers explained 'why the government
lacked the strength necessary to prevent armed uprisings'. In 1872, of
6,100 regular soldiers, 1,700 had already fulfilled their contract and were
retained by force; recourse was thus made to the national guard, as they
were cheaper than the professional army. 'This feeling of repugnance towards military service is not something that should be underestimated in
men who would voluntarily rush to fight for their caudillo and, in the absence of other evidence, it would seem to show that an excess of bellicosity
was not the main cause of the civil wars suffered by Argentina.'[54]

---

[51] For Colombia, see Deas, 'Pobreza, guerra civil y política', pp. 121–3.

[52] Alvarez, *Las guerras civiles*, p. 6.

[53] Alvarez, *Las guerras civiles*, pp. 4–5.

[54] 'Towards 1825, the army consumed more than one million *pesos fuertes* out of a total
expenditure of 2,292,452 pesos. By 1834 ... the disordered state of public finance was the
exclusive result of the "illegal, excessive, ruinous" expenses incurred by the war budget ...

Nevertheless, despite all his quantitative aspirations, Alvarez devoted the last chapter of *Guerras civiles* to suffrage and state education and thus drew closer to the problematic which most politicians and intellectuals of the period associated with revolutions. The history of suffrage in Argentina began in 1810, although on that occasion the only people to vote were 'certain political cronies' since, according to Alvarez, the 'semibarbarous majorities' were excluded from the elections, as they would have destroyed the undertaking when it first came up for renewal. For the same reasons the 'inhabitants of the country who were sympathetic to the enemy' also found themselves excluded.

The *Cabildo Abierto* that ended colonial government in 1810 was not formed by the majority of the citizens of Buenos Aires, but by 'some hundreds of people invited *ex profeso*'. Of the 450 who were invited, 251 attended and 224 voted, 79 of whom cast their vote for the victorious option. It was that 'illustrious and most healthy' section, linked to the *cabildos*, which elected the town deputies to the first General Congress. 'Once the plan had been adopted in February 1811 for the formation of provincial assemblies through indirect election, the summons was extended to all Spanish *vecinos*; but the circular warned that nobody expressing anti-government ideas should be designated.' After the coup that put an end to the first junta, the second junta was chosen theoretically through universal suffrage, though in practice the *cabildo* of Buenos Aires carried out the appointments by drawing lots.[55] To form the Assembly of Year XIII, the neighbourhood mayors were advised to call on their residents 'who were known to be bonded to the cause of America, not excluding military men, to publicly cast their vote, out loud, in support of people charged with the task of electing deputies who had proved their allegiance to the political regime in power'.[56]

The Constitution of 1826 did not establish universal suffrage, since the *jornaleros* had no vote and, after a certain date, neither did the illiterate. A number of provincial constitutions prior to 1853 denied the vote to farm labourers and workmen and the 1821 *Reglamento Provisorio* of Córdoba required a voter to be in possession of capital amounting to 400 pesos.[57] According to Alvarez it was Rosas, in his message of 1

(and) the entire revenue in 1833 from direct contributions was scarcely enough to defray the costs of a regiment. The army, in theory, should consist ... of 4,500 soldiers and 260 officers ... the real army, with less than 2,400 soldiers, boasted more than 700 officers. Instead of two generals, there were 13; 41 colonels, instead of seven; and 92 lieutenant-colonels, instead of the 17 officially authorised. Wages were not enough, land that was public property had to be distributed among devoted chiefs of staff and officials, and the fight for promotion came to be inseparable from civil war. At the beginning of 1865, right in the middle of internal reorganisation, there were still 30 generals on the books for an army of 8,000 men; and that year, the war with Paraguay once again made it impossible to reduce the numbers of high-ranking staff.' (Alvarez, *Las guerras civiles*, pp. 59–61.)

[55] The discussion concerning the democratic value of drawing lots as applied in primitive Greece is of importance. See Bernard Manin, *The Principles of Representative Government* (Cambridge, 1997).

[56] Alvarez, *Las guerras civiles*, pp. 133–5.

[57] *Ibid.*, p. 136.

January 1837, who laid the bases for the electoral laws that were applied
at that time in the whole country. Rosas said on that occasion:

> Much has been written and spoken among us on the subject of the constitu-
> tional system; but on the subject of elections, as in other areas, practice has
> shown itself to be very far from the most balanced doctrines. All previous gov-
> ernments, when they have interfered in the election of representatives within
> the terms of the law, have been reproached for this as if it were a crime, in their
> case, while their friends have been accused of showing signs of servility. This has
> given rise to a thousand subterfuges and the same corruption. The present
> governor, wishing to remove from our midst those beguiling theories that hy-
> pocrisy has invented, and to firmly establish a permanent legal guarantee for
> those in power, has sent lists to many respectable inhabitants and magistrates
> throughout the entire province. These lists contained the names of those citi-
> zens who, in his opinion, deserved to represent the rights of their nation, his
> intention being that those who received this information should lean towards
> the election of these candidates, if such was their will.[58]

Conclusions

It would not appear to be an overstatement to suggest that revolutions,
military *pronunciamientos* and uprisings were a constant which had an
important influence on Argentine politics in the nineteenth century.
The problem resides, precisely, in attempting to relate these variables in
a clear way. The early inclination of Juan Alvarez, tinged with positivist
influences, to link the civil wars with economic motivations, such as
drought or crop failures, left a very marked impression on later historiography. For a long time this led to precedence being given to social and
economic motivations when analysing these movements, and to confer-
ring on many of them, mistakenly, a clear character of opposition to the
system. Throughout the nineteenth century, these movements were
situated within the logic of the political system and those who participated in them were not excluded when they did not respect the rules of
the game. The ones who ended up on the outside were the losers, but
only for having lost, not for having attacked the logic of the system.

Now, as we have seen throughout this chapter, one of the main motivations of those who opted for these movements was power, understood in its
broadest sense. Insofar as elections had come to constitute a central element
for choosing governments and investing them with legitimacy, that is to say,
for distributing power between the different contending groups, it becomes
necessary to probe more deeply the relationship that existed between the
electoral processes and outbreaks of revolution. A two-pronged approach
could help us, on the one hand, to determine how far elections and their out-
comes, concrete or possible, became the trigger for revolutions and, on the
other, to link the latter to electoral reforms, which means approaching the

---

[58] Rosas, cited in Alvarez, *Las guerras civiles*, pp. 136–7.

problem the other way round. In this way we can enter the interstices of the political system and its mode of functioning, understanding the reforms, or projects for reform, as the desire of the different political actors to neutralise unrest and make the system more accountable. This can be seen clearly, for instance, in the writings of Carlos Pellegrini or Joaquín V. González.

Another concern of this study is related to the recurrence of revolutionary phenomena during the nineteenth century. On this point there is no doubt that the small price to be paid by those involved in armed insurrection guaranteed that revolt happened again and again, though it must not be forgotten that this small price refers to both the human losses among the insurrectionists and the political and penal repercussions that their actions involved. As we have observed, the number of victims in the majority of these revolutions was relatively low in relation to the magnitude of the political phenomena that were taking place, though there were the inevitable exceptions. This circumstance also explains the idealism and romanticism of those who took up arms in defence of their ideals.[59] In a certain sense, it would not be too far removed from reality to suggest a comparison with duels. In a duel one always ran the risk of dying, but in general it was a question of *playing* with death, despite the existence of some unfortunate cases. On the other hand, it was understood that, in general, although this was not always the case, duels, like politics, were a matter for gentlemen.

Nevertheless, we must also consider that the limited repercussions to be borne by participants in these uprisings were reinforced by a shared sensation of the weakness of the state and its repressive apparatus. For this reason, it is increasingly necessary to analyse how the 'forces of order' functioned. That image of weakness, shared by all sides involved, was to favour the recourse to revolution, since according to the rebels' appreciation of things, resistance was not likely to be fierce. Prison and exile were experienced as part of the adventure and the chance of a timely amnesty helped them to cherish the hope that sooner or later all would be forgotten and that even in the worst of cases, most of the military men who had been expelled could, at the proper time, return to ranks. This situation had its roots in a double reality. On the one hand, the judiciary were unable to deal in their entirety with trials relating to the punishment of revolutionaries. On the other hand, the political system itself implied that the authorities of today might be tomorrow's rebels, so there was no point in burning all one's boats when they might be needed in a possibly desperate situation in the future. Just as electoral fraud was practised by all, so revolutions were,

---

[59] Alfredo Alzugarat (ed.), *Desde la otra orilla (documentos inéditos y olvidados de la revolución de 1897)* (Montevideo, 1996) offers numerous examples of personal testimony of this kind. His point of reference is a conflict in Uruguay, but the testimony could be applicable to other cases elsewhere. The following gives us a sample: 'Various batallions that were training in Palermo and Belgrano have already set off. Others have stayed and many of us lads are waiting for the leader I told you about to teach us some discipline and then lead us away, either to die a brave death, or to triumph.' (p. 15).

paradoxically, a weapon within the reach of all the parties that aspired to achieve power by electoral means.

Nevertheless, the situation began to change at the end of the nineteenth century, as new political options appeared on the scene accompanied by the parallel strengthening of the apparatus of the state, which led to a toughening of repression. The emergence of options that were *dangerous* for the governability of the country and public peace, alongside the new international conjuncture, which was marked by an increase in the struggles of the European proletariat and the left in general, together with the outbreak of the First Russian Revolution, meant it was no longer possible to distinguish between good and bad revolutions. From this point on, any armed uprising was potentially dangerous for the system. And it was at this moment that the meaning of the word 'revolution' began to change profoundly in political language and in Argentine political history.

CHAPTER 3

Civil Conflict in Independent Mexico, 1821–57: An Overview

Will Fowler

Introduction[*]

Although a number of studies in early republican Mexico have started to dispel many of the myths and inaccuracies that have been inherited in the historiography over the last 150 years from the biased interpretations of Lucas Alamán and José María Luis Mora,[1] and above all, from the historians of the Porfiriato such as Justo Sierra and Enrique de Olavarría y Ferrari,[2] one issue which has continued to elude any serious attention from scholars is civil conflict.[3] To quote Michael Costeloe, 'An incalculable number of revolts, or *pronunciamientos*, took place ... so many [in fact] that nobody has yet counted them'.[4] Alamán's bold assertion that the first decades of national

---

[*] This chapter was written with financial assistance from the University of St Andrews and the Carnegie Trust for the Universities of Scotland.

[1] For review essays on recent studies on this period see Timothy E. Anna, 'Demystifying Early Nineteenth-Century Mexico', *Mexican Studies/Estudios Mexicanos*, vol. 9, no. 1 (1993), pp. 119–37; Donald F. Stevens, 'Autonomists, Nativists, Republicans, and Monarchists: Conspiracy and Political History in Nineteenth-Century Mexico', *Mexican Studies/Estudios Mexicanos*, vol. 10, no. 1 (1994), pp. 247–66; Barbara A. Tenenbaum, 'Mexico: So Close to the United States: Unconventional Views of the Nineteenth Century', *Latin American Research Review*, vol. 30, no. 1 (1995), pp. 226–35; Will Fowler, 'Introduction: The Forgotten Century, 1810–1910', *Bulletin of Latin American Research*, vol. 15, no. 1 (1996), pp. 1–6. For a bibliographical summary on recent studies on the period also see Linda Arnold, *Política y justicia. La suprema corte mexicana (1824–1855)* (Mexico City, 1996), pp. 11–2.

[2] See Josefina Zoraida Vázquez, 'Los años olvidados', *Mexican Studies/Estudios Mexicanos*, vol. 5, no. 2 (1989), p. 313.

[3] Although a comprehensive study of civil conflict in Mexico for this period is yet to be written, a number of studies have been published on regional and rural conflicts. See Moisés González Navarro, *Raza y tierra: la guerra de casta y el henequén* (Mexico City, 1970); Leticia Reina, *Las rebeliones campesinas en México, 1819–1906* (Mexico City, 1980); John Tutino, *From Insurrection to Revolution in Mexico: Social Bases of Agrarian Violence, 1750–1940* (Princeton, 1986); Friedrich Katz (ed.), *Revuelta, rebelión y revolución: La lucha rural en México del siglo XVI al siglo XX*, 2 vols (Mexico City, 1990); and Jaime E. Rodríguez O. (ed.), *Patterns of Contention in Mexican History* (Wilmington, 1992). An important contribution to the historiography which has provided much of the historical data discussed in this study is Ernesto de la Torre Villar et al. (eds.), *Planes de la nación mexicana* (Mexico City, 1987), 5 vols. An initial chronology of major revolts and *pronunciamientos* for the years 1821–53 can also be found in Will Fowler, *Mexico in the Age of Proposals, 1821–1853* (Westport, CT, 1998), pp. 277–87.

[4] Michael P. Costeloe, *The Central Republic in Mexico, 1835–1846. Hombres de Bien in the Age of Santa Anna* (Cambridge, 1993), pp. 2, 9. (Since Costeloe wrote these lines an initial chronology has been ventured. See note 3.)

life could be defined as one of 'revolutions'[5] and Sierra's Porfirian view that
Mexican history, prior to the establishment of General Díaz's allegedly stable and law-abiding liberal dictatorship, was merely an 'age of chaos',[6] continue to be reiterated in the historiography. However, a closer look at the
nature of the numerous rebellions which took place between the War of Independence (1810–21) and the mid-century War of the Reforma (1858–61)
poses a number of questions which this chapter aims to survey, in the hope
of highlighting: (1) the need for further research into the civil conflicts
which allegedly characterised this period, and (2) the extent to which such
research might in fact show that, with the exception of the Federalist Revolt
of 1832 and the Revolution of Ayutla (1854–55), the majority of revolts,
pronunciamientos and skirmishes which took place between 1821 and 1857
were not as significant as we have been led to believe, either in causing the
instability which has generally been perceived to have been widespread and
endemic in the politics of independent Mexico, or in affecting the everyday
lives of the majority of Mexicans who lived during this period.

This chapter proposes that the majority of revolts were not as important as the historiography has led us to believe, provided the civil
conflict they unleashed is qualified. Such qualification must take into
consideration: (1) the percentage of the population affected by the revolts; (2) the levels of violence these represented, and (3) their impact on
national politics. By 'civil conflict' what is understood here is a particular
kind of political violence that affects the everyday lives of the civilian
population of a particular country. Purely military clashes do not necessarily represent civil conflict, especially when these took place in the
countryside and did not involve direct civilian participation, nor does
the term 'civil conflict' refer to wars with other nations such as Spain,
France or the United States. As will be seen, the nature of military recruitment in nineteenth century Mexico (civilians were, in some cases,
forced to join the regular army) means that it would be artificial to make
a sharp distinction between those conflicts fought exclusively by soldiers
and those that involved civilians. Nevertheless, even when this is taken
into consideration, it remains the case that there were surprisingly few
revolts in early national Mexico that involved large segments of the civilian population, entailed large-scale fighting and had any impact on
national politics. To verify this controversial point, this chapter focuses
on the nature of civil conflict from 1821 to 1857 and then analyses the
different types of civil conflicts that surfaced, namely military, indigenous, regional and agrarian. It considers the issue of banditry as a possible element of civil conflict and concludes by arguing that only the civil
wars of 1832 and 1854–55 truly qualify as civil conflicts. The chapter

---

[5] Lucas Alamán, *Historia de Méjico*, vol. 5 (Mexico City, 1969), p. 434.
[6] Josefina Zoraida Vázquez, 'De la difícil constitución de un estado: México, 1821–1854', in
Josefina Zoraida Vázquez (ed.), *La fundación del estado mexicano, 1821–1855* (Mexico City,
1994), p. 9.

also includes a chronology of major revolts and *pronunciamientos*, which highlights those events that resulted in death-tolls of over 20, which led to a change in government or which were characterised by significant levels of civilian participation.

The nature of civil conflict in Mexico, 1821–1857: a survey

While it cannot be denied that 'military action by ambitious army officers became the normal method of expressing dissent or pursuing policy change',[7] the notion that Mexico was riddled with civil conflict during its early national period begs clarification. This becomes particularly evident if the term *civil* is used to refer to these conflicts, as this implies that the revolts involved a high level of civilian participation. A closer look at the most significant revolts from 1821 to 1857 (see Appendix) illustrates the extent to which the majority were inspired, led and fought by the military without the participation of the civilian population.[8] This fact, which has not been emphasised enough in the historiography, was stated time and again by contemporary politicians who either lamented or expressed relief that the majority of the population appeared to have no interest in the many political revolts which a wide spectrum of military officers orchestrated during these years.[9]

For example, in 1833, the radical Lorenzo de Zavala arrived at the conclusion that if 800 regular troops had in 1829 been able to dominate Yucatán, with a population of up to 700,000 inhabitants, this was because '400,000 degraded Indians do not experience any change in their way of being or lifestyle'. He then went on to lament that the indifference of the masses was inevitable when their situation did not change, regardless of whichever new form of government was promised.[10] Similarly, the *santanista* General José María Tornel came to believe 20 years later that the 'people had remained silent and obeyed, just as they have always obeyed and remained silent, without there having been a single stimulus which could have shaken the cold indifference with which they have seen so

---

[7] Costeloe, *The Central Republic*, p. 2.

[8] The army was not yet a clearly defined, professional institution. The fact that chain gangs were used to recruit unwilling civilians (i.e. Indians) by force to form the rank and file of the troops does beg the question of whether it is artificial to distinguish between strictly military conflicts and civil conflicts for this period. See Waddy Thompson, *Recollections of Mexico* (New York, 1847), pp. 168–74. However, recruitment statistics from the 1846–48 war with the United States suggest that this distinction is valid. At a time when one might have expected a significant rise in recruitment, the regular army failed to muster more than 20,000 men, although Mexico had a population of over seven million. In other words, the army did not represent more than 0.28 per cent of the population at large. Josefina Zoraida Vázquez, *La intervención norteamericana 1846–1848* (Mexico City, 1997), p. 112.

[9] Notwithstanding the apparent apathy of the masses, most of the governing factions found themselves attempting to co-opt the support of this 'silent' majority. See Torcuato S. Di Tella, *National Popular Politics in Early Independent Mexico, 1820–1847* (Albuquerque, 1996).

[10] Lorenzo de Zavala, *Obras* (Mexico City, 1969), pp. 457–8.

many revolutions take place'.[11] It is important to note that this was not a view sustained solely by Mexican politicians, who clearly had marked interests when writing about the political behaviour of the masses. The Scottish-born Fanny Calderón de la Barca, who lived in Mexico in the 1840s, could not help expressing her amazement at the people's indifference to the 1840 July Revolt:

> The tranquillity of the sovereign people during all this period is astonishing. In what other city of the world would they not have taken part with one or other side? Shops shut, workmen out of employment, thousands of idle people, subsisting, Heaven only knows how, yet no riot, no confusion, apparently no impatience. Groups of people collect on the streets, or stand talking before their doors, and speculate upon probabilities, but await the decision of their military chiefs, as if it were a judgement from Heaven, from which it were both useless and impious to appeal.[12]

In contrast to the high levels of civilian participation during the War of Independence (1810–21),[13] and later on, in the mid-century Civil War of the Reform (1858–61), the majority of revolts and conflicts which emerged during the early national period did not involve or affect the population at large. Furthermore, the apparent importance of the few notable exceptions is diminished when we consider the effect such revolts had at a national level. The majority of civil conflicts (i.e. those which involved the participation of the masses at a village level) were of a specific regional nature and, moreover, generally involved either local grievances or racial issues. In particular, the majority of the civil conflicts which were recorded to have erupted throughout this period in the present-day northern states of Sonora, Sinaloa, Chihuahua, Coahuila, Nuevo León, Tamaulipas, Durango and even Zacatecas, including the central Sierra Gorda, and in the southern states of Oaxaca, Chiapas and Yucatán were what the Creole elite came to define as 'caste wars'. Although these indigenous revolts were often bloody,[14] their impact on

---

[11] José María Tornel y Mendívil, *Breve reseña histórica de los acontecimientos más notables de la nación mexicana* (Mexico City, 1985), p. 12. For two recent studies on Tornel see: María del Carmen Vázquez Mantecón, *La palabra del poder. Vida pública de José María Tornel (1795–1853)* (Mexico City, 1997); and Will Fowler, *Tornel and Santa Anna. The Writer and the Caudillo, Mexico 1795–1853* (Westport, CT, forthcoming).

[12] Fanny Calderón de la Barca, *Life in Mexico* ([1843] repr. London, 1987), p. 246. Doña Calderón de la Barca, as the Spanish Ambassador's wife, was no less biased in her descriptions of the behaviour of the Mexican lower classes, but, as she was not herself a political actor, her memoirs reveal different biases from those of Zavala or Tornel.

[13] It is estimated that prior to 1816, at the height of Morelos' leadership of the campaign for Independence from Spain, there were approximately 40,000 civilians fighting for the insurgency. See Ernesto de la Torre, *La independencia de México* (Madrid, 1992), p. 99. This figure does not take into consideration all of the recorded 281 communities (cities, towns and villages) that fought for Independence. See Juan Ortiz Escamilla, *Guerra y gobierno. Los pueblos y la independencia de México* (Seville, 1997), pp. 179–83.

[14] This contrasts with the majority of internal conflicts fought by the army during this period, which, on the whole, seldom led to much loss of life. See Will Fowler, *Military Politi-*

national politics was remarkably insignificant. An analysis of the annual ministerial reports of the ministers of war from 1822–53 illustrates clearly that these revolts were not perceived to be a threat to the well-being of the nation. The indigenous rebels were repeatedly character-ised as 'barbarians' (*indios bárbaros*) and were generally repressed by regiments made up of criminals, deserters and levied Indians whose punishment consisted in being sent to those frontier posts.[15] In other words, defeating these rebels was not thought to require the better-equipped troops who were destined to guard the more respectable gar-risons in the main cities, and to fight in the more 'important' conflicts that entailed safeguarding national sovereignty (the wars against Spain [1829], France [1838–39] and the United States [1846–48]) or which were considered to threaten peace and order within the more central and prosperous regions of the Republic (present day Mexico, Puebla, Veracruz, Jalisco, Guanajuato, Querétaro, Zacatecas, Aguascalientes, Morelos, Michoacán and Hidalgo).

Those civil conflicts which did cause a significant change in govern-ment can in fact be reduced to five: the revolt of La Acordada (1828), the Federalist revolt against the Bustamante government of 1832, the Texan Revolt (1835–36),[16] the Revolution of the Three Hours (1844) and the Revolution of Ayutla (1854–55).[17] These are the only cases of re-volts which had a major impact at a national level and which involved a high level of civilian participation. *Pronunciamientos* such as Casa Mata (1823), Jalapa (1829), Cuernavaca (1834), Guadalajara, Ciudadela and Perote (1841), San Luis Potosí (1845), Polkos (1847) and Jalapa (1853) that resulted in a change of government were all led and fought by the military and did not involve significant civilian participation. Further-more, of these five mentioned civil revolts, only two involved large scale fighting throughout the republic. The Revolt of La Acordada and the

---

cal Identity and Reformism in Independent Mexico. An Analysis of the Memorias de Guerra *(1821–1855)* (London, 1996), pp. 16–21.

[15] See footnote 9.

[16] The Texan campaign did not result in a change of government. The interim president, José Justo Corro remained in office until the elections of 1837 brought General Anastasio Bustamante back to power. Moreover, the 1836 Constitution known as *Las Siete Leyes* remained in effect until it was overthrown by the Bases de Tacubaya of 1841. However, the Battle of San Jacinto did involve the capture of the Republic's president, General An-tonio López de Santa Anna, and as a result, brought a temporary end to the influence that had been exerted by the *santanistas* since 1834. Santa Anna was not able to regain the presidency until 1839.

[17] In all these examples the military were also involved. It would be wrong to assume that there was a clear divide between military and civilian politicians, but revolts have been labelled as civil conflicts when there were civilians amongst the ringleaders of the revolts and when civilians were involved in the fighting. It should also be noted that the civic militias which played a key role in the revolts of 1832, 1844 and 1854–55 have been classified as civilian forces. If one were to define the civic militias as military forces (i.e. as analogous to the regular professional army), then the instances of civilian participation in revolts during this period would become even more insignificant. In that case, it could be said that only the civil conflicts of 1828 and 1835–6 had any impact on government.

Revolution of the Three Hours affected Mexico City only and were of a very short duration. The Texan Revolt, notwithstanding its historical and political importance, did not affect the population at large (at least in terms of who was involved in, or was directly affected by, the fighting), given the remoteness of its location.

Therefore, the majority of the conflicts that surfaced during this period involved only a limited section of the population: namely the military, which represented approximately 0.28 per cent of Mexico's overall population.[18] However, even in the case of military revolts, a study of their individual duration, the effects they had at a national level and the percentage of the population which was affected by them might prove that the generally-held view that the early national period in Mexico was plagued by military interventions is not altogether accurate. As Josefina Zoraida Vázquez noted recently, although 'there were a great number of plans ... only a handful of them were significant'.[19] This is confirmed, in terms of national politics, by the fact that in a period which spanned over 36 years, only seven military-inspired uprisings led to a change of government (Casa Mata, 1823; Jalapa, 1829; Cuernavaca, 1834; Guadalajara, Ciudadela and Perote, 1841; San Luis Potosí, 1845; Polkos, 1847; and Jalapa, 1853). Moreover, if one takes into account the five aforementioned civilian-led revolts, of which one did not actually involve a change of government (the Texan Revolt), it becomes evident that the idea that after Independence, 'the quarrels between liberals and conservatives would repeatedly plunge the country into civil war' is not only inaccurate but greatly exaggerated.[20] During 36 years, only 12 revolts seriously affected national politics. Furthermore, of these 12 revolts, only two involved large scale fighting at a national level (Federalist Revolt, 1832 and Ayutla, 1854–55). The Texan Campaign, which gave rise to three major battles (El Alamo, Goliad and San Jacinto), affected only the underpopulated region in question and those regular troops sent to fight the rebels.[21]

Furthermore, seven of these conflicts did not lead to any deaths at all (Casa Mata, 1823; Cuernavaca, 1834; Guadalajara, Ciudadela and Perote, 1841; Three Hours, 1844; San Luis Potosí, 1845; Polkos, 1847; and Jalapa, 1853). In the case of the revolt of La Acordada (1828) only a handful of individuals were killed. In the case of the revolt of Jalapa (1829) although no blood was shed in the actual overthrow of General Vicente Guerrero's government, it is not included as a bloodless revolt because the year-long resistance Guerrero went on to mount in the south against General Anastasio Bustamante's government did involve

---

[18] See footnote 9.

[19] Josefina Zoraida Vázquez, 'Political Plans and Collaboration Between Civilians and the Military, 1821–1846', *Bulletin of Latin American Research*, vol. 15, no. 1 (1996), pp. 21–2.

[20] Edwin Williamson, *The Penguin History of Latin America* (Harmondsworth, 1992), p. 259.

[21] Apart from the Indian tribes there were around 40,000 inhabitants in Texas in 1836. This constituted approximately 0.006% of the population in Mexico at the time. See Vázquez, *La intervención norteamericana*, p. 29.

fighting (albeit sporadic), ending with the notorious and atypical execution of Guerrero on 14 February 1831.[22]

Apart from the Texan campaign and the regional/indigenous/agrarian conflicts in Sonora, Sinaloa, Yucatán, Oaxaca and Sierra Gorda, only two others involved full-scale battles, namely Governor Francisco García's federalist revolt in Zacatecas of 1835 (Battle of Guadalupe), and General José Urrea and Colonel José Antonio Mejía's federalist revolt in Tamaulipas of 1839 (Battle of Acajete). As was the case with the Texan Campaign, neither of these conflicts affected the nation at large in terms of where the fighting was located. Moreover, in both cases, the government succeeded in quelling the revolts and their impact on national politics was minimal.

The only other conflict that involved a relatively high death toll was General José Urrea's federalist revolt of July 1840. However, as a recent study of Urrea's *pronunciamiento* has shown, the deaths which were caused by this revolt were more the result of the random and intensive bombing to which the centre of the capital was subjected, than of any direct encounters between the rebels and the government troops.[23]

A superficial glance at any list of revolts for this period conjures up an image of chronic instability. The sheer number of revolts would suggest in itself that Mexico was immersed in constant turmoil during the first half of the nineteenth-century. Nevertheless, a closer analysis of their individual duration, the effects they had at a national level and the percentage of the population which was affected by them might provide a very different understanding of the ways in which these numerous internal conflicts affected Mexican society. In order to assess the impact these revolts had on the republic, this chapter will survey the different revolts in terms of the following categories: military conflicts, indigenous conflicts, regional/agrarian conflicts, banditry and finally, civil conflict.

Military conflicts

In many ways it would be misleading to suggest that the military conflicts of this period did not affect the civilian population. The most successful military uprisings were planned and carried out with the support, and at times, even at the instigation of civilian politicians.[24] To quote Brian Hamnett:

---

[22] Jan Bazant, 'From Independence to the Liberal Republic, 1821–1867', in Leslie Bethell (ed.), *Mexico since Independence* (Cambridge, 1992), p. 12.

[23] The civilians who died during the revolt were not killed deliberately because of their involvement in the fighting. The casualties were accidental, as they were the result of bombs that exploded in the city centre. To quote Fanny Calderón de la Barca, who witnessed the revolt: 'Both parties seem to be *fighting the city* instead of each other; and this manner of firing from behind parapets is decidedly safer for the soldiers than for the inhabitants'. Calderón de la Barca, *Life in Mexico*, p. 231. See also Michael P. Costeloe, 'A Pronunciamiento in Nineteenth Century Mexico: "15 de julio de 1840"', *Mexican Studies/Estudios Mexicanos*, vol. 4, no. 2 (1988), pp. 245–64.

[24] Vázquez, 'Political Plans', p. 19.

> In Mexico, perhaps more so than in other Latin American countries, the re-
> peated military interventions happened in a context in which the political is-
> sues were defined by civilians ... The intervention of military politicians was
> not motivated to promote the objectives of the army; it was determined by the
> nature of the constitutional conflict which existed between the civilians.[25]

Apart from the fact that it was civilian politicians who invited military
intervention, most of the successful revolts were financed by landowners
and businessmen who were not themselves members of the army.[26]
Nonetheless, most revolts were military conflicts in the sense that the
fighting was carried out by professional soldiers, rather than by armed
civilians. With the five exceptions noted earlier, and excluding, for the
time being, the indigenous/agrarian revolts which will be looked at further on, none of the seven remaining significant military revolts was
fought by civilians. In other words, there were in these cases no recorded instances of civilians becoming involved in the fighting.

In fact, there appears to have been, in the majority of military conflicts, a conscious effort on the part of the government troops and those
of the *pronunciados* to avoid any fighting at all, let alone to involve the
civilian population. Moreover, in those cases where conflict did lead to
fighting, it was remarkably tame, so long as the encounter was between
regiments of the regular army. In the words of Ruth Olivera and Lilian
Crété, 'Contrary to the rule elsewhere, Mexican revolutions were seldom
sanguinary. Contemporary observers even had the feeling that Mexicans
fired upon each other from safe distances in order to avoid casualties'.[27]

The key military revolts of Casa Mata (1823), Cuernavaca (1834),
Guadalajara, Ciudadela and Perote (1841), San Luis Potosí (1845),
Polkos (1847) and Jalapa (1853) took place without any violent clashes at
all. This can be explained if one considers that after the experience of
the 11-year War of Independence, the population at large, at least those
who belonged to those generations who had suffered and had lived
through the conflict, must have been weary of war.[28] The lack of bloodshed can also be explained by the way most of the military revolts were
executed. The conspiracies which preceded most of the *pronunciamientos* entailed a long correspondence which gave the rebels a fairly

---

[25] Brian Hamnett, 'Partidos políticos mexicanos e intervención militar, 1823–1855', in
Antonio Annino et al (eds.), *America Latina dallo stato coloniale allo stato nazione*, vol. 2
(Milan, 1987), p. 574.
[26] Vázquez, 'Political Plans', p. 23. Also, as an example of how a *pronunciamiento* was financed by civilian entrepreneurs, see Michael P. Costeloe, 'The Triangular Revolt in
Mexico and the Fall of Anastasio Bustamante, August-October 1841', *Journal of Latin
American Studies*, vol. 20 (1988), pp. 337–60.
[27] Ruth Olivera and Lilian Crété, *Life in Mexico under Santa Anna, 1822–1855* (Norman,
OK, and London, 1991), p. 167.
[28] This also applies to most of the agrarian revolts that surfaced during this period. To
quote John Tutino, 'agrarian conflicts did not engulf Mexico immediately after Independence. The defeats suffered by the insurgents of 1810 were still fresh memories.' See Tutino, *From Insurrection to Revolution*, p. 248.

sound idea of the kind of support their revolt would have.[29] This in turn meant that by the time the revolt was announced with its corresponding manifesto and *grito*, both the rebels and the government tended to be in a position where they could assess, depending on the number of plans of allegiance the revolt received, which of the sides had the greatest chance of winning the conflict.[30] In the cases of the revolts of Casa Mata (1823), Cuernavaca (1834), Guadalajara, Ciudadela and Perote (1841), San Luis Potosí (1845), Polkos (1847) and Jalapa (1853), the governments of Agustín de Iturbide (1821–23), Valentín Gómez Farías (1833–34), Anastasio Bustamante (1837–41), José Joaquín de Herrera (1844–45), Gómez Farías (1846–47) and Manuel María Lombardini (1853) surren-dered without mounting any significant resistance after realising that the regular army favoured the objectives of the rebels.

Although the changes in government brought about by these revolts, with their respective changes in policies (concerning issues such as the constitutional framework of the republic, taxation, education, land re-form, economic policy, freedom of the press and the role of the Church), affected the population at large, the lives of the majority of Mexicans were not interrupted by any noticeable form of politically-inspired *violence*. It could in fact be said that, with the exception of the revolts of 1832 and 1854–55, for the average civilian in the more populated central regions of Mexico, while changes in government might have affected his or her life, the violence which is generally associated with civil conflict did not.[31] As an example, a cobbler born at the end of the eighteenth-century and living in Mexico City would have witnessed fighting only in 1828 during the Revolt of La Acordada, in 1840 during the July Revolt and some rioting in 1844 during the Revolution of the Three Hours. In 1832, he might have heard the gunfire from the Rancho de Posadas during the last stages of the fed-eralist revolt against Bustamante's government. However, in this instance, the fighting did not actually reach the capital itself. If one adds together each one of these cases, the witnessed violence would have constituted no more than 20 days of his existence. He would also have seen the violence that preceded and followed the capture of the capital in September 1847 by the US army, but given that this was an international conflict, it does not enter the analytical parameters of this study. It should be stressed that the hypothetical cobbler from Mexico City was far more likely to have wit-

---

[29] For the characteristic steps that were taken in the preparation and execution of a typical pronunciamiento, see Vázquez, 'Political Plans', pp. 21–3.

[30] The traditional pattern of action was one in which those high-ranking officers who had been in correspondence with the rebels during the conspiracy phase, and who had previ-ously negotiated to support the revolt in exchange for privileges, pay rises, etc., in the event that the *pronunciamiento* was successful, published and circulated their respective plans of allegiance to the uprising in the days which immediately followed its eruption.

[31] In the mid-to-late1820s the city and state of Mexico together accounted for nearly 20% of the country's entire population of approximately 6.2 million people. The most populous states thereafter were Puebla (population 750,000) and Jalisco (population 650,000). See Timothy E. Anna, *Forging Mexico 1821–1835* (Lincoln, NE, 1998), pp. 101–2.

nessed political violence than an equivalent cobbler from the other central cities. The average civilian from the cities of Puebla, Morelia, Cuernavaca, San Luis Potosí, Querétaro, Veracruz, Jalapa, Guadalajara or Guanajuato, in contrast, did not witness any significant political military violence during this period, even during the revolts of 1832 and 1854–55.

In brief, the majority of military conflicts took place outside the main urban areas,[32] they were seldom bloody and they did not directly involve or affect the majority of the civilian population. They consisted more of shows of strength, which were resolved without fighting or popular involvement. Although further research needs to be carried out into each of these individual revolts before any firm conclusions can be reached, it would nevertheless appear to be the case from this preliminary survey that between 1821 and 1857, the more populated areas of central Mexico did not experience any significant politically-motivated displays of violence (with the exception of the conflicts of 1832 and 1854–55). However, it would be wrong to assume that this was the case throughout the republic. As will be seen in the following pages, a very different situation obtained in the more peripheral regions of Sonora, Sinaloa, Yucatán, Chiapas, Guerrero and Oaxaca, where larger indigenous populations resorted to almost constant raids on the properties of the land-owning Creole classes throughout this period. Although these conflicts did not cause noticeable changes in government policies and were not motivated by political division between liberals and conservatives, they nevertheless affected the lives of the population from these regions.

Indigenous conflicts

Carmen Vázquez Mantecón's historical maps of revolts and rebellions in the nineteenth century show the regions which were most affected by indigenous conflicts from 1821–57.[33] These were Sonora and Sinaloa (Yaqui wars: 1826–33, 1834–37, 1838–56),[34] Sierra Gorda (Xichu revolts: 1844, 1847, 1849, 1854–55)[35] and Yucatán (Maya revolts: 1847–52).[36] Furthermore, in the northern regions of Nuevo México and California

---

[32] Most battles and skirmishes were fought in the margins of the larger haciendas freqently found outside the main cities. A typical battle, the Battle of Tulancingo (7 January 1828) was fought on the outskirts of the hacienda of San Antonio Ahuehuetitla and in which only eight soldiers died, can be found in Tornel, *Breve reseña histórica*, pp. 201–3.

[33] Carmen Vázquez Mantecón, 'Rebeliones y revueltas. 1820–1910', hojas I y II, in *Atlas Nacional de México* (Mexico City, 1990).

[34] For the Yaqui Wars see Evelyn Hu-DeHart, *Yaqui Resistance and Survival. The Struggle for Land and Autonomy, 1821–1910* (Madison, 1984), in particular pp. 18–73; and Cecile Gou-Gilbert, *Una resistencia india. Los yaquis* (Mexico City, 1985).

[35] The second revolt of 1847, and those of 1849 and 1854–55 included the participation of military officers and resulted from a number of causes, of which the discontent of the indigenous population was only one. See Carmen Vázquez Mantecón, 'Espacio social y crisis política: La Sierra Gorda 1850–1855', *Mexican Studies/Estudios Mexicanos*, vol. 9, no. 1 (1993), pp. 47–70.

[36] Marie Lapointe, *Los mayas rebeldes de Yucatán* (Mexico City, 1983).

there were repeated clashes before 1848 between the few Mexican settlements which had been established there and nomadic tribes such as
the Yaquimas, Cayuses, Nez Percés, Navajos, Utes, Apache, Comanche,
Kiowa, Pawnees and Jicarillas.

Life in the peripheral regions of the north of the republic was one of
constant skirmishes between the Mexican settlers and the indigenous
tribes. To quote Evelyn Hu-DeHart, 'the Yaquis found themselves
locked in continuous, often violent, battle with the new Mexican republic
for control over land, water, their own labour power and, ultimately,
their community'.[37] However, these conflicts affected a very small percentage of Mexico's population. After all, as the minister of war noted in
1844, these revolts occurred because since Independence no Mexican
government had succeeded in populating Sonora and Sinaloa with
enough settlers for an orderly society to be established there.[38]

As for the Sierra Gorda, it is important to note that conflicts started to
erupt with a certain regularity only in the 1840s and 1850s. Nor were these
strictly indigenous conflicts. As was the case with states or departments such
as Sonora and Sinaloa, the populated areas of the Sierra Gorda were few
and very difficult to reach. It was precisely because of the region's inaccessi-
bility that it became a favourite hideout for fugitive rebels and criminals.[39]
Furthermore, of the nine revolts which took place in the Sierra Gorda between 1844 and 1854 (Xichu, 1844; Xichu, 1847; Tomás Mejía, 1847; Leonardo Márquez, 1849; Eleuterio Quiroz, 1849; Mariano Paredes y Arrillaga,
1849; Vicente Vega, 1854; Eulogio Contreras, 1854; and Gonzalo Vega,
1854), excluding the three last revolts which came to form part of the
Revolution of Ayutla which will be considered below, only one attracted the
intervention of government troops (Paredes y Arrillaga, 1849). The others
were fought out and resolved by the local communities and caciques who
were affected by them, without concerning the national government, or for
that matter, the Mexican population at large.

In the case of Yucatán, an important distinction also needs to be made
between the caste war of 1847–52, which was a bloody and devastating racial, social and political revolution and the numerous revolts which affected
the peninsula prior to 1847. The secessionist revolts of 1829, 1840–41,
1842–43 and 1844–46 were mainly led by the Creole elites in Yucatán who
wanted power to rest with them rather than with a government based in a
capital over 1,500 kilometres away.[40] Although some fighting took place
during these secessionist revolts, the skirmishes were few and of minor sig-

---

[37] Hu-DeHart, *Yaqui Resistance*, pp. ix–x.
[38] British Library (henceforth BL) LAS 535 (8)3: José María Tornel y Mendívil, *Memoria del secretariado de estado y del despacho de Guerra y Marina, leída a las cámaras del congreso nacional de la República Mexicana en enero de 1844* (Mexico City, 1844), p. 52.
[39] Vázquez Mantecón, 'Espacio social y crisis', p. 51.
[40] Will Fowler, 'José María Tornel y Mendívil, Mexican General/Politician (1794–1853)', unpublished D.Phil diss., University of Bristol (1994), pp. 161–3.

nificance (with the exception of the battle of Tixkokob, 1843).[41] In fact, although the government of Santa Anna (1841–44) attempted to impose its will on the rebels, the conflict in Yucatán was not considered to be a major priority. In stark contrast to the military mobilisation which was ordered to quell General Mariano Paredes y Arrillaga's revolt of November 1844, in which Santa Anna himself abandoned the presidency to lead the attack on Guadalajara, most of the troops dispatched to Yucatán were criminals and deserters who were sent there as a form of punishment. The very composition of these troops meant that they often joined the rebels on arrival, rather than executing their mission of vanquishing the Yucatecans.

What emerges from this very general overview of the indigenous conflicts that surfaced during this period is that they did not transcend the regions in which they took place. As a result, they did not affect the more densely populated regions of central Mexico and they had a minimal impact on national politics, let alone on the lives of the majority of Mexicans. Moreover, while from the perspective of a settler in Sonora, these years must have been particularly turbulent, the same cannot be said for an average civilian in the Sierra Gorda or Yucatán. In the Sierra Gorda, violence played a significant part in everyday life only towards the end of the period which concerns this study. In Yucatán, with the exception of the battle of Tixkokob (1843) which affected only military forces, none of the secessionist revolts involved any serious fighting. It was only from 1847 to 1852 that the white community in the peninsula was faced with the horrors of a full-scale indigenous revolution.[42] Evidence that the different Mexican governments, and by extension the bulk of the population of the more populated central regions of the republic, did not accord much attention to these indigenous revolts can be found in the fact that there was no serious effort to appeal or listen to the indigenous communities' demands until the *porfiriato*. Even then, the policies implemented in response to indigenous grievances were barely significant. The 1910 Mexican Revolution would confirm this. Furthermore, bearing in mind the Mexican government's response to the 1994 Zapatista uprising in Chiapas, it is not difficult to appreciate that the indigenous revolts of the first half of the nineteenth-century were not perceived to be a major threat or even concern by the different governments of the period.[43] These conflicts did not affect national poli-

---

[41] For a gloating account of the defeat inflicted on General Matías Peña y Barragán's government troops by the Yucatecan Sebastián López de Llergo, see BL: 9771b33(3): *Desahogo de D. José M. Tornel bajo la firma de José López de Santa Anna* (Mérida, 1843).

[42] It is interesting to note that faced with the Maya uprising, those Creole elites from Mérida and Campeche who had previously struggled to consolidate the independence of Yucatán found themselves begging for military support not only from the central government, but also from the United States and the Spanish authorities in Cuba. Their situation had become so desperate that they preferred annexation by the United States, or even a return to Spanish colonial domination, to defeat by the Maya.

[43] It is interesting (and perhaps worrying) to note that a similar trend is emerging at present in the way that the Mexican government appears to be ignoring the conflict in Chiapas. In a recent

tics, in the same way that national politics failed to address the problems that caused them. As Anne Staples has noted recently, regarding the government's response to the protests of the different indigenous populations since Independence:

> the Indians live in regions which are far away from the seat of power; their contribution to the gross internal product is minimal; it is easy to forget them, for they neither have nor have had a voice (with which to express their discontent). As in the nineteenth century, it always comes as a shock when they demand to have the same rights as the rest of the population.[44]

Regional and agrarian conflicts

If a distinction is to be made between these indigenous revolts and those that might be considered regional and agrarian, this lies in the fact that the latter did not focus on racial issues. The majority of rural conflicts during this period arose from the same sorts of land-related issues that provoked the indigenous revolts. However, the demand for exclusion of citizenship in the Mexican state which characterised revolts such as Juan Banderas' Yaqui war (1826–33) did not feature among the reasons for the rural or agrarian rebellions which will be surveyed here. Instead these regional and agrarian conflicts arose either as a result of localised land disputes or a commercial need for greater autonomy on the part of the regional elites.

It needs to be stressed that these agrarian revolts did not really start to surface until the 1840s. As John Tutino noted:

> During the period after Independence, there was little sustained rebellious activity among estate dependants. The era of decompression in which estate production was turned over to many tenants — who gained autonomy that apparently compensated for persisting insecurities — relieved, or at least cushioned, the grievances of many estate dependants.[45]

It was only after the start of the Mexican–US War of 1846–48 that several significant rural insurrections exploded in Yucatán, the Sierra Gorda, Juchitán (Oaxaca) and in the Isthmus of Tehuantepec. However, with the exception of the noted Maya revolution in Yucatán, these agrarian revolts did not affect the majority of the population even in the areas in which they took place. They were sporadic and short-lasting uprisings in which the number of casualties was minimal. It was only in 1848 that numerous rural protests started to spread across the core of

---

letter, the Zapatista leader Subcomandante Marcos accused the Zedillo government of publicly ignoring the conflict and of carrying on as if Chiapas did not matter or exist. (See *La Jornada*, 11 September 1998. See also Will Fowler, 'Goatsuckers, Guerrillas and Democracy: Mexico in the 1990s', *Vida Hispánica*, no. 19 (March 1999), pp. 12–6.

[44] Anne Staples, 'Una falsa promesa: La educación indígena después de la independencia', in Pilar Gonzalbo Aizpuru and Gabriela Ossenbach (eds.), *Educación rural e indígena en Iberoamérica* (Mexico City, 1996), p. 63.

[45] Tutino, *From Insurrection to Revolution*, p. 247.

the central highlands, affecting modern states such as Mexico, Morelos and Hidalgo.[46] Nevertheless, these 'were not sustained mass insurrections such as those in the peripheral areas. They were lengthy protests, punctuated by sporadic violence.'[47]

Therefore, two key points need to be emphasised. The first is that agrarian conflicts did not characterise the first two decades of the early national period. They became an important feature in the countryside only in the late 1840s. The second point is that these conflicts cannot really be defined as civil wars. Although these conflicts were organised and fought out by the civilian population of the countryside, the scale of the violence was relatively minor. In other words, the late 1840s witnessed the emergence of significant social unrest in the rural regions of the republic, but not the emergence of anything that could be categorised as civil war. This unrest, paired with the national-political grievances exacerbated by the Santa Anna dictatorship (1853–54), led to the bloody Revolution of Ayutla (1854–55). However, it would be misleading to argue that prior to 1854 Mexico was riddled with significant or widespread agrarian revolts.

In terms of regional conflicts, with the exception of the 1832 federalist revolt, only four escalated into violent confrontations (Zacatecas, 1835; Texas, 1836; Tamaulipas, 1839; Yucatán, 1843). Relevant to the discussion of these revolts are the tensions which arose between the centralist tendencies of the more central regions, and the federalist tendencies of the more peripheral ones. As can be appreciated from the appendix, the great majority of the *pronunciamientos* that surfaced during this period were inspired by either the centralising or federalising shifts of the different governments that came to power between 1821 and 1857. Therefore, excluding the period of the Revolution of Ayutla which was not inspired solely by the centralist-federalist divide, the most conflictive years were 1832, 1835–36, 1839–41 and 1846. In other words, the numerous regional federalist revolts which erupted in 1832, 1835–36, 1839–41 and 1845–46 reflected, in the first instance, a strong rejection on the part of the more peripheral regions (Zacatecas, Aguascalientes, Jalisco, Texas, Durango, Tamaulipas, Nuevo León, Veracruz, Tabasco, Yucatán, Chiapas, Oaxaca and Guerrero) of the centralising tendencies of General Anastasio Bustamante's first government (1830–32) and the consolidation of a centralist constitution under General Santa Anna's government (1835–36)[48] and later, an equally strong drive on their part to end the Central Republic, thereby bringing about the return of the 1824 Federal Constitution (1839–41 and 1845–46). In contrast, 1834 and 1835 were years which were also characterised by numerous centralist *pronunciamientos* in the more central cities of Ori-

---

[46] For a study of agrarian unrest in the state of Mexico see Michael P. Costeloe, 'Mariano Arizcorreta and Peasant Unrest in the State of Mexico, 1849', *Bulletin of Latin American Research*, vol. 15, no. 1 (1996), pp. 63–79.

[47] Tutino, *From Insurrection to Revolution*, p. 256.

[48] Including the interim presidencies of General Miguel Barragán and José Justo Corro.

zaba, Toluca, San Luis Potosí, Puebla, Cuernavaca and Mexico City, all of which emerged as a means of pressuring the government into effecting the significant reform of the 1824 Constitution which led to the drafting of the centralist 1836 Constitution known as *Las Siete Leyes.*[49]

Another year in which there was an intense proliferation of regional *pronunciamientos* was 1834, in which numerous priests collaborated with the military garrisons of the provinces, both central and peripheral, in unanimously rejecting the reforms which were being discussed and proposed by the radical congress of Valentín Gómez Farías' interim presidency. This study will not explore in any depth the Catholic Church's role in these conflicts and instead supports the notion that the Church was used more as an excuse by both the military and civilian politicians who organised most of the so-called religious conflicts of this period, thereby rejecting the view that the Church was an active perpetrator of rebellions.[50] It is nevertheless evident that at least in the cases of the 1834 *pronunciamientos* which spread throughout the Republic in favour of 'Santa Anna y los fueros' and later in the case of the anti-Gómez Farías 1847 revolt of the Polkos, certain members of the Church were particularly active in financing the uprisings.[51]

However, in spite of the frequency of regional *pronunciamientos*, only four escalated into violent confrontations. Governor Francisco García's federalist revolt of 1835 led to the Battle of Guadalupe in Zacatecas; the Texan revolt of 1836 led to the noted battles of the Alamo, Goliad and San Jacinto; the 1839 federalist revolt of General José Urrea and Colonel José Antonio Mejía led to the Battle of Acajete in Tamaulipas; and the 1843 secessionist revolt of Yucatán led to the noted Battle of Tixkokob. However, the Battle of Guadalupe lasted only a few hours and did not entail many casualties, and the battles of the Alamo, Goliad and San Jacinto affected only the remote and relatively small Texan population and those government troops despatched to the north to fight the rebels. As for the battles of Acajete and Tixkokob, these were

---

[49] See Reynaldo Sordo Cerdeño, *El congreso en la primera república centralista* (Mexico City, 1993), pp. 174–97.

[50] See Josefina Zoraida Vázquez, 'Iglesia, ejército y centralismo', *Historia Mexicana*, vol. 39, no. 1 (1989), pp. 205–34.

[51] See Michael P. Costeloe, 'The Mexican Church and the Rebellion of the Polkos', *Hispanic American Historical Review*, vol. 46, no. 2 (1966), pp. 170–8. For the Revolt of the Polkos also see Pedro Santoni, *Mexicans at Arms. Puro Federalists and the Politics of War, 1845–1848* (Fort Worth, 1996), pp. 182–95. For the political activities of the Church see Anne Staples, *La iglesia en la primera república federal mexicana (1824–1835)* (Mexico City, 1976); Anne Staples, 'Clerics as Politicians: Church, State, and Political Power in Independent Mexico' in Jaime E. Rodríguez O. (ed.), *Mexico in the Age of Democratic Revolutions, 1750–1850* (Boulder, 1994), pp. 223–41; Brian Connaughton, *Ideología y sociedad en Guadalajara (1788–1853)* (Mexico City, 1992); Alvaro Matute, Evelia Trejo and Brian Connaughton (eds.), *Estado, iglesia y sociedad en México. Siglo XIX* (Mexico City, 1995); and Brian Connaughton and Andrés Lira (eds.), *Las fuentes eclesiásticas para la historia social de México* (Mexico City, 1996).

brief in their duration, they took place in under-populated peripheral locations and they affected only the military forces who fought them.

The majority of these 'revolts' were concerted and formalised protests which the different regional garrisons, churches, town halls and haciendas presented to the republic in the form of printed *pronunciamientos*, plans or *actas* which were publicised either in the form of pamphlets or in the national press. Much research needs to be carried out into what these actual *pronunciamientos* represented to the majority of the population of the different localities in which they surfaced. Nevertheless, an initial analysis might suggest that these *pronunciamientos* did not in any way amount to civil war. Moreover, what such research might also show is that it was never the intention of those individuals who drafted the texts of these *pronunciamientos* to encourage civil conflict. The majority of *pronunciamientos* should perhaps be seen as an early-nineteenth century equivalent of modern day lobbying. As such, they were an integral part of Mexican political culture during its early national period. In other words, for the average politician wishing to encourage political change, whether at a regional or national level, the *pronunciamiento* represented as good a constitutional means as the process of elections or congressional debate.[52] That the *pronunciamiento* was, paradoxically, a *constitutional* political strategy is suggested by the much publicised citizen's right to insurrection (*derecho de insurrección*) which was reiterated in the *catecismos políticos* children were expected to learn at school after Independence. In other words, if we interpret the *pronunciamiento* as a clear reflection of this constitutional *derecho de insurrección* (which all young citizens were taught as an integral part of their political culture), then we are not facing instances of armed revolts, but rather, examples of a political culture that accepted the *pronunciamiento* as a normal and, above all, constitutional means to fulfil the people's aspirations. It is interesting to note that by 1835, one of the main authors of the *Siete Leyes*, Francisco Sánchez de Tagle, attempted to make a distinction between what were, in his mind, acceptable examples of the right to insurrection ('positive resistance') from those cases which were not

---

[52] Xiomara Avendaño Rojas has recently illustrated the extent to which the 'right to insurrection' was publicised in the *catecismos políticos* and *cartillas del ciudadano* which children were expected to learn in school from as early as 1822. One of these *cartillas* stated: 'The right of insurrection is based on the same source of power, since nothing is more just and legitimate than disobeying the commands of those who, although empowered by the people to govern, neither carry out their duties nor satisfy the aspirations of the people: nothing is more just and legitimate than insurrection against those who attempt to impose their will on the people'. ('El derecho de insurrección se funda en el mismo origen del poder, pues nada más justo y legítimo que desobedecer los mandatos del que, facultado por el pueblo para dictarlos, no llena cumplidamente su encargo, ni satisface las aspiraciones del pueblo: nada más justo y legítimo que la insurrección contra el que trata de imponer su voluntad al pueblo.') See Xiomara Avendaño Rojas, 'La evolución histórica de la ciudadanía: un punto de partida para el estudio del Estado y la nación' in Luis Jáuregui and José Antonio Serrano Ortega (eds.), *Historia y nación. vol. 2, Política y diplomacia en el siglo XIX mexicano* (Mexico City, 1998), pp. 171–82.

('negative resistance').[53] In this sense, it might be productive in sociological, anthropological and political terms to study these *pronunciamientos* more as projects, proposals and requests than as calls to arms.[54]

Banditry

Another aspect of Independent Mexico which has attracted scant attention from scholars is banditry. While this initial survey suggests the need to revise the view that the period under study was characterised by civil conflict, an altogether different perspective emerges when the issue of banditry is taken into consideration. Unlike civil conflict, banditry was a regular feature of the republic during its early national period.[55] Any propertied person who decided to travel at the time either requested an escort or ran a high risk of being assaulted.[56] As was noted by the US minister plenipotentiary, Waddy Thompson, who was himself threatened by bandits on three separate occasions during the same journey to Puebla from Jalapa in 1842, 'In less than a month after this, five or six Americans left their arms in the stage at this same place, and they were robbed of everything they had with them'.[57] Fanny Calderón de la Barca similarly described how on one occasion her journey to Puebla was temporarily detained because her party did not have an adequate escort; a local from San Miguel de los Soldados 'seemed to think it extremely probable that we should be robbed, believed, indeed had just heard it asserted, that a party of *ladrones* were looking out for (us)... (An escort of) two men could be of no manner of use, as, in case of attack, resistance, except with a large escort, was worse than useless.'[58] It comes as no surprise that one of the main reasons used by the Minister of War in 1835 to justify having a large army was so that the roads were not used solely by bandits.[59]

---

[53] Francisco Sánchez de Tagle, *Refutación de las especies vertidas en los números 21, 22 y 23 del periódico titulado "El Anteojo" contra el proyecto de la primera ley constitucional que presentó al Congreso la Comisión de Reorganización* (Mexico City, 1835) quoted and analysed in Alfonso Noriega, *El pensamiento conservador y el conservadurismo mexicano,* vol. 1 (Mexico City, 1993), pp. 134–40.

[54] Will Fowler, *Mexico in the Age of Proposals.*

[55] It is thus not surprising that two of the most significant realist novels about the 1840s–60s written in Mexico in the late nineteenth century were about banditry: Manuel Payno, *Los bandidos de Río Frío* (Mexico City, 1996) (originally published in Barcelona, 1891); and Ignacio M. Altamirano, *El Zarco* (Mexico City, 1984) (originally published in Mexico City, 1901).

[56] For example, General Tornel refused to return to Mexico City from Morelia in 1848 until he was guaranteed an escort of 20 dragoons from the state military authorities, 'as the road is full of thieves' ('por estar el camino lleno de ladrones'). Archivo Histórico Militar de la Secretaría de la Defensa Nacional (Mexico City), expediente XI/III/I–93, Tornel to Minister of War General Pedro Anaya, 30 May 1848.

[57] Thompson, *Recollections of Mexico*, p. 21.

[58] Calderón de la Barca, *Life in Mexico*, pp. 40–1.

[59] BL: L.A.S. 535/2 (8): José María Tornel y Mendívil, *Memoria del secretario de estado y del despacho de guerra y marina, leída en la cámara de representantes en la sesión del día veinte y tres de marzo y en la de senadores en la del veinte y cuatro del mismo mes y año de 1835* (Mexico City, 1835), p. 3.

Banditry was of considerable concern to the Mexican elite, who constantly reiterated their anxieties in their personal correspondence, in the articles they published in the press and in their political demands for more effective policing. Banditry posed a threat to their lifestyles and properties, but denunciations of banditry also served other purposes. The elite used the term to categorise many of the political conflicts of the period. In other words, they described many revolts as being nothing other than the despicable activities of ruthless bandits. For example, the Yaqui caudillo Manuel María Gándara who led the Yaqui revolt of 1843, and who has recently been analysed as a political leader,[60] was described in General José María Tornel's ministerial report of 1844 as a 'dreadful man' (*hombre funesto*), who having once been a law-abiding citizen (he was named governor of Sonora in 1841), had become a bloodthirsty bandit at the head of an army of barbaric Indians.[61] By describing its leader as a simple bandit, Tornel stripped Gándara's revolt of political content.[62]

Needless to say the elites' obsession with safeguarding their properties was accompanied by a particularly emphatic fear of social dissolution.[63] The memory of the rampages which characterised the initial stages of the War of Independence and the scenes of popular violence which accompanied the Revolt of La Acordada, leading to the riot of the Parián market in 1828, haunted and traumatised the political elites during the first three decades of national life.[64] Thus the need to create a law-abiding and orderly society with a strong government was one of the political aspirations which was shared by all of the political factions.[65] Paradoxically, while this fear determined or at least justified the gradual exclusion of the less affluent members of society from participating in the political process, limiting the suffrage first in the 1836 Constitution, and subsequently even further in the 1843 Constitution and during the Dictatorship of 1853–55, the elites remained ostensibly scandalised by the lack of interest the masses showed in politics.

Although it needs to be noted that the countryside in particular was seriously affected by banditry, the numerous clashes that are recorded as

---

[60] Hu-DeHart, *Yaqui Resistance*, pp. 59–74.

[61] Tornel Y Mendívil, *Memoria del secretariado de estado y del despacho de guerra … 1844*, pp. 50–2.

[62] This is not dissimilar to the way Pancho Villa was branded as a 'bandit' by his political adversaries, while his supporters considered him to be a great revolutionary leader. See Friedrich Katz, *The Life and Times of Pancho Villa* (Stanford, 1998).

[63] Will Fowler, 'Dreams of Stability: Mexican Political Thought During the "Forgotten Years". An Analysis of the Beliefs of the Creole Intelligentsia (1821–1853)', *Bulletin of Latin American Research*, vol. 14, no. 3 (1995), pp. 287–312.

[64] For the riot of the Parián market see Silvia M. Arrom, 'Popular Politics in Mexico City: The Parián Riot, 1828', *Hispanic American Historical Review*, vol. 68, no. 2 (1988), pp. 245–68.

[65] A recent study on the success of Santa Anna and the *santanistas* stresses the extent to which the general's popularity was based on the perception that, unlike his contemporaries, he led a faction that was particularly tough on criminals. See Will Fowler, 'The Repeated Rise of General Antonio López de Santa Anna in the So-Called Age of Chaos' in Will Fowler (ed.), *Authoritarianism in Latin America since Independence* (Westport, CT, 1996), pp. 1–30.

having taken place between the propertied classes, the military escorts and the small gangs of bandits composed of deserters and members of the dispossessed classes cannot be defined as civil conflicts given that the skirmishes, albeit numerous, had no immediate political significance.

Civil conflict: the 1832 Federalist Revolt and the Revolution of Ayutla, 1854–55

The only clear examples during this period of civil wars which were long-lasting, affected national politics, and involved the population at large were the 1832 Federalist Revolt[66] and the Revolution of Ayutla, 1854–55.[67] In both cases, the revolts involved large scale fighting with high tolls of casualties; they were characterised by the participation of civilian militias, and they affected a wide number of regions. This is not the place for a detailed analysis of these revolts (why they erupted, how they developed, etc.). However what needs to be highlighted is the extent to which these revolts, unlike the majority of conflicts which have been surveyed in this study, can be categorised as major civil wars.

The 1832 Federalist Revolt entailed, together with numerous skirmishes, four particularly bloody battles. Given that the majority of conflicts during this period were seldom sanguinary, further research needs to be carried out into why in 1832 the revolt degenerated into such violent conflict. The battle of Tolomé (located in Veracruz, 3 March 1832) between General Calderón's government regular troops and General Santa Anna's federalist civil militias lasted seven hours and resulted in over 100 casualties. Santa Anna's regiment of 800 infantry and 600 cavalry suffered a death toll of 80, and a further 528 of his men were taken prisoner.[68] The Battle of Gallinero (located between San Miguel de Allende and Dolores Hidalgo, 18 September 1832) between General Anastasio Bustamante's government regular troops and General Ignacio Moctezuma's federalist civil militias resulted in over 969 casualties.[69] Ac-

---

[66] On the 1832 Federalist Revolt see, Frank Samponaro, 'La alianza de Santa Anna y los federalistas, 1832–1834. Su formación y desintegración', *Historia Mexicana*, vol. 30, no. 3 (1981), pp. 359–80; Michael P. Costeloe, *La primera república federal de México (1824–1835)* (Mexico City, 1983), pp. 327–51; Jaime E. Rodríguez O., 'The Origins of the 1832 Rebellion' and Josefina Zoraida Vázquez, 'Los pronunciamientos de 1832: aspirantismo político e ideología' both in Jaime E. Rodríguez O, *Patterns of Contention*, pp. 145–62 and pp. 163–86 respectively.

[67] On the Revolution of Ayutla see General Doblado, *La Revolución de Ayutla* (Mexico City, 1909); Fernando Díaz Díaz, *Caudillos y caciques. Antonio López de Santa Anna y Juan Alvarez* (Mexico City, 1972); Jan Bazant, *Antonio Haro y Tamariz y sus aventuras políticas, 1811–1869* (Mexico City, 1985); Carmen Vázquez Mantecón, *Santa Anna y la encrucijada del Estado. La dictadura (1853–1855)* (Mexico City, 1986), pp. 281–96; and Anselmo de la Portilla, *Historia de la Revolución de México contra la dictadura del General Santa Anna, 1853–1855* (Mexico City, 1993).

[68] Costeloe, *La primera república federal*, p. 333.

[69] 'Oficio del cura de la villa de Dolores Hidalgo, en que da noticia del número de muertos que se sepultaron en su parroquia, después de la acción del Gallinero' (Dolores Hidalgo,

cording to another account 2,000 of Moctezuma's men were killed, and 1,200 were taken prisoner.[70] The battle of San Agustín del Palmar (located in Puebla, 29 September 1832) between General José Antonio Facio's government regular troops and General Santa Anna's federalist civil militias resulted in over 200 casualties and the subsequent seizure of Puebla.[71] The battle of the Rancho de Posadas (located in the Valley of Mexico, 6 November 1832) between General Bustamante's government regular troops and General Santa Anna's federalist civil militias resulted in also over 200 casualties and was described by José María Bocanegra as 'very bloody' (*muy sangrienta*).[72]

The lives of the majority of the population in the central regions of the republic were seriously affected by the conflict. The fighting involved the participation of a high percentage of civilians who, deciding to support the revolt by joining the federalist militias, abandoned families, jobs, fields and properties in order to bring down Bustamante's government. This disposition on the part of the civilian population to abandon the security of their homes and lifestyle and to risk their lives fighting was uncommon during this period and needs serious study.[73] The deployment and billeting of government troops also affected many communities, which found themselves having to cope with the sudden arrival of entire regiments in their vicinity. Finally, the rebels' control of the key port of Veracruz and those regions north-west of Zacatecas, paired with the longevity of the conflict, had a major impact on the republic's trade and economy, unlike the majority of revolts which surfaced during this period.[74]

While the reasons for the high levels of violence which characterised the 1832 Federalist Revolt still need to be fully explained, the violence which featured prominently in the Revolution of Ayutla (1854–55) is easier to understand. In the context of increasing agrarian unrest, coinciding with a dramatic polarisation of politics following the formalisation of political parties in the late 1840s, Santa Anna's dictatorship, in particular after the deaths of Alamán and Tornel in June and September 1853, became so extreme both in its repressive nature and in its autocratic pseudo-monarchic form of government that conservatives, moderates and radicals alike found themselves uniting to overthrow him.

---

23 Sept. 1832), in José María Bocanegra, *Memorias para la historia de México independiente, 1822–1846*, vol. 2 (Mexico City, 1987), p. 339.

[70] F. de P. Arrangoiz, *México desde 1808 hasta 1867*, vol. 2 (Madrid, 1872), p. 211.

[71] See 'Parte oficial de la derrota que sufrieron las fuerzas al mando de D. Antonio Facio' in Bocanegra, *Memorias*, vol. 2, pp. 341–4.

[72] Bocanegra, *Memorias*, vol. 2, pp. 316–7.

[73] This is particularly the case as the policies pursued by Bustamante's government (1830–32) were not fundamentally different from those adopted by the previous governments of generals Guadalupe Victoria and Vicente Guerrero. See Will Fowler, *The Liberal Origins of Mexican Conservatism, 1821–1832* (Glasgow, 1997), pp. 32–41.

[74] Barbara A. Tenenbaum, *México en la época de los agiotistas, 1821–1857* (Mexico City, 1985), p. 60.

Nevertheless, it needs to be noted that, as yet, no historian has written a full and comprehensive study of this revolution.

More so than in the case of the Federalist Revolt, the Revolution of Ayutla was characterised by intense popular participation. Under the leadership of Juan Alvarez the entire south of the Republic rose in arms against Santa Anna. The villages and towns of Michoacán were equally quick to respond in rising against the dictatorship following the proclamation of the Plan of Ayutla (1 March 1854). Santa Anna, at the head of 5,000 men, was unable to defeat General Ignacio Comonfort at the Battle of Acapulco (20 April 1854). As an expression of his frustration, his army assaulted and destroyed all the villages and haciendas it passed through on its retreat to the capital. Following this defeat, the revolution spread throughout the republic with violent uprisings erupting in the states of Tamaulipas, Guanajuato, San Luis Potosí and even Mexico. The violent nature of this civil conflict was such that Santa Anna decreed that 'every single village which manifests itself on the side of the rebels against the supreme government must be burned to the ground'. Moreover, he ordered that all rebel leaders be executed. Compared to previous conflicts, in which rebel leaders were seldom executed, Santa Anna's response to the rebellion was particularly brutal. Furthermore, in contrast to the Federalist Revolt of 1832, when despite high levels of civilian participation fighting was limited to specific battles which took place outside major urban areas, the Revolution of Ayutla was characterised by widespread fighting in towns, villages and cities where garrisons loyal to the regime attempted to repress the rebellious civilian communities by burning and ransacking their properties. General Comonfort's correspondence during the war highlights only too well the extent to which the fighting became uncontrolled. Unlike 1832, when organised militias led by regular generals and high-ranking officers fought the government troops in specific locations, the Revolution of Ayutla witnessed the random pillage and destruction of communities which were not necessarily directly involved in the conflict. Comonfort was particularly emphatic in stressing that it was imperative that the revolutionary forces behave in a civilised manner. He wrote time and again to his subordinate officers to demand that any acts of gratuitous violence be punished by death: 'no excesses will be tolerated, nor will we allow bandits to claim they defend the glorious revolution which is costing us so many sacrifices'.[75]

In brief, while the Federalist Revolt was the first major civil conflict to erupt in Mexico after Independence, the Revolution of Ayutla represented the first major revolution or civil war of this period, involving not so much straightforward battles as violent outbreaks throughout the central and southern regions of the republic which affected the civilian population at large.

---

[75] Comonfort to General Antonio Díaz Salgado, Las Balsas, 22 May 1855, in Doblado, *Revolución de Ayutla*, p. 81.

Conclusion

Instability, like time, is relative. It depends almost entirely on perception rather than on concrete facts. While throughout this period the political elites were consistent in lamenting the extent to which independent Mexico was afflicted by civil conflicts, they were equally consistent in lamenting that none of the so-called revolutions which erupted after 1821 involved or affected the majority of the population. In other words, their perception of instability only concerned the higher echelons of the political ladder. It was the elites who could not come to a significant agreement either on the form of government which was most appropriate for Mexico or on which caudillos were best suited to lead the new nation. Their perception of instability (with the exception of their obsession with banditry and their fear of social dissolution) did not take into account the political activities of the masses. The masses were perceived to be indifferent.

In essence, this survey of Mexican national politics in the more populated central regions of the republic suggests that, in general, only high-ranking officers and members of the political elite were involved in the conflicts which surfaced during this period. In other words, the history of the *pronunciamientos* of the first national decades is, with the exceptions of the 1832 Federalist Revolt and the Revolution of Ayutla (1854–55), the history of the elites' struggle to impose or consolidate their hold on power in a context of intensely heterogeneous and deeply divided factions. The ideological, personalist, regional, social and economic divisions which splintered the various political movements into numerous bitterly opposed factions prevented these elites from reaching a consensus through which the interests of their own social class, that of the *hombres de bien*, could have been better served. Nevertheless, while there is no doubt that these bitter struggles for power and to establish a long-lasting constitutional framework were one of the reasons why this period has been characterised as politically unstable, it is equally true that few of these upheavals affected the everyday lives of the majority of the population. It is interesting to note Fanny Calderón de la Barca's perception of the Triangular Revolt of 1841: 'This revolution is like a game at chess, in which kings, castles, knights and bishops are making different moves, while the pawns are looking on or taking no part whatever'.[76] The majority of the political revolts were instigated, organised and carried out by the political elites without involving the people.

Moreover, the great majority of these so-called civil conflicts were in reality nothing other than formalised complaints or political proposals that did not involve or even intend to involve any serious fighting. It is time for a distinction to be made between what a *pronunciamiento*, as opposed to a revolt or revolution, actually meant. When fighting did

---

[76] Calderón de la Barca, *Life in Mexico*, p. 412.

take place it was seldom sanguinary, and it generally affected only the rank and file of the army, without bringing the civilian population into the fray. Between 1821 and 1857 only two revolts erupted which could properly be defined as civil conflicts and which affected national politics and the population at large, namely the Federalist Revolt of 1832 and the Revolution of Ayutla (1854–55). The other instances of civil conflict, in the peripheral regions of Yucatán, Sonora, Sinaloa and Texas, albeit violent, were relatively insignificant in terms of their individual duration, the effects they had at a national level and the percentage of the population which was affected. Although it would be absurd to argue that this was a period of stability, or that there was little political unrest, it is evident from this initial survey that further research needs to be carried out into the nature of the revolts which emerged between 1821 and 1857 before we can fully comprehend the extent to which this was, in reality, a period of significant political violence. However, it is clear from this preliminary overview that the traditional view which we have inherited from Lucas Alamán, and which continues to be upheld even in the work of notable intellectuals such as Enrique Krauze that this was a period of revolutions needs to be dramatically revised.[77]

---

[77] Enrique Krauze, *Siglo de caudillos* (Barcelona, 1994), p. 128.

Chronology of Major Revolts and Pronunciamientos in Mexico, 1821–57

Conflicts that resulted in death-tolls of over 20 have been highlighted in bold. <u>Revolts that led to a change in government are underlined.</u> *Revolts that were characterised by significant civilian participation are italicised.*

1821   24 February: Plan of Iguala: General Agustín de Iturbide

      24 August: Treaties of Córdoba: Signed by Iturbide and Viceroy Juan O'Donojú

      28 September: Declaration of Independence (Mexico City)

1822   18 May: <u>Iturbidista Coup</u> (Mexico City) [Mexico became an Empire]

      22–26 September: Revolt of Brigadier Felipe de la Garza (Soto de la Marina)

      6 December: Plan of Veracruz: Generals Antonio López de Santa Anna and Guadalupe Victoria

1823   5 January: Pronunciamiento of Generals Nicolás Bravo and Vicente Guerrero

      1 February: <u>Plan of Casa Mata</u>: General José Antonio Echévarri (Veracruz) [Brought about the end of Agustín I's Mexican Empire in March 1823]

      23 February: Plan of Jalisco (Guadalajara)

      5 June: Federalist Plan of San Luis Potosí: Santa Anna

      22 December: Revolt of General José Antonio Echévarri (Puebla)

1824   17 January: Plan of Francisco Hernández (Puebla)

      23 January: Revolt of Colonel José María Lobato (Mexico City)

      8–11 June: Iturbidista Plan of Guadalajara: Generals Luis Quintanar and Anastasio Bustamante

      August: Anti-Spanish Revolt: Colonels Manuel and Antonio León (Oaxaca)

1825–1833 *Juan Banderas led indigenous rebellion in the then Estado del Occidente at the head of Yaqui, Maya, Pima and Opata Indians (involved 15 battles with federal troops and 34 major attacks on local settlements)*

1827 12 January: Pro-Spanish Plan of Juan Climasco Velasco (also known as Plan of Father Arenas)

27 March: Plan of Tlaxcala

31 July: Plan of Veracruz: Colonel Manuel Rincón

23 December: Escocés Pronunciamiento of Montaño (Otumba). To be led thereafter by General Nicolás Bravo

24 December: Escocés Revolt of José Nuño de Rivera (Texcoco)

1828 7 January: Battle of Tulancingo [Estimated eight casualties]

12 September: Pro-Guerrero Pronunciamiento of Perote: Santa Anna (Perote)

16 September: Plan of Perote: Santa Anna (Perote)

30 November: *Revolt of La Acordada*: Lorenzo de Zavala (Mexico City) [led to overthrow of constitutionally elected presidential candidate, General Manuel Gómez Pedraza, replacing him with General Vicente Guerrero]

4 December: *Riot of the Parián Market* (Mexico City)

1829 6 November: Centralist Pronunciamiento of Campeche: Commander Ignacio de la Roca (Campeche) and subsequent revolt in Yucatán

4 December: Plan of Jalapa: Sebastián Camacho to be led thereafter by General Anastasio Bustamante [led to overthrow of Guerrero's government]

17 December: Bustamantista Plan of Tehuantepec

19 December: Bustamantista Plan of San Luis Potosí

23 December: Bustamantista Plan of Mexico City

24 December: Bustamantista Plan of Jalisco (Guadalajara)

26 December: Anti-Bustamantista Plan of Jalapa: Santa Anna

1830 3 January: Revolt in Ciudad Victoria

13 January: *Federalist Plan of San Luis Potosí*: Governor Vicente Romero (San Luis Potosí)

10 February: *Federalist Plan of Michoacán*: Governor Salgado (Morelia)

February: Revolt of Vicente Guerrero in the south begins (Acapulco, Guerrero)

11 March: Plan of Codallos: Juan José Codallos (Santiago Fort, Barrabás)

March: *Revolt of Governor Salgado* (Zamora, Michoacán)

June: Pro-Guerrero Revolt of Juan Nepomuceno Rosains, Francisco Victoria and Cristóbal Fernández (Puebla)

June: Pro-Guerrero Revolt of José Márquez (San Luis Potosí)

June: Pro-Guerrero Revolt of José María Méndez and Gregorio Mier (Morelia, Michoacán)

18 August: Pronunciamiento of Officer Felipe Codallos (Mexico City)

30 September: Battle of Texca (between Guerrerista rebels and government troops) [Estimated eight casualties]

1831 14 February: Execution of Vicente Guerrero (Oaxaca)

15 April: Juan Alvarez surrenders ending Guerrero Revolt in the south

1832 ***Federalist Civil War Against the Government of General Anastasio Bustamante***

2 January: Plan of Veracruz: Santa Anna (Veracruz) [led to overthrow of Bustamante's government after a year of civil conflict]

6 January: Federalist Plan of Alvarado

10 January: *Federalist Plan of Huamantla*

26 January: *Federalist Plan of Tarecuato*

1 February: *Federalist Plan of San Juan Bautista*

5 February: Federalist Plan of San Cristóbal

11 February: *Federalist Plan of Nuestra Señora de la Concepción Tonalapa*

12 February: *Federalist Plan of Teloloapan*

15 February: *Federalist Plan of San Miguel Tecomatlán*

15 February: *Federalist Plan of Ajuchitán*

15 February: *Federalist Plan of San Juan Bautista Tlalchapa*

21 February: *Federalist Plan of San Miguel Teloloapan*

22 February: *Federalist Plan of Hacienda de Cubo*

23 February: *Federalist Plan of Mineral de Tepatitlán*

26 February: *Federalist Plan of Mineral de Tetela*

28 February: *Federalist Plan of San Juan Bautista de Tehuehuetla*

2 March: *Federalist Plan of San Francisco Huahutla*

3 March: **Battle of Tolomé** (Veracruz) [estimated over 100 casualties in battle; the number of casualties rose to 1,000 as General Calderón's troops were forced to prolong their stay in the tropics]

3 March: *Federalist Plan of Tlacotepec*

4 March: *Federalist Plan of Tetela del Río*

5 March: *Federalist Plan of Santa María Xochitepec*

5 March: *Federalist Plan of San Pedro Pemapa*

6 March: *Federalist Plan of Santo Tomás*

6 March: *Federalist Plan of Santa María Xochicalco*

6 March: *Federalist Plan of Tulaltongo*

7 March: *Federalist Plan of San Miguel Sochitepec*

10 March: Federalist Plan of Tampico

13 March: *Federalist Pronunciamiento of Pueblo Viejo*

14 March: *Federalist Plan of Tampico*

25 March: *Federalist Plan of Huetamo*

March: Federalist Revolt: Colonel Antonio Barragán (San Luis Potosí)

March: *Federalist Revolts recorded in Toluca, Río Verde, Zacatecas, Durango, Texas*

8 April: *Federalist Pronunciamiento of Tancahuitz*

27 April: Revolt of Colonel Ignacio de Inclán, calling for return of Gómez Pedraza (Lerma)

19 May: *Federalist Plan of Zacatlán*

25 May: *Federalist Plan of Cuahuayutla*

1 June: *Federalist Plan of Tancanhiz*

3 June: *Federalist Pronunciamiento of Seris*

4 June: *Federalist Pronunciamiento of Tabasco*

17 June: *Anti-Federalist Pronunciamiento of Zacualtipan*

5 July: Plan of Veracruz, calling for return of Gómez Pedraza

10 July: *Plan of Zacatecas,* calling for return of Gómez Pedraza

12 July: *Federalist Revolt begins in Zacatecas:* Francisco García

12 July: *Federalist Plan of Puente Nacional*

13 July: Plan of Jalisco (Guadalajara)

16 July: *Federalist Plan of Santa María Tenistlán*

26 July: *Federalist Plan of Villa de Austin*

5 August: *Federalist Plan of San Luis Potosí*

5 August: *Federalist Plan of Guadalcazar*

12 August: Federalist Plan of Juan Alvarez (Acapulco)

17–19 August: Federalist Plan of Matamoros

3 September: *Federalist Plan of San Felipe*

4 September: Federalist Pronunciamiento of General Gabriel Valencia

6 September: *Federalist Plan of Temascaltepec del Valle*

18 September: **Battle of El Gallinero** (San Luis Potosí) [estimated over 969 casualties; 2,000 casualties according to one account]

19 September: *Anti-Federalist Plan of Huetamo*

24 September: *Anti-Federalist Plan of Zacapu*

26 September: *Federalist Pronunciamiento of Culiacán*

29 September: **Battle of El Palmar** (Puebla) [estimated over 200 casualties]

30 September: Federalist Plan of Guadalajara

4 October: Santanista Revolt of Yucatán (Mérida)

4 October: Santanista Revolt of Tabasco

4 October: Santanista Revolt of Chiapas

3 December: *Federalist Plan of Ixtapan*

6 December: **Battle of the Rancho Posadas** (Mexico) [estimated over 200 casualties]

7 December: *Anti-Federalist Pronunciamiento of Toluca*

11 December: Peace Treaty is signed in Puente de México between Bustamante and Santa Anna

13 December: *Federalist Pronunciamiento of Huachinango*

23 December: Convenios de Zavaleta are signed bringing the war to an end

1833   15 January: Pronunciamiento of Monterrey

26 May: Plan of Escalada: Colonel Ignacio Escalada (Morelia, Michoacán)

8 June: Plan of Arista: General Mariano Arista (Huejotzingo, Puebla)

9 June: Pronunciamiento of Texcoco

17 June: *Plan of Mineral de Nieves*

19 June: Pronunciamiento of Matamoros

22 June: Pronunciamiento of Campeche

23 June: *Pronunciamiento of Matamoros*

25 June: Plan of Villa del Carmen

25 June: Plan of Villa de Chilapa

26 June: Plan of San Felipe del Obraje

12 August: *Pronunciamiento of Arizpe*

19 October: *Pronunciamiento of Tlaxcala*

27 November: *Plan of San Cristóbal de Chiapas*

2 December: Plan of Chichihualco: General Nicolás Bravo

1834   2 February: Plan for a Monarquía Indígena: Priests Carlos Tepisteco Abad and Epigmenio de la Piedra

11 May: Revolt of Puebla: General José Mariano García Méndez

15 May: *Plan of Jalapa*

18 May: *Plan of San Agustín Tlaxco*

23 May: Pronunciamiento of Oaxaca: Manuel Gil Pérez

25 May: Plan of Cuernavaca: General José María Tornel [led to overthrow of Valentín Gómez Farías' administration]

May: Pronunciamientos supporting the Plan of Cuernavaca recorded in *Huitzuco*, *Chicnahuapan*, Huejotzingo, Zacapoaxtla, Mexico, Taxco, Huetuco, Tepecoacuilco, Iguala, *Ixtlahuaca*, San Felipe, *Temascaltepeque*, Mazatepec, *Santa María Nativitas*, Tlacotepec and Tenancingo

31 May: Pronunciamiento of Toluca: Colonel José Vicente González (Mexico)

June: Pronunciamientos supporting the Plan of Cuernavaca recorded in *San Salvador El Verde*, *Huezotla*, *San Martín Texmelu-*

can, Misantla, San Francisco, El Carmen, San Pedro Tolimán, Te-
cualoya, Teotitlán, San Andrés Tuxtla, Malinalco, Teziutlán, Tux-
pan, Colima, Teotihuacán, San Juan Aquixtla, Apam, Coronanco,
Totolapa, Todos los Santos (Cempoala), San Nicolás Ponatla, Jiute-
pec, Santiago Tetla, San Ildefonso Hueyotlipam, Cuautitlán, San
Andrés Chalchicomula, Tula, Tepeaca, Santa Ana (Montealto),
Iguala, Tlalmanalco, San Juan Bautista Tlayacapan, Tepotzotlán,
San Pedro Tlaxcoapan, Santa María Tultepec, San Miguel Xalto-
can, San Salvador Atenco, Ayotzingo, Tenango Tepopola, Conte-
pec, Santo Domingo Xochiltepec, Ixtapaluca, Ameca, San Juan
Tianguismanco, Zinguilican, Tecalli, Coyoacán, San Juan del Río,
Cadereyta, Mineral de Zimapan, Ixmiquilpan, Salamanca, Atlixco,
Santo Domingo Mixcoac, Mineral del Cardonal, San Juan Evan-
gelista Acatzingo, Atocpan, Santiago de Querétaro, Santiago Tulye-
hualco, San Agustín Tlaxco, Mineral de Pachuca, Celaya,
Huascasaloya, Irapuato, Atotonilco el Grande, Guadalajara, Mexico
City, San Francisco Soyaniquipan, Santa Catarina Mártir, Santo
Evangelio, Huachinango, Zinapécuaro, León de los Aldama, Azca-
potzalco, La Piedad, San Juan Jonotla, Santa Ana Sacatlalmanco,
Acapulco, San Juan Bautista Acatlán, San Martín Tucamapan,
Teloloapan, Guanajuato, Oaxaca, Morelia, San Nicolás Nochixtlán,
Santa Ana Tianguistenco, Etla, Michoacán, Matamoros, Purísima
Concepción de los Catorce, Analco, Jamiltepec, Tepeji, Santa Anna
de Tamaulipas, Tehuantepec, Rancho del Zapote, Chihuahua, Ori-
zaba, Córdoba, Tlaxco and Omotepec.

June: Colonels José Antonio Mejía and Gutiérrez's anti-
santanista revolt (Puebla and later Tehuacán, Veracruz)

June: Month-long siege of Puebla

19 June: *Federalist Plan Salvador*

July: Pronunciamientos supporting the Plan of Cuernavaca recorded in *Minatitlán, Jamiltepec, San Juan de los Llanos,*
Tenancingo, Colima, Morelos, San Cristóbal de Colima, Cam-
peche, Veracruz, Mineral de Temascaltepec, Santo Domingo
Ocotlán, Guadalcazar, Ciudad del Venado, Joquizingo, Po-
cyaxum, Villa de Salinas del Peñón Blanco, San Juan Teoti-
huacán, San Juan de Guadalupe, Villa del Carmen, Acámbaro,
Iguala, San Francisco de los Pozos, Xicalapa, Ozuluama, Tam-
pico, Mexico City, Cholula, Villa de Ramos, Río Verde, Ciudad
Fernández, Tomatlán, Villa de Natividad Cunduacán, San Fran-
cisco, Matehuala, Coyuca, Santo Domingo, San Juan Bautista,
Morelia, Tantoyuca, Monterrey, San Marcos Eloxoclutlán, Pun-
garabato, Montemorelos, Huetamo, Matamoros, Santa Can-
tarina de Pátzcuaro, Monclova, Puebla, Lagunillas, Chinameca,
San Juan Bautista Cuautla, San Buenaventura, Nadadores,

Guerrero, San Martín Atercal, San Miguel Acambay, Durango, Tepeji, Texas and *Ario.*

August: Pronunciamientos supporting the Plan of Cuernavaca recorded in *Zacatlán, Puebla de los Ángeles, Temapache, Cocupao, San José de Puebla, Lagos, Jalapa, Coatepec, Teocelo, Huimanguillo, Acatlán, Orizaba, Morelia, Mascota, Sinaloa, Colima, Coahuila, San Pedro Piedragorda.* Further plans of allegiance recorded in the states of Nuevo México, Querétaro, Guanajuato, San Luis Potosí, Michoacán, Nuevo León, Puebla, Yucatán, Jalisco and Chiapas.

1835   23 March: Plan of Texca: General Juan Alvarez

April–May: Federalist Revolt: Francisco García (Zacatecas)

11 May: **Battle of Guadalupe** [estimated 20 casualties]

18 May: Centralist Pronunciamiento of Nombre de Dios (Durango)

19 May: Centralist Pronunciamiento of Orizaba: Miguel Fernández

28 May: Centralist Pronunciamiento of Tlaxcala

29 May: Centralist Pronunciamiento of Toluca (Toluca)

30 May: Centralist Pronunciamiento of Zacatecas

30 May: Federalist Pronunciamiento of San Francisco

31 May: Centralist Pronunciamiento of Cuernavaca

June: Pronunciamientos supporting the Centralist Plan of Toluca recorded in Mineral de Veta Grande, Sombrerete, Fresnillo, Saín Alto, San Luis Potosí, State of Mexico, Mineral de Pánuco, San Juan Teotihuacán, Santa Ana Chiautempam, Zinacantepec, Mineral del Taxco, Tenango, Nativitas, San Juan Bautista de Teúl, Tlaltenango, San Juan Bautista de Tepetongo, Tepechitlán, Atolinga, Guadalupe (Zacatecas), Tlalpan, Momax, Jonacatepec, Mexico City, Jalapa, Morelia, Durango, Culiacán, Pueblo Viejo, Villa del Carmen, San Juan Bautista de Jonuta and Villa Parras.

June: Pronunciamientos opposing the Plan of Toluca's centralist demand for a constitutional change of government recorded in Austin, Campeche, Mérida, Sisal, Hool, Calkiní, Cahuich, Hecelchakan and Leona Vicario.

July: Pronunciamientos opposing the Plan of Toluca's centralist demand for a constitutional change of government recorded in Chiapas, Viesca, Mapimí, Tabasco, Villa Guerrero, Coahuila, Texas, Tepetitán, Allende and Macuspana.

16 August: Federalist Pronunciamiento of Tecpan

23 August: Federalist Plan of Oaxaca

6 September: Plan of the Junta Anfictiónica of New Orleans

7 November: Secessionist Pronunciamiento of Texas

November: José Antonio Mejía Federalist Revolt (Tampico)

1836 January–June: Federalist Revolts recorded in Huajuapam (Oaxaca), Zacatecas, Alta California, Chiapas and Papantla.

2 March: Declaration of Texan Independence

6 March: **Battle of El Alamo**

18 March: **Battle of Goliad**

21 April: **Battle of San Jacinto**

20 December: Plan of Captain Mariano Olarte

1837 26 January: Federalist Pronunciamiento of Alta California

14 April: Federalist Pronunciamiento of San Luis Potosí

6 May: Federalist Pronunciamiento of Río Verde

16 September: Secessionist Pronunciamiento of Sonora

9 October: Pronunciamiento of González and Fiz

1 December: Federalist Pronunciamiento of Aguililla (Michoacán)

26 December: Federalist Pronunciamiento of Arizpe: General José Urrea

1838 11 January: Federalist Pronunciamiento of Culiacán

16 January: Federalist Pronunciamiento of Sinaloa

3 June: Federalist Pronunciamiento of Monte Alto

3 September: Federalist Pronunciamiento of Arizpe

7 October: Federalist Pronunciamiento of Santa Ana de Tamaulipas: Longinos Montenegro

7 October: Federalist Pronunciamiento of Tampico: Colonel José Antonio Mejía and Valentín Gómez Farías

9 November: Federalist Pronunciamiento of Camargo

17 November: Federalist Plan of Opodepe

22 November: Federalist Plan of Rancho de Puntiagudo

12 December: Federalist Pronunciamiento of Ciudad Victoria

16 December: Federalist Revolt of Santa Ana de Tamaulipas begins: José Urrea

23 December: Federalist Plan of Alejo Espinosa

1839 19 January: Federalist Pronunciamiento of Monclova

22 January: Federalist Pronunciamiento of General José Urrea (Tampico)

27 February: Pronunciamiento of Montemorelos

28 February: Federalist Pronunciamiento of San Cristóbal de Hualahuises

3 May: **Battle of Acajete** [estimated 40 casualties; Mejía is executed]

1 June: Pronunciamiento of Misantla

11 June: Pronunciamiento of Rancho de San Francisco

13 December: Federalist Plan of Juan Pablo Anaya

1840 23 January: Federalist Plan of Casa Blanca

18 February: Secessionist Pronunciamiento of Mérida

25 February: Secessionist Pronunciamiento of Campeche

4 March: Secessionist Revolt in Yucatán begins

30 March: Federalist Pronunciamiento of San Andrés de Nava

30 March: Federalist Pronunciamiento of Santa Rita de Morelos

30 March: Federalist Pronunciamiento of San Pedro de Gigedo

1 April: Federalist Pronunciamiento of Valle de Santa Rosa

13 May: Pro-government Pronunciamiento of Camargo

17 May: Pro-government Pronunciamiento of Ciudad Guerrero

17 May: Pro-government Pronunciamiento of Villa de Mier

17 May: Pro-government Pronunciamiento of Villa de la Purísima Concepción de Mier

30 May: Pro-government Pronunciamiento of San Fernando de Rosas

16 July: Federalist Revolt: José Urrea and Valentín Gómez Farías (Mexico City)

19 July: Federalist Plan: José Urrea and Valentín Gómez Farías (Mexico City)

9 August: Pronunciamiento of Turicato (Michoacán)

1 October: Pronunciamiento of Valle de Aguililla

7 December: Pronunciamiento of Pichucalco

28 December: Pronunciamiento of San Pedro Michoacán

1841   14 January: Secessionist Declaration (Yucatán)

1 February: Yaqui Secessionist Plan of Independence: Manuel María Gándara (Sonora)

1841–44 Third Major Yaqui Revolt

8 May: Secessionist Plan of Independence (Chiapas)

10 May: Pronunciamiento of Landa (Querétaro)

30 July: Pronunciamiento of Capula

August–October: <u>Triangular Revolt</u>: Generals Mariano Paredes y Arrillaga, Santa Anna and Gabriel Valencia (Guadalajara, Veracruz and Mexico City) [led to overthrow of Bustamante government]

8 August: <u>Plan of Guadalajara</u>: General Mariano Paredes y Arrillaga (Guadalajara)

23 August: Pronunciamiento of Northern Army seconding that of Guadalajara: General Mariano Arista

4 September: Pronunciamiento of La Ciudadela: General Gabriel Valencia (Mexico City)

5 September: Pronunciamiento of Santa Anna de Tamaulipas

9 September: <u>Pronunciamiento of Perote</u>: Santa Anna (Perote)

9 September: Pronunciamiento of Santiago de Querétaro

11 September: Pronunciamiento of Veracruz

11 September: Pronunciamiento of Durango

12 September: Plan of General Anastasio Bustamante (Mexico City)

14 September: Pronunciamiento of Saltillo

14 September: Pronunciamiento of Monterrey

15 September: Pronunciamiento of Tlaxcala

15 September: Pronunciamiento of Santa Anna Chautepam

17 September: Pronunciamiento of Orizaba

28 September: Plan of Tacubaya

1 October: Federalist Pronunciamiento (Mexico City)

2 October: Pronunciamiento of General Valentín Canalizo

3 October: Centralist Pronunciamiento of Morelia

4 October: Pronunciamiento of Pátzcuaro

5 October: Pronunciamiento of Acuitzio

6 October: Pronunciamiento of Apatzingán

6 October: Federalist Pronunciamiento of Morelia

7 October: Pronunciamiento of Tacámbaro

9 October: Pronunciamiento of Aguililla

9 October: Pronunciamiento of Tangancícuaro

10 October: Pronunciamiento of Zamora

10 October: Pronunciamiento of Chilchota

10 October: Pronunciamiento of Mineral de Zacualpan

12 October: Federalist Revolt of Durango

20 October: Federalist Pronunciamiento of Estancia de Juchitán

20 October: Pronunciamiento of Florentino Villar

22 October: Pronunciamiento of General Nicolás Bravo (Chilpancingo)

22 November: Pronunciamiento of Acapulco: General Juan Alvarez

1842   9 December: Plan of San Luis Potosí

11 December: Pronunciamiento of Huejotzingo: General José María Tornel (Puebla)

December: Over 100 Anti-Congress Pronunciamientos were recorded in the states of Jalisco, Zacatecas, Michoacán, Querétaro, Veracruz, Oaxaca and Aguascalientes.

1843   1 January: Pronunciamiento of Tapachula

March–May: Juan Alvarez led revolt in the south

23 September: Plan of Opedepe

1844   Xichu Revolt in the Sierra Gorda

2 November: Pronunciamiento of Guadalajara: General Mariano Paredes y Arrillaga (Jalisco)

6 November: Pronunciamiento of Aguascalientes

8 November: Pronunciamiento of Zacatecas

9 November: Pronunciamiento of General Lino J. Alcorta

12 November: Pronunciamiento of General Pedro Cortázar

15 November: Pronunciamiento of Querétaro

18 November: Pronunciamiento of San Luis Potosí

22 November: Pronunciamiento of Pátzcuaro

6 December: <u>Revolution of the *Tres Horas*</u> (Mexico City) [led to overthrow of Santa Anna's government]

December: Anti-santanista pronunciamientos recorded in San Fernando de Guaymas, Hermosillo, San Cristóbal, Ures, Seris, Camargo, Tlaxcala, Oaxaca, Jiloltepec, Tejupilco, San Francisco Tepeyanco, Santa Inés Zacatelco, Tabasco, Tuxpan, Veracruz, Armada Nacional, Saltillo, Nuevo León, Sabinas, San Juan de Ulúa, Morelia, Zitácuaro, Michoacán, Hacienda del Mortero, Durango, Tampico, Perote, Guanajuato, Santa Lucía Coyuca, Chihuahua, Yucatán and Amatlán.

1845   21 January: Pronunciamiento of Santa Fe

7 June: Federalist Revolt: Valentín Gómez Farías (Mexico City)

14 June: Federalist Revolt of Tabasco: General Ignacio Martínez (Tabasco)

15 June: Federalist Revolt of Juchitán (Oaxaca)

14 December: <u>Pronunciamiento of San Luis Potosí</u>: General Manuel Romero. Thereafter led by General Mariano Paredes y Arrillaga [led to overthrow of General José Joaquín de Herrera's government]

1846   5 February: Pronunciamiento of Maztlán

April: Juan Alvarez anti-Paredes Revolt (Guerrero)

20 May: Pronunciamiento of Guadalajara

31 July: Pronunciamiento of Veracruz and Ulúa

4 August: <u>Plan of La Ciudadela</u>: General Mariano Salas and Valentín Gómez Farías (Mexico City) [led to overthrow of Paredes y Arrillaga's government]

11 August: Federalist Pronunciamiento of Durango

12 August: Federalist Pronunciamiento of Zacatecas

12 August: Federalist Pronunciamiento of San Luis Potosí

16 August: Federalist Pronunciamiento of Colima

4 September: Pronunciamiento of Santa Anna de Tamaulipas

19 November: Federalist Pronunciamiento of San Juan Bautista (Tabasco)

1847   Second Xichu Revolt in the Sierra Gorda

Revolt of Tomás Mejía in the Sierra Gorda

16 February: Clerical Pronunciamiento of Oaxaca

26 February: <u>Revolt of the Polkos</u> [led to overthrow of Valentín Gómez Farías's administration]

21 December: Revolt of the Repúblicas Indígenas de Campeche begins

1847–1852 Caste War in Yucatán

1848   15 June: Monarchist Pronunciamiento of General Mariano Paredes y Arrillaga

1849   11 February: Pronunciamiento of Sierra Alta

Santanista Revolt of Leonardo Márquez (Sierra Gorda)

Revolt of Eleuterio Quiroz (Sierra Gorda)

1851   8 January: Plan of Guanajuato

26 July: Pronunciamiento of San Juan de Tierra Adentro

3 September: Plan of the Campo de la Loba

1852   July: Revolt in Mazatlán

26 July: Plan of Blancarte

14 December: Pronunciamiento of Durango

23 December: Pronunciamiento of Chihuahua

28 December: Pronunciamiento of Veracruz

1853   2 January: Pronunciamiento of Orizaba

19 January: Pronunciamiento of Mexico City

26 January: Pronunciamiento of San Juan Bautista

1 April: <u>Santanista Pronunciamiento of Jalapa</u>: Tornel (Jalapa) [led to overthrow of Manuel María Lombardini's government]

14 December: Pronunciamiento of Santa María de Zoquizquiapan

1854   24 February: ***<u>Revolution of Ayutla</u>***: General Juan Alvarez (Guerrero) [led to overthrow of Santa Anna's government after a year and a half of civil conflict]

February: Generals Juan Alvarez and Ignacio Comonfort led revolt in the south

1 March: Plan of Ayutla: Juan Alvarez

Revolts recorded in Guerrero and Michoacán

April: Revolt of Vicente Vega (Sierra Gorda)

April: Revolt of Gonzalo Vega (Sierra Gorda)

20 April: **Battle of Acapulco** (estimated 1,000 casualties)

Santa Anna's army destroyed and pillaged all the villages it crossed on its retreat to Mexico City from Acapulco

Sporadic fighting erupted throughout the Republic

December: Revolt of Eulogio Contreras (Sierra Gorda)

1855   13 August: Plan of San Luis Potosí: Antonio Haro y Tamariz

13 August: Pronunciamiento of Mexico City

4 October: Revolution of Ayutla ended with Juan Alvarez's rise to the presidency

12 December: Pro-clerical Revolt (Puebla)

12 December: Plan of Zacapoaxtla: Priest Ortega y García

19 December: Second Plan of Zacapoaxtla

1856   16 January: Siege of Puebla

21 January: Puebla surrenders to the rebels led by Antonio Haro y Tamariz

23 March: Ignacio Comonfort's government troops retake Puebla

CHAPTER 4

On the Origins of Civil War in Nineteenth-Century Honduras

Darío Euraque

Introduction

This chapter is primarily a historiographical essay. I am interested less in advancing a particular interpretation of nineteenth-century Honduran politics than in presenting the Honduran case within the Central America context. During the 1980s and early '90s, many collections of scholarly essays on 'Central America' published outside Honduras excluded Honduras from discussion, or asserted only that Honduras 'was and is' the 'first', 'exemplary', 'classic' 'Banana Republic', bereft, it seemed, of the nineteenth-century coffee tradition that made comparisons among Guatemala, El Salvador, Nicaragua and Costa Rica viable.[1] Yet at the same time, in Honduras itself, the work of scholars has not only enriched the study of the country's twentieth century history, but has perhaps also made it possible to position Honduras within the comparative study of nineteenth-century Central American political history.

This chapter has three objectives. First, it will make some broad observations about the character of the civil wars that plagued Honduras during the last century, at least insofar as the existing historiography allows. Second, the chapter will summarise the main arguments of what are, in my opinion, the two most important recent contributions to the study of nineteenth century Central American history, works which transcend the essays collected in the Cambridge series published in the mid-1980s.[2] I am referring to works of Robert G. Williams, and Lowell Gudmundson and Héctor Lindo-Fuentes.[3] Finally, this chapter will discuss the most recent and best Honduran historiography on the nineteenth century, considering in particular whether it illuminates the questions about politics and civil war raised in Williams's *States and Social Evolution*, and Gudmundson and Lindo-Fuentes' *Central America, 1821–1871*.

---

[1] Jeffery Paige, *Coffee and Power: Revolution and the Rise of Democracy in Central America* (Cambridge, 1997), p. 6.

[2] Leslie Bethell (ed.), *Central America since Independence* (Cambridge, 1991).

[3] R.G. Williams, *States and Social Evolution: Coffee and the Rise of National Governments in Central America* (Chapel Hill, 1994); and Lowell Gudmundson and Héctor Lindo-Fuentes, *Central America, 1821–1871: Liberalism before Liberal Reform* (Tuscaloosa, 1995). The Gudmundson and Lindo-Fuentes book, it should be noted, is a synthesis of work published first in volume three of the six-volume *Historia General de Centroamérica* published in 1993 in Madrid by Facultad Latinoamericana de Ciencias Sociales (FLACSO) and the Sociedad Estatal Quinto Centenario.

The civil wars of Honduras in the nineteenth century

Before engaging with Robert Williams's *States and Social Evolution* and Gudmundson and Lindo-Fuentes's *Central America,* I will consider the scope and character of the so-called civil wars of Honduras, drawing mainly on the 'great caudillo' approach to nineteenth century politics that was dominant in the historiography as recently as the 1960s. This will entail the examination of some very rough statistics on the incidence of 'civil wars': the number of people killed, the national governments overthrown and re-constituted and the role of political parties in par-ticular electoral contexts.

Table 4.1 Estimated Population of Central America, 1820–90 (by thousands)

Country	1820	1830	1840	1850	1860	1870	1880	1890
Honduras	135	152	178	203	230	265	307	399
El Salvador	248	271	315	366	424	493	554	758
Costa Rica	63	72	86	101	115	137	182	243
Guatemala	595	670	751	847	951	1,080	1,225	1,365
Nicaragua	186	220	242	274	278	337	N/A	360
Central America	1,227	1,385	1,572	1,791	1,998	2,312	2,268	3,125

Sources: Ralph Lee Woodward, 'The Aftermath of Independence, 1821–c. 1870'; and Ciro F.S. Cardoso, 'The Liberal Era, c. 1870–1930'; both in Leslie Bethell (ed.), *Central America since Independence* , pp. 8, 39.

This is relevant because a central historiographical issue concerns the depth of the 'political anarchy' that occurred both after political inde-pendence from Spain in 1821 and following the formal demise of the Central American Federation in 1842. However, even the period of the Central American Federation, which endured from 1824 to 1842, is said to have been marred by military strife. According to rough calculations, about 7,000 Central Americans died in military engagements between 1821 and 1842. This amounted to about 0.6 per cent of Central America's population in 1821 and 0.4 per cent of the 1840s population.[4] During this period some 700 Hondurans were killed, in 27 battles. These deaths rep-resented about 0.39 per cent of the country's population in the 1840s, and about 0.51 per cent of the population in the 1820s (See Table 4.1).[5] It ap-pears to have been rare for military engagements during this period to produce more than 50–100 deaths. This was probably true for most con-flicts between 1827 and 1879 in Honduras.

---

[4] A. Marure, *Efemeridades de los hechos notables acaecidos en la República de Centro América* (Guatemala, 1895, 1994 reprint), pp. 149–54.

[5] Marure, *Efemeridades*, pp. 141, 154.

The assumption that, until the relative stability of the 'liberal' *Reforma* years (1877–91), the post-federation period was more 'anarchic' than the period of the federation does not seem warranted, at least in terms of the numbers of battles that are reported to have occurred. During almost any 20-year period between 1840 and 1900, with the exception of 1860–80, the number of battles that occurred was roughly equal to the 30-odd conflicts reported for the 1820–40 period (see Table 4.2). The number of casualties did increase, probably due to more deadly firepower, about which we know very little.[6]

Table 4.2 Estimates of Dead and Wounded in the Civil Wars of Honduras 1820–90 (by decades)

Decades	Dead	% of Pop.	Injured	% of Pop.	Number of Battles
1820	161	0.11	24	0.01	15
1830	179	0.11	57	0.03	19
1840	1,165	0.65	110	0.06	17
1850	61	0.03	22	0.01	14
1860	165	0.07	57	0.02	45
1870	487	0.11	138	0.05	65
1880	N/A	N/A	N/A	N/A	3
1890	5,000	1.25	N/A	N/A	19
Total	7,218	–	408	–	187

Sources: A. Vallejo, *Compendio de la historia social y política de Honduras* (Tegucigalpa, 1882), pp. 413–20; and F. Díaz Chávez, *Sociología de la desintegración regional* (Tegucigalpa, 1972), p. 457. The 1890 figure is from Despatch 219, George T. Summerlin, US minister in Tegucigalpa, to US Secretary of State, 6 March 1928, US National Archives (Washington, DC), Record Group 59, 815.00/4188.

The claim that the post-1840 period represented a long decline into political anarchy usually rests on the belief that governments were continually constituted and re-constituted, as power was transferred to temporary *jefes de estado* whenever the legitimate *jefe* took to the battle field. Actually, as Charles A. Brand reminded us in the 1970s, between 1820 and 1838, when Honduras seceded from the Central American Federation, 'only one of its five *jefes primeros* was overthrown by force'.[7] The modern institution of the presidency began in Honduras in 1841, after formal secession from the federation, and the institution thereafter witnessed relative stability, regardless of whether the state was at war. Brand asserted that between 1841 and 1903, 'fourteen presidents served a total of 58

---

[6] S. Webre, 'Central America', in David G. LaFrance and Errol D. Jones (eds.), *Latin American Military History: An Annotated Bibliography* (New York, 1992).

[7] Charles Brand, 'The Background of Capitalist Underdevelopment: Honduras to 1913', unpublished D.Phil. dissertation, University of Pittsburgh (1972), p. 40.

years, with an average and median of four years'. What is more, only 'three of them served for less than two years and were among the four forcefully evicted from office. In every case, defeat was primarily caused by foreign intervention, [mostly Central American]'.[8]

On the other hand, this relative stability did not represent a form of popular electoral democracy. Formal constitutional restrictions on citizenship and electoral participation as candidates and voters remained in force until the 1890s.[9] As late as 1877, only 7.25 per cent of the population could vote, and suffrage was restricted entirely to men. Women did not receive the right to vote in presidential elections until 1955.[10]

Moreover, the so-called 'relative stability thesis' does not deny the use of violence and force at the moment of elections in order to ensure overwhelming electoral victories. The use of electoral violence was even more common during the supposedly more 'stable' *Reforma* and post-*Reforma* era. This period saw the first emergence in Honduras of political groupings resembling modern political parties. Known as 'electoral clubs', they developed within the elite groupings that were allowed to participate formally in the political system (see Table 4.3).[11]

Table 4.3 Presidential Elections in Honduras, 1877–1902 (votes cast for each party)

Year	Liberal Party	%	National Party	%	Other Parties	%	Total Vote
1877	16,603	81	–	–	4,032	9	20,635
1880	24,521	82	–	–	5,274	8	29,795
1883	3,500	8	40,598	92	–	–	44,098
1887	5,326	12	38,394	88	–	–	43,720
1891	12,300	26	34,362	74	–	–	46,662
1894	42,667	99+	–	–	499	–	43,166
1898	36,746	85	–	–	7,834	5	44,580
1902	27,195	36	42,234	55	7,008	9	76,437

Sources: For the 1877–98 period, F. Salgado, *Compendio de historia de Honduras* (Comayaguela, 1928), pp. 156, 158, 163, 166, 170, 203, 209. For 1902, S. Suazo Rubí, *Auge y crisis ideológica del Partido Liberal* (Tegucigalpa, 1991), p. 219.

[8] Brand, 'The Background of Capitalist Underdevelopment', p. 41.
[9] Marvin A. Barahona, 'Honduras: el estado fragmentado', *Paraninfo*, no. 7 (1995).
[10] Enrique Ochoa, 'The Rapid Expansion of Voter Participation in Latin America: Presidential Elections, 1845–1986', in Richard Wilkie and David Lorey (eds.), *Statistical Abstracts of Latin America*, vol. 25 (Los Angeles, 1987), p. 886.
[11] Marvin A. Barahona, 'Caudillismo y política en Honduras (1894–1913)', *Paraninfo*, no. 9 (Tegucigalpa, 1996) pp. 1–25.

When given the chance, parties used almost any means, including force or fraud, to impose these overwhelming victories, in large part, as William S. Stokes astutely asserted in a classic study, because all Honduran constitutions since 1824 insisted 'that a presidential candidate receive an absolute majority for election'.[12] In the case of pluralities, Congress selected a winner among the candidates. When candidates winning pluralities did not receive a favourable vote in Congress, they almost invariably revolted, although not always successfully.

Engaging the political history of nineteenth-century Central America

As noted earlier, two recent monographs offer broad arguments and research agendas in which to locate a discussion of the historiography of politics in nineteenth century Honduras: Robert G. Williams, *States and Social Evolution: Coffee and the Rise of National Governments in Central America*, and Lowell Gudmundson and Héctor Lindo-Fuentes, *Central America, 1821–1871: Liberalism before Liberal Reform*. Williams's book is a weighty tome grounded in archival research throughout Central America; the short book by Gudmundson and Lindo-Fuentes is a synthetic analysis based on the historiography produced during the last 15 years. Both offer approaches and findings that challenge the 'dependency perspective' to history which so dominated Central American scholarship in the 1970s and 1980s, especially the brilliant rendition by Edelberto Torres-Rivas.[13] What is more, the ideas offered by Williams and Gudmundson and Lindo-Fuentes can also help to frame questions and answers which were not addressed by pre-dependency approaches that focused on narratives and counts of battles, coups, counter-coups and changes in government. The Honduran historiography has a venerable tradition along these lines.[14]

---

[12] W. Stokes, *Honduras: An Area Study in Government* (Madison, 1950), p. 104.

[13] See Edelberto Torres-Rivas, *Interpretación del desarrollo social centroamericano* (San José, 1971). Chapter one, covering the pre-1870s period, is entitled '*La Anarquía*'. Other historians who study the 1820s–1840s period from the perspective of dependency theory are Ralph Lee Woodward Jr, 'The Liberal-Conservative Debate in the Central American Federation, 1823–1840', in V. Peloso and Barbara Tenenbaum (eds.), *Liberals, Politics and Power: State Formation in Nineteenth-Century Latin America* (Athens, GA, 1996); and Julio Pinto Soria, 'La Independencia y la Federación (1810–1840)', in Edelberto Torres-Rivas (ed.), *Historia general de Centro América*, vol. 3 (Madrid, 1993). A Honduran example of dependency theory is provided by Rodolfo Pastor Fasquelle, *Historia de Centro América* (Mexico City, 1988).

[14] The key Honduran authors are Antonio R. Vallejo (1844–1914); Rómulo Durón (1865–1942); Esteban Guardiola (1867–1953); Eduardo Martínez López (1867–1954); Félix Salgado (1872–1945); Rubén Barahona (1893–?); Lucas Paredes (–1970s?) and Victor Cáceres Lara (1915–94). Recent works in this tradition are René Vallejo Hernández, *Crisis histórica del poder político en Honduras* (Tegucigalpa, 1990); and Alexis Argentina González de Oliva, *Gobernantes hondureños: siglos XIX y XX* (Tegucigalpa, 1996).

Williams's *States and Social Evolution*

Williams's monograph is a major contribution to the historiography of modern Central America. It offers wide-ranging historical research while drawing on important theoretical traditions in an effort to explain the origins of the different political cultures, political systems and modes of governance within Central America, especially those constituted between the 1840s and 1900.

Most generally, Williams argues that the different intra-regional political cultures and government structures that exist in twentieth century Central America exhibited 'patterns of governance' founded during the 'moment of construction of Central American states', i.e. when 'coffee townships' emerged as politically dominant, between the 1840s and 1900, the period during which coffee became the principal export in most countries in Central America, excluding Honduras. Williams also argues that after the 1870s local elites and patriarchs frustrated by the 'limits of accumulation' within the coffee township boundaries coordinated cross-regional politics against the pre-coffee national governments, which were largely legacies of the late colonial period. He notes that a key element in this process was the use of police and military forces to impose labour discipline, which also had the effect of institutionalising violent, elitist and exclusivist 'patterns of governance', especially in Guatemala, El Salvador and Nicaragua.

More specifically, Williams contends that the precise relationships and timing of land, labour and capital inputs prior to elite cross-regional coffee township alliances explain the divergent paths taken by political institutions in different Central America countries. His detailed analysis offers a critical innovation, namely the notion that 'coffee patriarchs', in the context of local variations of land, labour and capital, used the municipal power of coffee townships as a first stage to eventual national power, reached circa 1900. This he calls 'nation building from the bottom-up'.[15] It occurred in El Salvador, Guatemala, Nicaragua and Costa Rica, with the latter's coffee townships and patriarchs establishing patterns of governance different from those in the former countries (the Honduran case will be addressed later).

Williams, however, does not reduce the resultant character of the states to different relationships of land, labour and capital as they developed between the 1840s and 1900. He recognises that each country contained 'pockets of coffee production' with 'highly distinct structural arrangements', regardless of the prominence of certain coffee townships. In short, he asks:

> With so many different models [of land tenure and labour relations in coffee production] to choose from, why did states end up favouring one over the others? In particular, why did the governments of Guatemala, El Salvador and Nicaragua enact national land, labour and capital laws that reinforced

---

[15] Williams, *States and Social Evolution*, p. 225.

the large plantation model, while the national government of Costa Rica encouraged the formation of family-sized farms in the coffee districts?[16]

His answer is that 'The adoption of national policies that favoured large plantations was determined by the existence of a potential Indian labour force. Because of the power of Indian community structures, coffee growers needed a strong counterforce to help them pry labour and land from those communities'.[17] Thus, Costa Rican governments, lacking the 'Indian problem', as others have called it, and enjoying a formidable agricultural frontier, could promote family-size farms in the coffee districts. Ultimately, this led to a more open political system in Costa Rica and a state less repressive and dependent on its coffee oligarchy.

Is this vision of nation-building and state formation supported by the existing historiography on nineteenth-century Honduras? Obviously, as Williams admits, the Honduran case requires detailed archival work at the municipal level, some of which has already begun. However, if Williams's elegant argument is to be shown to be correct in the Honduran case it will need substantial new archival research in municipal documents and particularly in the judicial archives of the nineteenth century. Two areas in particular must be addressed: first, and of major interest here, the politics of the period must be examined, especially the extent to which cross-regional alliances actually took place from coffee township to township. Secondly, a military and police historiography must be created, not only regarding the 'labour disciplining' aspect of the new states but also the resistance they encountered. The extent to which this context will help us to understand the origins of the civil wars in nineteenth century Honduras remains to be seen.

Gudmundson and Lindo-Fuentes's *Central America: 1821–1871*

Gudmundson and Lindo-Fuentes have written an important little book. Its significance derives from a number of factors. First, its authors address a hitherto almost totally neglected era of modern Central American social historiography. Secondly, the authors are representative of the new and innovative research now being conducted on this period. Equally important, they are familiar with historiographic trends outside their particular country of expertise, which for Gudmundson is Costa Rica and for Lindo-Fuentes, El Salvador.

Gudmundson and Lindo-Fuentes challenge the accepted liberal and often excessively rigid Marxist interpretations of the relationship between pre- and post-1870s Central American history. Underwriting this general purpose, although not systematically addressed in deference to the general audience for which the volume was written, is a wider objective: to offer a case study in which to deploy broader international historiographic trends, particularly efforts to reconceptualise the relations between civil society and

---

[16] *Ibid.*, p. 226.
[17] *Ibid.*, p. 232.

state formation. Given these broad agendas, and given the poor historiographies with which they had to work, the authors correctly see their slim text as a vehicle for provoking new research.

The specific arguments most relevant to this chapter that Gudmundson and Lindo-Fuentes detail are the following: First, Central American elites — whether liberal or conservative — deployed liberal policies towards Church, state, land and people long before the Liberal Reform period of the 1870s that promoted the so-called 'coffee and banana republics' established thereafter. Secondly, this occurred by the 1850s and 1860s, not because of a unified commitment to liberalism, but rather, because of local responses to the new incentives offered to export agriculture. These included political stability and the stimulus and cost-savings offered by maritime transportation on the region's Pacific coast, itself a process linked to the demands of the California Gold Rush of the late 1840s. The adoption of liberal policies occurred, that is, in the midst of the so-called general economic stagnation often attributed to the anarchistic era after the disintegration of the Central American Federation.[18]

If this broad argument is valid, suggest Gudmundson and Lindo-Fuentes, it means that a number of issues must be re-evaluated, especially if a new generation of historians is to be freed from the liberal and rigid Marxist views regarding relationships between civil society, the economy and the state prior to the 1870s. The authors thus offer a number of different theses that challenge the existing historiography.[19] These include the following points, which of course do not apply universally to all regions in Central America, and for which some work is available in the Honduran context:

1. The main obstacle to coffee exports before the 1870s was not land or peasant land tenure, but access to credit and labour.

2. Land privatisation, begun in the 1830s, intensified in the 1850s and 1860s, during the supposed period of stagnation and anarchy, not simply after the 1870s.[20]

3. The most forceful national identities assumed by the majority of Central Americans after Independence were rooted in conservative protection of Church ideology, not Church property or ecclesiastical economic influence.[21]

---

[18] An important economic history of nineteenth-century Honduras supports the Gudmundson and Lindo-Fuentes thesis. See Francisco Guevara-Escudero, 'Nineteenth-Century Honduras: A Regional Approach to the Economic History of Central America, 1839–1914', unpubl. D.Phil. dissertation, New York University (1983).

[19] See also J.L. Mahoney, 'Radical, Reformist and Aborted Liberalism: Origins of National Regimes in Central America', unpubl. D.Phil. dissertation, University of California (1997), pp. 1–79.

[20] For the application of this idea to Honduras, see both Guevara-Escudero, 'Nineteenth-Century Honduras'; and also Porfirio Pérez Chávez, 'Estructura económica de Honduras: gobierno del General Francisco Ferrera (1833–34, 1841–45, 1847)', unpublished *licenciatura* thesis, Universidad Nacional Autónoma de Honduras (1996).

[21] For Honduras, see also L. Oyuela, *Honduras: religiosidad popular, raíz de la identidad* (Choluteca, 1995); and Rolando Sierra Fonseca, 'Manuel Subirana y el movimiento me-

4. Ethnic identities, *indígena* and others, did not disappear quickly in the early to mid-nineteenth century, or even in the early twentieth century.[22]

5. Finally, and of great importance here, Gudmundson and Lindo-Fuentes argue that the civil wars in Central America before the dominance of coffee originated in 'an intraclass struggle among elites and would-be elites'. When considering this claim it is useful to bear in mind the model offered by Frank Safford many years ago for the early Latin American Independence period, namely, that the elite-dominated city-states 'near the colonial centres of privilege' defended the conservative cause, while 'all those on the periphery of power' sided with the liberal cause.[23]

One might quarrel that a number of points, some more significant than others, have been neglected in this book.[24] For example, the authors' argument would benefit from keeping state formation prior to coffee more directly relevant to their analysis. Historians elsewhere in Latin America have done so very effectively.[25] In this vein, Gudmundson and Lindo-Fuentes could profit from Robert G. Williams's concern with locating the origins of state formation under the auspices of coffee exports in the municipal structures inherited from the colonial period, particularly given the municipalities' general local sovereignty over issues of land. Even if we assume that credit and labour (issues not directly controlled at the municipal level) were the key factors in promoting coffee exports, the political origins of the coffee oligarchies that the authors believe emerged after the 1870s do need to be located at the municipal level.

Honduran historiography and Central America in the nineteenth century

To what extent does the existing historiography on nineteenth-century Honduras help us address the explanatory paradigms available in the work of Robert Williams and Lowell Gudmundson and Héctor Lindo-Fuentes, especially those issues on which their works converge? Let us first identify these points of overlap, since in many ways the texts by Williams and Gudmundson and Lindo-Fuentes diverge significantly. One issue on which all three authors seem to agree is the importance of bridging the chasm between pre-1870 and post-1870 history established

---

sianico en Honduras, 1857–1864', paper presented at the Museo de la República, Instituto Hondureño de Antropología e Historia, Tegucigalpa, Honduras, 20 Sept. 1996.

[22] For Honduras see Darío Euraque, 'La historiografía hondureña y el caudillismo indígena: entre Lempira y Gregoria Ferrera', paper presented to the Tercer Congreso Centroamericano de Historia, San José, Costa Rica, 15–18 July 1996; and Darío Euraque, *Estado, poder, nacionalidad y raza en la historia de Honduras: ensayos* (Tegucigalpa, 1996).

[23] Gudmundson and Lindo-Fuentes, *Central America*, p. 82; and Frank Safford, 'The Bases for Political Alignment in Early Republican Spanish America', in Richard Graham and Peter Smith (eds.), *New Approaches to Latin American History* (Austin, 1974), pp. 71–111.

[24] Women, politics and violence receive almost no comment. An interesting Honduran contribution that does examine these issues is Rocío Tabora, *Masculinidad y violencia en la cultura política hondureña* (Tegucigalpa, 1995).

[25] See for example Peloso and Tenenbaum (eds.), *Liberals, Politics and Power.*

by an older historiography, for which the coming to power of the liberal regimes of the 1870s represented a major rupture with the post-federation 'chaos', 'instability' and 'economic stagnation'.[26] While each author's general narratives offer distinct justifications for suggesting a continuity between pre- and post-1870s history, all underplay the supposed rupture between the anarchy of the 1840s–60s, and the stability of mono-export agriculture associated with coffee after the 1870s.

Williams, on the one hand, seems to offer a 'structural basis' for political conflict in nineteenth-century Central America, one grounded in elite cross-regional coffee township alliances seeking state power in order to further coffee production. Gudmundson and Lindo-Fuentes, on the other hand, draw on the Saffordian model mentioned earlier, that locates the social bases of war between a 'liberal' periphery, and a 'conservative' centre positioned near the colonial nucleus of privilege. Advances in Honduran historiography shed some light on these issues. Let us look first at Williams's thesis, which I have elsewhere addressed directly using Honduran sources, both primary and secondary.[27]

'Unlike the other countries', Williams suggests, 'Honduras did not develop a national class of coffee growers capable of building a national state.'[28] What is more, 'without an active class of agricultural entrepreneurs to push the reforms from below, the actions of the liberal state scarcely penetrated beyond the capital city'. Finally, 'although legislation was passed giving the facade of a liberal, secular state, the Honduran government continued the colonial tradition of living off concessions to *aguardiente* producers and foreign companies'.[29] In the end, 'in Honduras a national coffee elite did not emerge to influence the formation of the national state during the late nineteenth and early twentieth centuries'.[30]

This does not mean, Williams argues, that Honduras remained totally marginal to the region-wide effort to produce coffee, and that somehow the country lacked coffee elites and important coffee townships. According to Williams, 'capitalist agriculture penetrated the Honduran coffee economy during the nineteenth century, but it did best in areas that had already been carved out for haciendas'.[31] Furthermore, 'most of the land suitable for coffee ... was located in areas previously dominated by peasant agriculture', including in the richest coffee areas, Santa Bárbara and Comayagua.[32] And since the 'national state was unable (and, perhaps, unwilling at times) to in-

---

[26] One of Honduras's most prominent historians addressed this issue many years ago. See Mario R. Argueta, *Cronología de la reforma liberal hondureña* (Tegucigalpa, 1982), Colección Cuadernos Universitarios no. 23.

[27] Darío Euraque, *Reinterpreting the 'Banana Republic': Region and State in Honduras, 1870s–1972* (Chapel Hill, 1996), pp. 10–13.

[28] Williams, *States and Social Evolution*, p. 210.

[29] *Ibid.*

[30] *Ibid.*, p. 324, note 22.

[31] *Ibid.*, p. 97.

[32] *Ibid.*, p. 97.

tervene on their behalf, capitalists investing in coffee had to go through lo-cal institutions to gain access to land'.[33]

Although it is not clear how it happened, 'the exception in Honduras [from this pattern]', argues Williams, 'was in the [southern] department of Choluteca, where capitalist agriculture preceded the introduction of coffee, and the more commercialised townships privatised the surrounding lands'.[34] However, while 'in southern Honduras, merchants and landowners had suf-ficient clout in the commercial township of Choluteca to secure the land at higher elevation suitable for coffee ... they did not have colleagues in a similar position in other towns to form a lobbying force at a national level'.[35] Thus, in stark contrast to the other countries in Central America, 'Honduras retained a state that lived of concessions, [and] the government was run by a succession of generals and lawyers, and only one president, Luis Bográn (1883–91), be-came a coffee planter in 1892'.[36]

This interesting analysis leaves open the critical question as to why the bottom-up state-building theory Williams posits for the other countries in Central America may not apply to the Honduran case. Williams notes, for example, that 'the empirical focus on coffee alone ... prevents this study from uncovering the forces that did shape the evolution of the Honduran state', that is, that state 'incapable' or at times 'unwilling' to intervene on be-half of 'capitalists investing in coffee' in places like Santa Bárbara and Co-mayagua.[37] In Williams's view, to apply his theory of state formation to the Honduran case, 'one would have to examine the municipal records of commercial townships located in zones other than the peasant-dominated coffee areas'. In fact, Williams suggests, 'it would be interesting to see to what extent local elites on the North Coast, cattle barons in Olancho and mining officials or merchants in the major mining centres played a positive role in the development of national state institutions in Tegucigalpa, using their local townships as a springboard for national action'.[38]

I have addressed Williams's suggestion by drawing on research in the San Pedro Sula region of the banana-growing North Coast during the cru-cial era between the early 1870s and 1900, that is, before the direct invest-ments made by the foreign companies in railroads and land for banana exports and cultivation. I also connect my new research in that region not only to the specific issues addressed by Williams's thesis, but also to his par-ticular contention that the weak concessionary state in Honduras originated 'in the colonial era [when] functionaries of the state ... enrich[ed] them-selves by granting mining and timber concessions to foreign enterprises'.[39]

[33] *Ibid.*, p. 192.
[34] *Ibid.*, p. 101. Young Honduran scholars have offered some research on the question. See José Barahona G. et al., 'La evolución de la propiedad privada terrateniente en el mu-nicipio de Choluteca, 1865–1891', unpublished *Licenciatura* thesis, Universidad Nacional Autónoma de Honduras (1989).
[35] Williams, *States and Social Evolution*, p. 211.
[36] *Ibid.*, p. 219.
[37] *Ibid.*, p. 192.
[38] *Ibid.*, p. 324, note 22.
[39] Williams, *States and Social Evolution*, p. 92.

Finally, I offer another reading to why Santa Bárbara and Comayagua elites, coffee or otherwise, did not consider potential alliances with their counterparts in Choluteca.[40]

First, let me consider the concession enjoyed between the 1890s and 1912 by Washington S. Valentine over the Inter-Oceanic Railroad, Honduras's only railroad at the time. What was this mining tycoon based in Tegucigalpa transporting during almost two decades? Mostly bananas, bananas which provided a small export tax to a state deeply indebted to British bondholders since the 1870s. This fact must in turn be tied to Williams's recognition that 'Honduras was the last of the Central American countries to embrace the coffee boom and the last to have a commercial bank, [the Banco de Honduras]'.[41] Moreover, Williams also indicates that, 'even after 1888 when the first Honduran bank was chartered, long-term lending to agriculture (including coffee) was impeded by the durability of a peasant-based land tenure system'.[42]

Consider an alternative approach to the lack of a 'long-term lending to agriculture' problem, namely that the 'durability of a peasant-based land tenure system', even in the rich coffee areas of Santa Bárbara and Comayagua, was not the *key* problem that explains why the Banco de Honduras 'failed' to offer long-term credit to coffee cultivators. The land-tenure system remained an issue, but in my view the main difficulty turned on the role of the silver boom and its relationship to the founders of the bank itself. To begin with, most of the founding members of the Banco de Honduras enjoyed intimate commercial relations with the mining boom, both as shareholders in major companies and as ministers in the *Reforma* state.[43]

Therefore, in Honduras 'long-term lending to agriculture' and the 'durability of a peasant-based land tenure system' were not necessarily connected. The bankers associated with the mining boom between 1880 and 1900, including President Luis Bográn (1883–91), who owned shares in Honduras's first private bank, were not interested in 'long-term lending to agriculture'.[44] In fact, one scholar has argued that Bográn, unlike President Marco Aurelio Soto, 'actively supported the *ejidal* system', distributing communal lands at a time when in El Salvador and Guatemala the opposite was taking place.[45] There, coffee-promoting executives were slowly attacking communal properties.[46] In Honduras, the *Reforma* presidents profited immensely from mining and commerce, including Marco Aurelio Soto, who was a major shareholder in the New York and Rosario Mining Co., owned in part by Washington S. Valentine.

---

[40] See Euraque, *Reinterpreting the 'Banana Republic'*, pp. 9–13.

[41] Williams, *States and Social Evolution*, p. 185.

[42] *Ibid.*, pp. 211, 219.

[43] Guillermo Molina-Chocano, 'La formación del estado y el orígen minero-mercantil de la burgesía hondureña', *Estudios Sociales Centroamericanos*, no. 25 (1980); and Ammarella Vélez O. and Ivan Herrera, 'Historia de la municipalidad de Tegucigalpa, años 1870–1903', unpublished *Licenciatura* thesis, Universidad Nacional Autónoma de Honduras (1982).

[44] Brand, 'The Background of Capitalist Underdevelopment', p. 80.

[45] *Ibid.*, p. 237, note 364.

[46] Shelton H. Davis, 'Agrarian Structure and Ethnic Resistance: the Indian in Guatemala and Salvadoran National Politics', in Remo Guidieri et al. (eds.), *Ethnicities and Nations* (Austin, 1988).

Indeed, one of Soto's sons married one of Washington S. Valentine's daughters.[47] In short, the 'durability of a peasant-based land tenure system' did not represent an 'impediment', because in the 1880s and 1890s the bankers and the liberal reformers effectively abandoned the coffee option.

The serious study of the emerging role of banana cultivation in Honduras between the 1870s and 1900 in the context of Williams's argument does not amount to over-emphasising world system forces to the detriment of local conditions, pre-coffee or otherwise. It instead entails emphasising the fact that the North Coast's most prominent landed families had emigrated to that region from the coffee-growing regions of Santa Bárbara and Comayagua, and that the process of migration intensified precisely during the decades when the state in Tegucigalpa began to encourage not only the export of coffee, but export agriculture in general.

The reason why elites began abandoning two of the most important coffee growing regions in Honduras for the North Coast in the 1880s and 1890s had little to do with 'impediments' they might have confronted when considering the coffee-export option. The problem was not the 'durability of a peasant-based land tenure system', as Gudmundson and Lindo-Fuentes agree. Instead, the commercial and even landed elite had more to gain from relatively easy access to the banana lands and commercial opportunities than from coffee. In the long run, Honduras did not have a coffee oligarchy, with its attendant ultra-authoritarian and exclusivist state.

Where does this leave the Honduran case in Williams's overall argument? First, his contention that state building in Honduras did not follow the 'coffee township to national stage scenario' evidenced elsewhere in Central America between the 1840s and 1900 is correct. On the other hand, his model unfortunately offers no perspective for explaining the course and character of civil wars in nineteenth-century Honduras as outlined earlier in the chapter. Does the Honduran historiography shed light on this problem? Does the existing Honduran historiography support the alternative Saffordian model offered in the work of Gudmundson and Lindo-Fuentes?

Some important work on nineteenth-century Honduras has in varied ways addressed the problems with the Williams thesis and, at the same time, by drawing on new archival research, has shed light on the viability of the Saffordian model for the Honduran context. One such study represents an innovative approach to the transition between late colonial Honduran history and the civil war period of the post-1840s. A second work explores the existence of a Honduran 'oligarchy' prior to the 1870s. Finally, another work, currently in progress, addresses the character of the political rivalries between two supposedly 'conservative' and 'liberal' city-states, Comayagua, the colonial capital and capital of the state of Honduras until 1881, and Tegucigalpa, associated with the ascendance of late nineteenth-century positivist liberalism.

Leticia Oyuela's *Un siglo en la hacienda: estancias y haciendas en la antigua Alcaldía Mayor de Tegucigalpa (1670–1850)* analyses the rela-

---

[47] Brand, 'The Background of Capitalist Underdevelopment', p. 242, note 414.

tion between the history of Honduran *estancias* and haciendas and the cultural *mentalité* of their owners during this period.[48] She develops various arguments, some of more direct relevance here. According to Oyuela, by the late eighteenth century, the slow acquisition of land by the descendants of the conquistadores in Honduras, now *criollos*, produced a particular '*mentalidad criolla*' in and around what Gudmundson and Lindo-Fuentes call the Tegucigalpa city-state.[49] This *criollo mentalité* consolidated around the silver mining nexus in and around Tegucigalpa, because many of the colonial *hacendados* enjoyed investments in the mining industry.[50]

Equally important, this *criollo* mentality found broader legitimacy in the formation of a *criollo*-dominated local Catholic hierarchy, especially around aesthetic and cultural practices, often patronised by ecclesiastical personae connected by kinship ties with the mining-hacienda elites near Tegucigalpa.[51] Moreover, this cultural power enjoyed a political institutionalisation in the municipality of Tegucigalpa. Finally, these *criollo* elites promoted and secured an inter-ethnic conciliation by manipulating patron-saint celebrations, and other public Church rituals.[52] In this way, the *criollos* managed to establish alliances with urban *castas* who had played a key role in the pro-Independence process.[53]

What happened after Independence? Contrary to the claims of the traditional historiography, and seemingly unsupportive of the Saffordian model, Honduras's civil wars did not represent a conflict between city-states such as Comayagua and Tegucigalpa. Rather, the cultural *mentalité* of the *criollos*, whether in Comayagua or Tegucigalpa, a cultural *mentalité* feudal at heart, misread the liberalism of the Enlightenment, and their political leaders joined forces with non-*criollo* descendants of the *castas* in the conflicts of the 1840s and 1850s noted earlier.[54] The civil wars of this period, and those of the 1860s and 1870s, did not represent conflicts between liberals and conservatives, but rather intra-elite conflicts among the descendants of *criollos*.

Oyuela's work is an interesting hypothesis that is addressed in work by Jeff Samuels, Oscar Zelaya and others. Samuels views the post-Independence rivalry between Comayagua and Tegucigalpa 'in the context

---

[48] Leticia Oyuela, *Un siglo en la hacienda: estancias y haciendas en la antigua alcaldía mayor de Tegucigalpa (1670–1850)* (Tegucigalpa, 1994).

[49] Also see Marvin A. Barahona, 'La alcaldía mayor de Tegucigalpa bajo el régimen de intendencias (1788–1812)', *Estudios Antropológicos e Históricos*, no. 11 (Tegucigalpa, 1996) pp. 1–38.

[50] Luis Taracena Arriola, 'Minas, sociedad y política: la alcaldía mayor de Tegucigalpa', unpublished M.A. thesis, Universidad Nacional de Costa Rica (1993).

[51] Also see Leticia Oyuela, *Historia mínima de Tegucigalpa* (Tegucigalpa, 1989).

[52] Kevin Avalos, 'Fiestas y diversiones urbanas: una ventana a las mentalidades colectivas de la época colonial', *Paraninfo*, no. 8 (Tegucigalpa, 1995) pp. 57–74.

[53] This view challenges two important perspectives on this issue: Marvin A. Barahona, *La evolución de la identidad nacional* (Tegucigalpa, 1991) and Marielos Chaverri, 'La protesta social en Honduras colonial', *Paraninfo*, no. 10 (Tegucigalpa, 1996) pp. 15–34. These authors argue that no 'inter-ethnic conciliation' occurred during the colonial period.

[54] Echoes of this approach are evident for the Central American region as a whole in A. Bonilla, 'The Central American Enlightenment, 1770–1838', unpubl. D.Phil. diss., University of Manchester (1996).

of the liberal-conservative dichotomy'.[55] Samuels's work remains unfinished, but he offers some points of relevance here. For example, he too challenges the liberal-conservative ideological axis of conflict in the nineteenth century, and instead suggests that the civil wars be seen more as struggles 'among regions than an ideological struggle between political philosophies'.[56]

On the other hand, some work does suggest a regional basis to liberalism, however not in the peripheral sense, but in an economic sense. Gene R. Muller argued years ago that many of the elite liberal and anti-clerical attitudes prevalent in Honduras early in the nineteenth century originated with cattlemen opposed to Church tithes since 'the livestock producers' contributions comprised the majority of the tithe gross amounts each year'.[57] Was this liberalism regionally distinctive?[58] How did this earlier liberalism, the sort advocated by Francisco Morazán, affect the liberalism of the *Reforma* period?

At any rate, it seems that the regional focus that Samuels suggests is more particular than the Saffordian model, since it is not dichotomised around 'central' and 'peripheral' areas, but rather around municipalities within central and peripheral areas. According to Samuels, 'the argument is essentially that the level of societal organisation affecting most of the population in the nineteenth and early twentieth century was the municipality, and not necessarily the department or state level'.[59] In this way, Samuels's work may fill the gap left by the fact that Robert G. Williams's thesis does not deal with the dynamics of Honduran history before the 1870s.

Oscar Zelaya's work on the Honduran 'mining-hacienda' oligarchy that consolidated its hold on the municipality of Tegucigalpa between the 1840s and 1870s seems supportive of Samuels's concerns with grounding the social bases of Honduran civil wars in this period in regional antagonisms that lacked the ideological cohesion along a liberal-conservative axis assumed in the older historiographies.[60] The fact is that the families whose economic power is detailed by Zelaya represented a sector of the *criollos* whose *mentalité* is discussed by Oyuela.[61]

On the other hand, while Samuels's focus on municipal regions might enrich the lacunae in Williams's thesis as applied to Honduras, it, like Williams's analysis, fails to link interesting social and economic histories to political analy-

---

[55] Jeff Samuels, 'Another Tale of Two Cities: Political Rivalry and Economic Change during the Decline of Comayagua and the Rise of Tegucigalpa, 1821–1876', dissertation prospectus, Tulane University (1990).

[56] Jeff Samuels, 'Zonas regionales en la historia de la formación del estado de Honduras: 1830s–1930s: la zona central', paper presented at the Conference of the Latin American Studies Association, Los Angeles, 25 Sept. 1992.

[57] Gene Muller, 'The Church in Poverty: Bishops, Bourbons and Tithes in Spanish Honduras, 1700–1821', unpubl. D.Phil. diss., University of Kansas (1982), p. 184, note 32.

[58] Some work on the Olancho civil wars in the 1860s suggest it was. See José Sarmiento, *Historia de Olancho* (Tegucigalpa, 1990).

[59] Samuels, 'Zonas Regionales en la Historia', p. 13.

[60] Oscar Zelaya, 'Tipificación del grupo social dominante en el antiguo Departamento de Tegucigalpa, 1839–1875', unpubl. *Licenciatura* thesis, Universidad Nacional Autónoma de Honduras (1992).

[61] Also see Oscar Zelaya, 'La alcaldía de Tegucigalpa y su desarrollo poblacional', *Paraninfo*, no. 10 (1996), pp. 145–56.

sis and narrative. This, of course, is a major problem in the overall Latin American historiography on politics in the nineteenth century. In other words, while the historiography that emerged as dominant in the 1970s displaced the 'great man' approach, thereafter few studies tried to address directly the political history of the nineteenth century in ways that viewed the great caudillos and their entanglements in civil wars in the contexts of regional economic and social histories.[62] In short, there is much to be done if Honduran political history of the nineteenth century is to rival advances made elsewhere in Latin America.[63]

---

[62] Exceptions in the historiography of Honduras are Kenneth Finney, 'Rosario and the Election of 1887: The Political Economy of Mining in Honduras', *Hispanic American Historical Review*, vol. 59, no. 1 (1979); Sarmiento, *Historia de Olancho;* Robert H. Holden, 'Caudillos, Partidos, elecciones y guerras: hacia un entendimiento de la violencia en la historia política centroamericana', paper presented to the Tercer Congreso Centroamericano de Historia, San José, Costa Rica, 15–18 July 1996; and Robert H. Holden, 'El carácter del ejército de Honduras en los finales del siglo XIX: bandos armados o institución nacional?', *Revista de Historia*, no. 9 (Nicaragua, 1997).

[63] For example, writing on Honduras has nothing to equal Donald F. Stevens, *Origins of Instability in Early Republican Mexico* (Durham, NC, 1991); Ralph Lee Woodward Jr., *Rafael Carrera and the Emergence of the Republic of Guatemala, 1821–1871* (Athens, GA, 1993); and Gilbert Joseph and D. Nugent, *Everyday Forms of State Formation: Revolution and the Negotiation of Rule in Modern Mexico* (Durham, NC, 1994).

CHAPTER 5

Cautionary Tale: A Radical Priest, Nativist Agitation and the Origins of Brazilian Civil Wars

John Charles Chasteen

Nothing was dearer to Brazil's nineteenth-century elite than the image of Brazilian institutional stability amid Spanish American civil wars. Nonetheless, Brazil's civil wars define an epoch of the country's political history — a tumultuous generation following Independence — very much as in Spanish America. Extended outbreaks of fighting occurred in the Amazonian north (1835–40), on the plains of Rio Grande do Sul (1835–45), in and around the capital of Bahia (1837–38) and in the backlands of Maranhão (1839–40), with briefer eruptions in São Paulo (1842), Minas Gerais (1842) and Pernambuco (1848). For several years, the accumulation of these revolts threatened to fragment Brazil, and they figure in standard narratives as 'the most radical and violent rebellions in Brazilian history, before or since'.[1] In the other hand, some of these 'wars' lasted only months, few spilled much outside the borders of a single province and none ever threatened to overthrow the central government. They pale, it must be admitted, beside the Spanish American version. After a few unpredictable years in the mid 1830s, the imperial state inexorably gained the upper hand, consolidated its grip and eventually won its vaunted reputation for seemingly imperturbable stability during the close-to-half-century rule of Pedro II.[2]

Taken singly, none of these regional or liberal rebellions (as they are collectively known) has much claim on the attention of Brazilian historians, but taken together, they pose an interpretative challenge. Their synchronous timing despite widespread distribution — north, north-east, centre, south — strongly suggests linked origins. Were these rebellions parallel manifestations of the same, general Brazilian phenomenon, and if so, how? Certainly, the weakened monarchical legitimacy of the regency years (1831–40) must begin such a general explanation. Beyond that, however, collective assessments of the revolts have tended to dwell on the political economy that made each distinctive. For example, some seemed to threaten the hierarchical social order, others merely to defend a particular version of it. Powerful landowners spearheaded the rebellion in some provinces and opposed it in others. One began as a strictly urban barracks revolt, one in the remote backlands, and so on. Meanwhile, the crucial question of common origins usually gets an answer that can be

---

[1] Leslie Bethell (ed.), *Brazil: Empire and Republic, 1822–1930* (Cambridge, 1989), p. 68.

[2] Good overviews are Emilia Viotti da Costa, *The Brazilian Empire: Myths and Histories* (Chicago, 1985), pp. 53–77; Roderick J. Barman, *Brazil: The Forging of a Nation, 1798–1852* (Stanford, 1988), pp. 161–216; and Leslie Bethell and José Murilo de Carvalho, '1822–1850', in Bethell (ed.), *Brazil: Empire and Republic*, pp. 58–75.

paraphrased as follows: during the early 1830s, decentralising reforms of liberal inspiration devolved too much political power to provinces and localities, allowing petty factionalism to spin out of control.[3] This answer is presented today without evidence, enthusiasm or elaboration, and is the legacy of a much older historiography: the consensual narrative of the winners, an apology for centralised rule. Brazilians, reads the unexamined subtext of this version, were simply not yet ready for liberty.[4]

There is a lot wrong with this explanation, yet it does take the most logical starting point. Not for nothing are these known as liberal revolts. With minor exceptions, all the rebel movements were loosely identified with liberal ideas like popular sovereignty, limited monarchy, social contract and more adventurously, federalism or even republicanism. While contemporaries did not call these various movements by any collective name, few rebels would have objected to being called liberal. They shared a common political vocabulary and saw themselves engaged in national political issues. But do republicans really share an ideology with proponents of limited monarchy? Can slave-owners be true liberals? Concentrating on the programmatic particulars of liberal ideologies does not lend much coherence to Brazilian political history in the period, except in the broadest sense, because early Brazilian liberalism was too inchoate, too various, too quickly evolving and also too full of contradictions. In addition, most Brazilians who joined liberal rebellions seem to have paid little mind to debates over forms of government. On one matter, however, they tolerated no ambivalence. Liberals were Brazilian patriots, committed to independence, steadfastly opposed to everything Portuguese: hierarchical absolutism, the threat of recolonisation and, most especially, the fellow with his thumb on the scales down at the corner store.

Specifically anti-Portuguese nativism was a standard theme of the liberal journalism that characterised Brazilian public life in the 1830s and, because newspapers were widely circulated and copied from each other, lent it unity. Unlike the rarefied debate over forms of government, the simple message of nativist agitation — 'Brazil should be for the Brazilians' — had explosive populist resonances.[5] Nothing political could more quickly bring an angry crowd into the street (as happened countless times throughout urban Brazil during these years) than the nativist 'hot button issue'. Anti-Portuguese name-calling by violent mobs may seem an unpromising place to look for major themes in Brazilian political history. My real interest is in nativism as proto-nationalism. Nativism was not a complex intellectual elaboration of national character, nor a

---

[3] Viotti da Costa, *Brazilian Empire*, pp. 68–9; Barman, *Brazil*, pp. 179–80; Bethell and Carvalho, '1822–1850', p. 68.

[4] This elite consensus is described by Richard Thomas Flory, *Judge and Jury in Imperial Brazil, 1808–1871: Social Control and Political Stability in the New State* (Austin, 1981), pp. 137–56. For its expression in national master narratives, see João Pandia Calogeras, *A History of Brazil* (New York, 1963), first published 1929, as well as the general overviews cited above.

[5] Slogan in the masthead of a nativist paper of Recife, *A revolução de novembro*, 1850. 'Panfletários da Revolução Praieira', *Revista do Arquivo Público*, Recife (Dec. 1976), p. 55.

project of nation-building. It had an immediate, tactical and mostly partisan emphasis. Importantly, though, it promoted new, territorially defined political identities, a crucial dimension of modern nationalism.[6]

The other side of the anti-Portuguese coin was pro-Brazilian. When nativist leaders began to formulate the terms of conflict as Portuguese versus Brazilian, they created the possibility of political alliances spanning divisions of race and class among the native born. Here lay the potential radicalism and also the practical magic of nativism, the magic that Spanish American Creoles had used to stir and direct mass mobilisation during the Wars of Independence.[7] In Brazil, liberalism, nativism and mass mobilisation got a later start and developed as political forces largely *after* independence. And that, I contend, is the most revealing light in which to view the liberal rebellions of 1835–48.

As had occurred in Spanish America, in Brazil the process of mass mobilisation sometimes unleashed destructive popular energies quite frightening to the elite, and even to the leaders who originally let the genie out of the bottle. The civil war that rocked the province of Pará between 1835 and 1840 constitutes a striking example of the nativists' ability to create an alliance across lines of race and class, a notable example, too, of destructive power unleashed.[8] To that example we now turn, beginning the narrative, as the nativists of Pará inevitably did, with the events of Brazilian Independence. One could not wish a better protagonist for this story than the Paraense nativist movement's unrivalled leader, a radical priest and publisher named João Batista Gonçalves Campos.

Batista Campos was white, a rural-born local boy, ordained at the seminary in Belém, capital of the province, in 1805. The origin of his political radicalism is a mystery. With a population of only about 24,000, Belém was hardly a metropolis, so Batista Campos must have met his fellow cleric Luiz Zagala, a French priest from Cayenne who spent more than a year in Belém, between 1815 and 1817, before being deported for his seditious ideas. Campos was also influenced by Felipe Alberto Patroni, a Paraense who was studying at Coimbra when Portuguese liberals made their 1820 revolution. Patroni, then an ardent 22 years old, left school and returned immediately to Pará, where he raised support for the liberal revolution. Brazilian provincial capitals now entered an

---

[6] I follow Roderick Barman and Richard Thomas Flory in highlighting nativism, but differ in considering it proto-nationalism. Barman sees provincial nativism as anti-nationalist, because loyalty to province crosscut loyalty to Brazil as a whole (Barman, *Brazil*, p. 111) while I am interested in what the two share: the concept of a territorially defined 'people'.

[7] In other words, I regard early nineteenth-century nativism as a crucial step in 'imagining' a national community. Benedict Anderson, *Imagined Communities: Reflections on the Origin and Spread of Nationalism* (London, 1983), of course supplies this concept, but his application of it to Spanish America and Brazil overemphasises the role of colonial newspapers and bureaucratic careers and misses the importance of mass mobilisation accompanying the process of Independence itself.

[8] For regional background and a relevant discussion of the social construction of race, see David Cleary, '"Lost Altogether to the Civilized World": Race and the Cabanagem in Northern Brazil, 1750 to 1850', *Comparative Studies in Society and History*, vol. 40 (1998), pp. 109–35.

uncertain — and, for some, heady — time of *conselhos abertos* (the precise equivalents of the Spanish American *cabildos abiertos* of 1810) and locally elected provisional juntas, an aspect of the Independence process that is obscured by the general tendency to focus on events in Rio.[9]

In April 1822, after participating in the formation of Brazil's first such provisional junta, Batista Campos helped Patroni found the radical liberal *O Paraense*, the first newspaper in Pará. The reaction was not long in coming. In May 1822, Patroni was arrested and deported, leaving Batista Campos to take over *O Paraense* and the leadership of Belém's radical liberals, despite repeated jailings and harassment from the largely conservative local authorities. For the next 15 years, Batista Campos stood clearly at the centre of a conflictive popular movement in Belém. From prison, in internal exile, at the barricades and always by means of the radical press, Campos announced his cause as the vindication of Brazilian Independence, a struggle against the recolonising conspiracies of the Portuguese party.[10]

It is easy to see how the nativist priest got started on this road. In September 1822, when news reached Belém of Pedro I's call for Independence, Campos published it in *O Paraense* and got two weeks in jail for his insolence from the authorities of Belém. Loyalist tendencies were strong in Belém, a city of paved principal streets, an impressive governor's palace, large churches and convents, a seminary and botanical garden. Prevailing winds and currents gave Belém better communications with Lisbon than with Rio. Furthermore, the strategic importance of the Amazon region made for a strong (and generally loyalist) Portuguese military presence in the city, and there were also many Portuguese wholesale merchants who dealt in nuts and other fruits of the forest. Independence came to Belém from without, in the form of a warship sent from Rio de Janeiro. Overnight, the Portuguese province became part of independent Brazil, with its Portuguese — now 'adopted Brazilian' — rulers still in place.[11]

Campos and his movement questioned the patriotism of the provincial government and demanded a new, native Brazilian one. Only then did the social turmoil of Independence really begin in Pará. In October 1823, revolting soldiers forcibly ousted the offending Portuguese-born officials and named Batista Campos the new provincial president. The rebellion was put down by marines from a Brazilian brig whose commander (an English mercenary) mistrusted the unruly patriotic mob. The naval commander had Batista Campos held against the mouth of a cannon (its fuse lit to dramatise matters) before sending him in chains to

---

[9] Pasquale di Paolo, *Cabanagem: a revolução popular da Amazônia* (Belém, 1990), pp. 89–100; and Barman, *Brazil*, p. 88.

[10] Without question the richest published source is Domingos Antônio Raiol, *Motins políticos, ou história dos principais acontecimentos políticos da Província do Pará desde o ano de 1821 até 1835*, 3 vols (Belém, 1970), which first appeared between 1865 and 1890.

[11] On Portuguese loyalism in the north, see Barman, *Brazil*, pp. 102–6.

Rio. The soldiers whose barracks revolt had placed Campos so briefly in power were not so lucky. Five were chosen at random for exemplary execution, then 256 others were packed so closely into the hold of the *Palhaço* (the 'Clown,' as the vessel was ironically named) that they all smothered in one night of suffocating Amazonian heat.[12]

Twelve years later, as Batista Campos led the Paraense nativist movement to the brink of the most devastating civil war in Brazilian history, the 'Brazilian Party' and the 'Portuguese Party' were still divided along essentially the same lines. By 1833, a contemporary account referred to 'an inveterate hatred that has long existed between the two parties'.[13] The Brazilian Party was still talking about the *Palhaço*. How often would not the participants in mid-nineteenth-century civil wars have recounted similar antecedents for their conflicts all over Latin America? I refer here not only to a continuity of political cleavages and leadership, but specifically to the war stories, the tales of martyrdom, the cries for vengeance that made up so much partisan discourse in the nineteenth century. These narratives most frequently start with Independence, and combatants in these wars often made sense of them in this way, a circumstance which we must take into account, along with attention to the political economy that contemporaries often excluded from their explanations. Overall, the locations of greatest conflict in Brazil at the time of Independence correlate strongly with the scenes of later civil wars.[14]

Batista Campos was, above all, a political journalist. Shockingly little appears to have survived to represent the writing of a man who wrote so much. I have not yet found a single copy of any of his newspapers, though I suspect some exist outside Belém and Rio. Nothing of what survives, however, suggests an unusually powerful bent as a political ideologue. Batista Campos was an influential writer for reasons that had little to do with his originality or persuasiveness. Writing his pamphlets, broadsides and periodicals allowed this radical priest to participate in a national political discourse, located him in a specific quadrant of it and thus gave him prospective allies throughout Brazil and, above all, in Rio de Janeiro. Although there were no nationally organised parties, Brazilian nativism created a broad sense of national alignments. As a radical liberal who defended the interests of native-born Brazilians against the Portuguese-born (and their fellow travellers), Campos was clearly a potential ally for nativists who wielded significant influence in the National Assembly during the 1820s.[15] Precisely for that reason, although he was sent as a pris-

---

[12] Di Paolo, *Cabanagem*, pp. 102–13.

[13] Instituto Histórico e Geográfico Brasileiro, Rio de Janeiro (hereafter IHGB), Coleção Alencar Araripe, Ofício do Governador do Pará, José Joaquim Machado de Oliveira ao Governo Imperial, ofício, 11 May 1833.

[14] Greatest Portuguese resistance to Independence occurred in Pará, Maranhão and Bahia, scenes of three of the four major civil wars: Barman, *Brazil*, pp. 104–5.

[15] According to Flory, *Judge and Jury*, the men who dedicated themselves to journalism in the period were almost always liberals, and by 1827, 'liberal reformism and revolutionary nativism had become identified (pp. 5–14).

oner to Rio on two occasions, he returned each time in triumph to Belém
thanks to the efforts of political allies at the imperial court.

Take, for example, the pamphlet entitled 'Apology for João Batista Gonçalves Campos, Canon of the Cathedral of Pará, currently a prisoner in Rio
de Janeiro, To serve as refutation against the boorish calumnies with which
the enemies of the EMPEROR and of Brazil have tried to lower the well-
deserved reputation of this virtuous man, Written by a lover of the truth
and an admirer of the patriotism constantly evident among the clergy of
Pará'. The author describes Campos as 'the principal stay of Independence,
the bulwark of justice and column of provincial prosperity' in Pará. This
pamphlet also contains a series of addenda transcribing sworn testimonies
taken in Pará, to the effect that Batista Campos was a defender of Brazilian
Independence against its enemies.[16] The opening passage of another pamphlet (I will omit the title this time) gives a further sense of the mechanics
and tenor of this national political discourse in which 'character issues'
loomed large. The target here is the governor who imprisoned Campos
and sent him to Rio on the second occasion:

> Provoked ... by José d'Araujo Rozo, ex-president of Pará, with an article
> that appeared in the *Spectador* [sic] on the sixteenth of last month, sup-
> posedly copied from the London periodical *Padre Amaro* (but actually
> sent there from Pará by Rozo, because otherwise that journalist [the
> author of *Padre Amaro*] would not prostitute his pen nor risk his credi-
> bility with vague accusations completely lacking foundation and patently
> false anyway), I am obliged to entreat, once again, the attention of the re-
> spectable public, briefly describing the public life of this despicable indi-
> vidual [Rozo] as president of Pará, and without touching on his domestic
> or private life, not only because I decline to descend to his level, but from
> a desire not to offend the reader's Christian moral standards.[17]

The pamphlet (signed with the initials JBCG but probably not written by
Campos) goes on to accuse Rozo of blocking the practical implementa-
tion in Pará of the new Brazilian constitution. Batista Campos soon returned in triumph to Pará with a commendation from the emperor, but
his struggles as a nativist journalist had hardly begun.

Nativism and the periodical press arose together in the late 1820s and
early 1830s. This proliferation of partisan print media in a society formerly
without printing is a phenomenon worth pondering. There was not a single
press functioning anywhere in Portuguese America before 1808. Only a
handful of newspapers existed in all Brazil before Independence — exactly
two in 1814, both published in Rio. The first uncensored paper appeared
only in 1821. Censorship was reimposed from 1822 to 1826 (though defied in

---

[16] *Apologia de João Batista Gonçalves Campos, Cônego da Catedral do Pará, atualmente
preso no Rio de Janeiro. Para servir de refutação as grosseiras calumnias com que se tem
esforçado os inimigos do IMPERADOR e do Brasil a deprimir o bem merecido conceito
d'aquele virtuoso varão. Feito por um amante da verdade e admirador do patriotismo brasileiro devisado constantemente no Clero do Pará* (Rio de Janeiro, 1824).
[17] *Desagravo do Arcipreste João Batista Gonçalves Campos contra José d'Araujo Rozo* (Rio
de Janeiro, 1825).

Pernambuco by another radical priest and publisher, the famous Frei Caneca), slowing the expansion of printing, an activity still limited at that time to half a dozen provinces. The first presses arrived in the provinces of São Paulo and Rio Grande do Sul, for example, only in 1827. In the next four years, however, the number of periodical publications in Brazil more than quadrupled, totalling 54 by 1831. In the province of Bahia alone, no fewer than 60 short-run titles had appeared before 1837, and nativist journalism seems to have reached its most intense activity throughout the country precisely on the eve of the first regional revolts.[18] Quite suddenly, the radical liberal discourse that had formerly been confined to narrow channels (especially to French books smuggled into Brazil with false covers) was splashed within reach of anyone literate and, consequently, within hearing of many who were not. 'Nowadays there is no shoemaker, no barber, etc. who does not speak of the sovereignty of the people', sneered one conservative.[19]

'The blacks talk of nothing but Batista Campos and his party', echoed a Belém official in an 1831 report to the Minister of Empire.[20] But how did nativist discourse reach them, given that very few poor people of any colour could read? Some heard the paper read aloud, no doubt. For the most part, though, the press served to articulate a discourse of opposition among the literate across space, and then they delivered their own version of it to the illiterate majority by word of mouth. Sold by subscription, not in the street, political sheets like *O Paraense* (and later other Campos publications such as *Orfeu paraense*, *O publicador amazonense*, and *Paraguassú*)[21] preached to the choir. They sought not to convince readers so much as to supply them with convincing arguments for oral delivery. The frequent adoption of colourful personas who announce political opinions in colloquial language must have facilitated the transfer of political rhetoric from print to speech, and the common dialogical format, dramatising a political debate among various acquaintances, is suggestive in that regard as well.[22]

Nativist rags used the familiar language of liberal patriotism (seemingly staid, utterly generic and mostly unconvincing today) salted with anti-Portuguese invective of a tellingly colloquial tone: '*Eu sou o galego / La da botica / Sou muito amante / De quem m'enrica*'.[23] And, in a famil-

---

[18] Nelson Werneck Sodré, *História da imprensa no Brasil* (Rio de Janeiro, 1966), pp. 97, 134–5, 153, 213; Barman, *Brazil*, pp. 77–79.

[19] Flory, *Judge and Jury*, pp. 18–9. On the profound implications of the new partisan journalism for Brazilian political culture, see Sodré, *História da imprensa*, pp. 179–80; and Hélio Vianna, *Contribução a história da imprensa brasileira (1812–1869)* (Rio de Janeiro, 1945), p. 121.

[20] IHGB, Coleção Instituto Histórico, Marcelino José Cardoso to Ministério e Secretário do Estado dos Negócios do Império, 9 Sept. 1831.

[21] Ernesto Cruz, *Temas da história do Pará* (Belém, 1960), pp. 212–3.

[22] Vianna, *Contribução a história da imprensa*, pp. 137–41, 182.

[23] Epigraph of a satirical nativist paper, *O gallego* (Recife, 1849–50): 'Panfletários da Revolução Praieira', *Revista do Arquivo Público*, Recife (Dec. 1976), p. 55. Freely translated, the verse reads: 'I'm the Galician/From the corner store./When you make me richer,/I love you more'. Whether 'Galician' here extends vaguely to northern Portugal is a

iar reflex action, Brazilian nativists inverted the racial slurs proffered by their enemies. Although in most cases only rhetorically, they raised African and indigenous affiliations as a point of pride, as is evident in periodical titles like *O Mulato, O Cabrito,* and *O Indigena do Brazil.*[24] As one nativist orator announced to the Portuguese Côrtes in 1822: '*Mulatos, cabras,* and *crioulos; índios, mamelucos,* and *mestiços* are all our people ... Whatever their colour, whatever their status, they were born in Brazil' — in sharp contradistinction to those who 'left their umbilical cords in the lands of Portugal'.[25] Men born in Portugal still enjoyed power and wealth in Brazil long after most Spaniards had fled Spanish America. The Portuguese presence, representing the perpetuation of colonial hierarchies, became a defining factor of political life and birthplace provided a handy lever for challengers eager to pry powerful men out of government positions. Thus, in provinces like Pará, where men born in Portugal retained strong economic and political control after Independence, the nativist dichotomy was invoked most starkly and most vociferously by the native elite. This tactical situation, not an ideological mutation of nativist thought, made the movement radical in Pará.

As Brazilian nativism reached its zenith at the national level in the early 1830s, violent clashes began in Belém. News of the abdication of Pedro I — an abdication responding, in the immediate term, largely to nativist agitation against his 'Portuguese cabinet' — arrived in Pará a month and a half after the fact in the form of a newspaper brought from Maranhão. The April Revolution, as the nativists called the abdication, had unseated a monarch and heartened the revolutionaries particularly by suggesting the efficacy of popular mobilisation. After all, when Pedro famously declared that 'he would do anything for the people, but nothing they forced him to', the force in question was a menacing crowd that had gathered in Rio's Campo de Santana and refused to disperse over several days, demanding reinstatement of a 'Brazilian cabinet.[26] Batista Campos was the leader of analogous crowds in Belém. Now nearly 50, he had continued to hold notable ecclesiastical charges and to publish opposition papers. At the time of the April Revolution, he was a member of the Pará president's advisory council, with a significant personal following described in a hostile report to the central government as 'almost all of low condition' and including 'disreputable mulattos and blacks'.[27]

---

moot point, but as European outsiders, a Galician and a Minhoto (someone from Minho, in northern Portugal) were interchangeable.

[24] Sodré, *Historia da imprensa,* pp. 181–91.

[25] The quotations are from E. Bradford Burns, 'The Intellectuals as Agents of Change and the Independence of Brazil, 1724–1822', in A.J.R. Russel-Wood (ed.), *From Colony to Nation: Essays on the Independence of Brazil* (Baltimore, 1975), pp. 239–40; and Domingos Antônio Raiol, *Motins políticos,* vol. 3, p. 833. Terms describing Brazilians of mixed race are defined in Table 1.

[26] Barman, *Brazil,* p. 159.

[27] IHGB, Coleção Instituto Histórico, Marcelino José Cardoso to Ministério e Secretário do Estado dos Negócios do Império, 9 Sept. 1831

The April Revolution's repercussions in Pará put the radical priest again at the centre of the conflict. Given nativist influence in the regency, conservatives expected the worst from the new provincial president who arrived from Rio in July 1831. Meanwhile, the number of votes Campos had received in the election of the president's advisory council made him, effectively, the vice-president of Pará. By 7 August 1831, the new president had given such proof of his nativist sympathies that the conservative military commander of the province clapped him in prison and sent him back to Rio. Knowing better, at this point, than to send Batista Campos to Rio, the military commander destined him for *internal* exile on the Madeira River, deep in the Amazon basin. But the irrepressible Campos soon recovered his freedom of movement and used his trip up the river for political organising. He was recognised as the legitimate vice-president of the province in Obidos and Santarem, the only two towns of any political importance up river, and when the regency finally managed to put a new provincial president in place after about half a year, the radical priest was invited back to Belém and given a hero's welcome.[28]

If Batista Campos and his nativist motifs seemed welcome up river, it can also be said that nativism played well in the backlands generally, and that the insurgent forces that began Brazilian civil wars often gathered their strength from the hinterlands far from the major cities and plantation belts. The general characteristics of frontier life explain why. The population of Brazilian frontiers was strongly indigenous, with fewer whites or blacks and a lot of white/indigenous mixing among the landowning families. In addition, social distances (even the divide between master and slave) seemed more easily bridged on the frontier because disparities of wealth appeared less glaring in the rude conditions of daily life that all shared. Such social characteristics lent credence to the basic nativist claim that all Brazilians had something 'native' in common.

The parts of Pará that Batista Campos visited during his internal exile constituted the most indigenous lands in Brazil, a maze of rivers, great and small, with the inhabitants of the province living almost exclusively along the riverbanks, about 100,000 of them altogether, scattered across a subcontinent. Many of the people of Pará were *tapuios*, indigenous people who had lost their tribal culture (especially through missionisation) and now spoke Nheengatu, a generic form of Tupi and essentially the last remnant of the famous *lingua geral* of colonial Brazil. The *tapuios* fished, cultivated a bit of manioc, collected the bounty of the forest and came and went as they pleased: a floating population, in all senses of the word. This way of life was shared by many of mixed ancestry — *mamelucos*, *pardos* and *cafuzes* — likely to speak Portuguese in addition to Nheengatu. Although there were some sugar plantations not far from Belém and cattle ranches here and there, the landowners of Pará were not numerous or prosperous or powerful. The rural popula-

---

[28] Di Paolo, *Cabanagem*, pp. 127–8.

tion of the province lived mostly by subsistence agriculture, fishing and gathering (cacao, Brazil nuts, rubber) on land for which no legal title existed. The bureaucrats, military officers and wholesale merchants who composed the Portuguese party almost all lived in Belém. Thus, the few thousand *paraenses* up river who maintained some tenuous connection to Brazilian public affairs might easily welcome Batista Campos and embrace the principle of Brazil for the Brazilians, but they did not bring with them much political support. Even the sugar planters of Pará, some of whom belonged to the Brazilian Party, lacked the large retinues of social dependents typical of plantations elsewhere.[29]

So it was that the Portuguese Party, which loomed large in the streets of Belém, maintained the upper hand in the provincial government of Pará during the late 1820s and early 1830s, even with nativism ascendant in Rio. For example, the creation of a National Guard throughout Brazil (to undercut the power of a centrally controlled army) constituted an important part of the nativist project at the national level. In Pará, paradoxically, it was the Portuguese Party that, because of its predominant influence in the provincial government, managed to create the National Guard in its own image, filling it with 'adopted Brazilians' who refused to wear the national emblem. (One attempt to force them to wear it led them to depose the provincial president.) In response to this pre-emptive move by the Portuguese Party, the Brazilian Party formed its own militia, called the Municipal Guard. In the conflictive wake of the April Revolution, these two groups — whether or not operating formally as such — came to blows with increasing frequency on the streets of Belém. On 16 August 1833, 'with incredible velocity, rumours spread throughout the districts surrounding [Belém] saying that a faction composed of Portuguese and "adopted" Brazilians was conspiring against native-born Brazilians in order to destroy Independence'. On that day a pitched battle between the two sides left 95 dead.[30]

The bloody clash of 16 April 1833 represents another standard element of the origins of Brazilian civil wars. At issue, specifically, in the bloody streets of this small provincial city was not a policy but a person: the provincial president. This time it was Campos and his party who expected the worst of a new appointee who had not yet arrived, so they organised a petition drive, then a *conselho aberto*, to keep the current president, while the Portuguese Party rallied around his yet-to-arrive replacement. No single flashpoint appears more often or more crucially in the events leading to the liberal rebellions than disputes over who would be named, retained or ejected from the office of provincial presi-

---

[29] On rural Amazonia in the period, see John Hemming, *Amazon Frontier: The Defeat of the Brazilian Indians* (London, 1987); José Veríssimo, 'As populações indígenas e mestiças da Amazônia, sua linguagem, suas crenças, e seus costumes,' *Revista do Instituto histórico-geográfico brasileiro*, vol. 50 (1887), pp. 295–390; and Ernani Silva Bruno, *Amazônia (Acre — Amazônas — Pará — Territórios)*, vol. I of *História do Brasil — Geral e regional* (São Paulo, 1966).
[30] Quotation from IHGB, Coleção Alencar Araripe, José Joaquim Macedo de Oliveira, 11 May 1833 (discussing the events of 16 April 1833); Di Paolo, *Cabanagem*, pp. 128–33.

dent, and quite logically so. Given the overwhelming importance of patronage structures in political life, and the practical reality that the law
did not apply to one's friends, people really did matter more, in practical terms, than did policies.[31]

The president whom the Brazilian Party championed in April 1833
was a moderate, but he was also a Mason, and so was the next provincial
president sent from Rio. This Batista Campos would not brook. There is
more than a whiff of opportunism in the nativists' anti-Masonic crusade
at this juncture, for Masonry had been around quite a while, and it was
far from being exclusively a reactionary affair. By raising the spectre of
an anti-patriotic Masonic cabal, Campos neatly tarred the provincial
president with the same brush he used for his local enemies, since *Mason* served effectively as a code word for 'adopted Brazilian'. In addition, the Church had always frowned on Freemasonry, and the clergy of
Pará — from the bishop down — sympathised strongly with Campos,
supplying many nativist militants.[32]

The national triumph of nativism during the regency had exhilarated
but also frustrated Campos. Since the late 1820s, nativist influence in the
National Assembly had contributed to a general devolution of power away
from the central government, true enough, but only into the hands of the
locally powerful. Campos must have known he was pushing the authorities hard when he brought in another famous firebrand journalist,
Vicente Ferreira de Lavor Papagaio from Maranhão to Belém, where he
published the *Maranhaense Sentinel on Lookout in Pará*. In the words of
the provincial president — referring both to their anti-Masonic populism
and to their 'subversive principles' (now including mention of a federal
republic) — the two partisan journalists worked to 'spread the most atro-
cious insults around the town' and 'attempted to twist the opinion of the
least educated class of society, preaching absolute equality'.[33] When news
of important constitutional amendments (the 'Ato Adicional') reached
Belém in mid 1834, Campos and Papagaio rejected them in terms that,
according to the military commander of the city, began 'disposing spirits
toward civil war'.[34] The furious president was more explicit (though perhaps less reliable), saying that Campos and Papagaio denied the authen-
ticity of the published amendments and promised their followers that the
true version included freedom for slaves, proclamation of a republic and
the expulsion of all Portuguese, along with the confiscation of their possessions, to be distributed to members of the Brazilian Party.[35]

The authorities now shut down the subversive press and moved to
arrest Campos and Papagaio, who fled to the plantation of a sympa-

---

[31] Richard Graham, *Patronage and Politics in Nineteenth-Century Brazil* (Stanford, 1990).
[32] Di Paolo, *Cabanagem*, pp. 135–8.
[33] IHGB, Coleção Alencar Araripe, Ofício do Governador do Pará, José Joaquim Machado
de Oliveira ao Governo Imperial, ofício, 11 May 1833.
[34] IHGB, Coleção Instituto Histórico, Joaquim José da Silva Santiago, Comando da Armas
do Pará, 24 Nov. 1834.
[35] IHGB, Coleção Instituto Histórico, Bernardo Lobo de Souza, 24 Nov. 1834.

thiser. As they gathered forces outside the city, the nativists began to be called 'Cabanos' — from *cabanas*, the simple dwellings of the country-side. Government intelligence reports from visitors to the Cabano camp described a strikingly multiracial gathering that seemed set principally on 'finishing off the Masons'. One spy reported seeing Papagaio.[36] When a military force took the rebel camp, however, its commanding officer captured neither of the journalists, but he found a grave, reportedly Papagaio's.[37] More likely, the man buried there was Batista Campos. His sudden death at the outbreak of the war, supposedly as the result of his cutting an infected boil while shaving, would seem to raise questions. No suggestion of foul play has entered the historical record, however.[38]

Certainly, his leadership would be missed. Batista Campos had determination and the common touch among Amazonians, as well as national political alliances. The inventory of his possessions (done in 1850, well after the war) shows a man of property, including a substantial house in Belém and even a modest sugar plantation. It also shows three slaves, and there were probably more before the war.[39] Like the Cabano leaders who succeeded him, and like all the other leaders of nativist movements throughout Brazil, Campos was a white man who occupied a place in the upper reaches of the social hierarchy. If social levelling entered his political discourse, it figured less notably in his personal life.

In full perspective, nativist politics was initiated by the elite and only occasionally stirred and harnessed popular energies. As had been true at the time of Independence, when nativism first developed, the main purpose of nativist politics was the empowerment of a native-born leadership through the creation of cross-class, multi-racial alliances. Such alliances were much more risky than the mobilisation of social clientele that the upper classes used most often when deploying armed force. When landowners led their peons to a fight, military order confirmed the social order. But when nativist leaders called forth the entire racial gamut of native-born Brazilians on the premise that all shared rich, white enemies aligned with Portugal, they might unleash the whirlwind. This is what happened in the Paraense civil war that began in 1835. Although the rebels twice captured Belém, they were unable to consolidate these victories. Their activities spread for a thousand miles up-river. Nevertheless, a concerted campaign by the imperial government crushed the last holdouts by 1840. As many as 30,000, a fifth of the population of the province, may have died in the war.

The foregoing narrative demonstrates the importance of nativist agitation in Pará, as well as its links to a national political process. In order to

---

[36] IHGB, Coleção Manuel Barata, from a handwritten reproduction of the *Correio oficial paraense*, 15 Nov. 1834, which transcribes an 'Ofício do Comandante das Armas'.

[37] IHGB, Coleção Manuel Barata, Acará, Francisco de Siqueira Monterroso e Melo, 9 Nov. 1834.

[38] Raiol, *Motins políticos*, supplies testimony of two women who nursed the dying Campos: pp. 539–40.

[39] IHGB, Coleção Instituto Histórico, Testamento e Inventário do Cônego João Batista Gonçalves Campos, Lata 178, Pasta 34.

fully establish the nature of Paraense nativism, however, we need to go beyond the persuasively repetitious but quite impressionistic and tendentious racist descriptions of imperial officials. 'Of all those fellows of the priest's party, very few were white', a military official might fume, but how reliably?[40] Fortunately, some unusual quantitative evidence is available.

During the course of the fighting, captured Cabanos were locked in a prison ship and the registers of prisoners include information on the race and occupation of each. The precision of the numbers is of course deceptive because we cannot know how faithfully the sample represents the makeup of the Cabano army, yet the broad outlines are unambiguous.[41]

Despite the frequent suggestions by imperial officials that 'the priest's party' was mostly black, rebel prisoners came in all colours and constituted a rough cross-section of Amazonian society, urban and rural. Escaped slaves were few, less than a tenth, outnumbered by whites, in fact. The list with most blacks and fewest whites shows 86 white artisans, planters, traders, even a judge or two, but only 46 black slaves. On the other hand, while whites held most leadership positions they remained a minority, and indigenous people and people of mixed race composed the great majority. About a quarter of the prisoners were urban artisans, seasoned in a decade of street skirmishes with members of the Portuguese Party.[42] Relatively free agents with aspirations for upward social mobility, they constituted part of the nativists' core constituency throughout Brazil.

The radical potential of the nativist coalition is demonstrated, above all, by the presence — along with middling or poor urban people such as artisans — of even larger contingents of middling and poor rural people. More than half the rebel prisoners were *lavradores* who lived an independent life along the river banks, fully running the gamut of Amazonian racial types, but most quite humble.[43] They constitute the great mystery of the revolution. Given what we know of their social milieu, few could have been

---

[40] IHGB, Coleção Instituto Histórico, José Manuel de Morais, Quartel do Comando das Armas, 7 Sept. 1831.

[41] To create this table, I tabulated and analysed the entries in three bound registers entitled 'Relação nominal dos rebeldes presos', Códices nos 972, 1130 and 1132 in the Arquivo Público do Pará (Belém) and the entries in similar register, 'Relação dos presos rebeldes falecidos a bordo da corveta defensora,' previously published by Carlos de Araujo Moreira Neto, *Indios da Amazônia, de maioria a minoria (1750–1850)* (Petrópolis, 1988), pp. 281–315.

White Cabanos must have been less likely to suffer summary execution when captured by government forces, causing them to be over-represented on lists of prisoners. In addition, whether because of worse treatment or due to their greater susceptibility to European diseases, indigenous people died after their imprisonment at a higher rate than people of other racial groups. (Thus, List A — an enumeration of prisoners who died on board prison ships — over-represents Indians, as is clear from comparison of this list with the others.) Conversely, better treatment for those at the top of the racial hierarchy enhanced their chances of survival on board.

[42] Arquivo Público do Pará (Belém), 'Relação nominal dos rebeldes presos,' Códice no. 972. Of 607 prisoners identified, more than 150 were of clearly urban occupation.

[43] Arquivo Público do Pará (Belém). 'Relação nominal dos rebeldes presos', códice no. 972. Of 607 total, 364 prisoners were *lavradores*: by race, 100 *índios*, 100 *pardos*, 56 *mamelucos*, 50 *brancos*, 29 *cafuzes* and 12 *pretos*.

brought into the fight by ties of patronage to a landowner. The forest was too dense, the land too vast, the fluvial maze too intricate to prevent their escape had they desired not to join the rebel army. Like the artisans, these partisans could not be compelled and had to be attracted.

Table 5.1 Lists of Cabano Prisoners, 1836–40. Percentages by Racial Classification

Race	List A	List B	List C	List D
	(N=228)	(N=607)	(N=429)	(N=141)
Whites	07	14	24	24
Mamelucos and *mestiços**	15	15	14	19
Pardos and *mulatos**	20	29	24	20
Cafuzos*	09	09	09	11
Indios and *tapuios**	45	24	22	21
Negros and *Pretos**	04	09	07	05
TOTAL	100%	100%	100%	100%

*Mamelucos and *mestiços* had mixed indigenous and European ancestry. *Pardos* and *mulatos* had mixed African and European ancestry. *Cafuzos* had mixed indigenous and African. *Indios* and *tapuios* were of purely indigenous ancestry. Negros and *pretos* were of purely African ancestry.

Sources: List A: 'Relação dos presos rebeldes falecidos a bordo da corveta defensora,' reprinted in Moreira Neto, *Indios da Amazônia*, pp. 281–315; Lists B, C and D: 'Relações nominais dos rebeldes presos,' Códices no. 972, 1130 and 1132 in the Arquivo Público do Pará (Belém). Lists B, C and D (enumerations of living prisoners) have been arrayed in chronological order, B having been elaborated in 1836, D in 1840, and C at some point in between. These lists seem to represent one changing group of prisoners rather than three entirely different groups. The second recapture of Belém by government forces in 1836 apparently produced the largest prison population, and that number declined thereafter (despite a few additions) as prisoners died or were released. So arranged, the lists seem fairly consistent and their variations logical.

Nativism, I have argued, provided the attraction. Among the many prisoners who died was one nicknamed 'Frigate,' a man incriminated by the report that he had sworn 'to drink the blood of whites and Masons'.[44] Obviously, there is some basis for the persistent later memories of the Paraense conflagration of 1835–40 as a caste war.[45] But caste wars are not waged by armies led by whites and broadly representative of the general population. On the other hand, neither was this an army of land-owning patrons and their rural clients. 'Frigate' had learned to rail against Freemasons from the nativist discourse that elided 'Masons' into 'Portuguese',

---

[44] Prisoner 104, a *pardo* nicknamed 'Fragata': 'Relação dos presos rebeldes falecidos a bordo da Corveta Defensora', in Moreira Neto, *Indios da Amazônia*, pp. 281–315.

[45] Tiago Throlby, *A cabanagem na fala do povo* (São Paulo, 1987), pp. 63–92.

and eliding both into 'white' constituted but one step further in the same direction. Thus were the nativist leaders hoist on their own petard. Least of all does our examination of Paraense nativism resemble the picture of a stable, patrimonial society which most historians of Latin America routinely assign to all imperial Brazil, as a sort of continuation of the colonial order. But were Batista Campos, his discourse, his nativist movement and the resulting civil war representative of Brazil as a whole?

Admittedly, events in Pará constitute an extreme, rather than a typical example. Nonetheless, they serve accurately to signal overall tendencies. Clergy like Batista Campos figure strongly, by all accounts, among Brazilian radicals of the early nineteenth century — more than 40 were indicted for participation in the Pernambucan sedition of 1817 alone — and they were present in all the liberal rebellions of the 1830s and 1840s. The brash new periodical press also played a role in all the liberal rebellions. At least 40 newspapers (*O Povo, O Americano, O Continentista*) had appeared by 1840 in Rio Grande do Sul, where one Padre José Antonio Caldas, another radical priest and publisher, served as the principal ideologue. Ninety-three radical liberal publications were associated with the 1848 liberal rebellion in Pernambuco, called the Praieira movement after the name of the street where many of them were printed. The nativist rebels of Maranhão took their name from a newspaper, those of Bahia, from an opposition journalist, and so on.[46] As for nativist themes, their centrality and intensity varied considerably, but they were everywhere present. They ranged from effusions about offences intolerable for 'truly Brazilian hearts', to simple name-calling and Portuguese-bating ('Masons,' 'sailors,' 'eagle beaks'), to detailed proposals that would ban all Portuguese from retail commerce, remove them from public employment, prohibit their bearing arms and deport those not married to Brazilian women.[47] Told that the nativist press taught hatred for Portuguese, a Pernambucan legislator of 1848 repeated for the record his conviction that, to the contrary, 'such aversion seemed to be innate among Brazilians'.[48]

Unsavoury sentiments of this kind, along with the ugly mob violence that sometimes accompanied them, have kept historians from paying early nineteenth-century Brazilian nativism the attention it deserves. Yet we need to look beyond the arbitrariness of birthplace as destiny to evaluate properly the role of nativism in the political development of Brazil. Of special importance was the way that the defining terms of

---

[46] Walter Spalding, *A epopéia Farroupilha (pequena história da Grande Revolução, acompanhada de farta documentação da época, 1835–1845)* (São Paulo, 1963), pp. 59–60; 'Panfletários da Revolução Praieira', *Revista do Arquivo Público*, Recife (Dec. 1976); Luiz Viana Filho, *A Sabinada (A república bahiana de 1837)* (Rio de Janeiro, 1938).

[47] Sérgio Buarque de Holanda (ed.) *História geral da civilização brasileira*, tomo II: *O Brasil monárquico*, vol. 2: *Dispersão e unidade*, second edition (São Paulo, 1967), p. 277; J.M. Pereira de Alencastre, 'Notas diarias sobre a revolta civil que teve lugar nas Províncias de Maranhão, Piauhy, e Ceará', *Revista Trimensal do Instituto Histórico Geográfico e Etnográfico do Brasil* (1872), vol. 35, p. 469; Hendrik Kraay, '"As Terrifying as Unexpected": The Bahian Sabinada, 1837–1838', *Hispanic American Historical Review*, vol. 72 (1992), pp. 507–8.

[48] Panfletários da Revolução Praieira', in *Revista do Arquivo Público*, Recife (Dec. 1976), p. 13.

conflict (Brazilian versus Portuguese) enabled political alliances spanning divisions of race and class among the native born, exactly as occurred in Spanish America during the Wars of Independence. Early
Brazilian nativism should be looked at as popular proto-nationalism, its
links with the expansion of the press examined particularly, its parallels
in Mexico and Argentina (to mention only two salient contemporaneous
examples) pondered thoughtfully. Was Brazil not yet ready for liberty,
as Brazilian elites consensually declared by 1850, with lasting historiographical effects? Or was it already a good bit readier than they liked?

CHAPTER 6

The War of the Supremes: Border Conflict, Religious Crusade or Simply Politics by Other Means?

Rebecca Earle

In the 70-odd years after Independence, Colombia experienced, by one count, nine national civil wars, two international wars, three army coups and several dozen more localised conflicts.[1] On average, a major war broke out every seven years. This is not a particularly inspiring record. As Rafael Núñez lamented, 'in the course of our independent political life the maintenance of public order has been the exception and civil war the rule'.[2] During the second half of the nineteenth century, Colombian politicians and other observers of the national scene looked back in their memoirs and other writings on the decades of unrest and political instability, casting around for explanations of the disorder they saw engulfing their country. The explanations they found tended to ascribe the civil wars that plagued Colombia to immature political and economic structures that made civil war the most reliable way for ambitious men to achieve wealth and power. In the words of José María Quijano Wallis, the stagnant post-colonial economy 'led the military caudillos ... to seek their livelihood and personal aggrandisement in the hazards of civil war, or in the intrigue and accommodation of politics'.[3] This common explanation for civil wars, in other words, stressed that these conflicts were essentially about achieving personal power. They were, in this interpretation, the consequence of an inadequate economic and political system, not the result of societal fragmentation or profound ideological difference. Indeed, observers often suspected that the political platforms put forward by politicians merely masked lust for power. The conservative historian José Manuel Restrepo hypothesised in his memoirs that the supposedly religious aims of the insurrection of 1839 'were probably nothing more than a pretext with which to deceive the villages. The true design of the shadowy ambitious men who promoted it was the dissolution of the republic under the guise of establishing a federal system, or rather anarchy, in this country.' A few pages later he noted 'What a pity that New Granada's peace is disturbed because a few ambitious men

---

[1] Alvaro Tirado Mejía, *Aspectos sociales de las guerras civiles en Colombia*, (Bogotá, 1976), pp. 12–3.

[2] Rafael Núñez, ' La ley o la libertad' (1891), in Rafael Núñez, *La reforma política en Colombia*, 7 vols. (Bogotá, 1946), vol. 4, p. 45.

[3] José María Quijano Wallis, quoted in Charles Bergquist, *Coffee and Conflict in Colombia, 1886–1910*, (Durham, NC, 1978), p. 4. Bergquist discusses this point more fully in *Coffee and Conflict*, pp. 3–17; and Frank Safford provides a rough sketch of the same argument in 'The Problem of Political Order in Early Republican Spanish America', *Journal of Latin American Studies*, vol. 24, special supplement (1992), pp. 91–2.

want to rule, usurping public authority ... So far [the insurrection's leader] Obando has not proclaimed any political principle, although [others] have spoken of religion. It is probable that Obando will adopt this same language, as he is a refined hypocrite.'[4] Nor has this view of Colombia's civil wars lost its freshness. A recent survey of Colombian history characterised the nineteenth century civil wars thus: 'Yet another feature of Colombian history is that even the most bloody conflicts cloaked themselves in legal principles, and naked ambitions confronted each other in the name of grand societal and constitutional projects.'[5]

Certainly this view has some appeal. No one can read the correspondence of José María Obando (caudillo extraordinaire and president of Colombia) without acknowledging that sheer lust for power played a significant role in nineteenth-century politics. Do we then find it convincing to ascribe the disorder of nineteenth-century Colombia to uncontrolled competition for public office? Perhaps not; certainly historians such as Charles Bergquist have offered very different, if controversial, readings of some of Colombia's civil wars. This chapter will explore the origins of one civil war, in an attempt to uncover the role of both naked political ambition and deeply-held social concern. It will examine the so-called *Guerra de los Supremos*, which broke out in 1839 and lasted until 1841.

I will start with a brief summary of the main events of this conflict. The primary purpose of the overview is not to transmit a detailed account of the central features of the Guerra de los Supremos, but rather to highlight that there are a number of different narratives that could be spun about this war. Any explanation of the origins of the conflict thus depends in part on which narrative one selects.

Narrative 1: *la Guerra de los Conventos*

In June 1839, the inhabitants of the Colombian city of Pasto took up arms against the government of Bogotá. Pasto, a provincial capital near the border with Ecuador, had a history of regionalist rebellion and a large indigenous population.[6] The cause of the unrest in 1839 was a law ordering the closure of all monasteries with fewer than eight members. According to one reading of the *Guerra de los Supremos*, this law was the origin of the entire civil war. For this reason, it is worth looking a little more closely at the evolution of this piece of legislation.

Although the order to suppress small monasteries had first been passed in 1821 by the Congress of Cúcuta, it had never been enforced in

---

[4] José Manuel Restrepo, *Diario político y militar* (Bogotá, 1954) vol. 3, pp. 144–5, 155–6.

[5] Jean-Pierre Minaudier, *Histoire de la Colombie de la conquête a nos jours* (Paris, 1992), p. 137.

[6] Late colonial rebellion in Pasto is discussed in Rebecca Earle, 'Indian Rebellion and Bourbon Reform in New Granada: Riots in Pasto, 1780–1800', *Hispanic American Historical Review*, vol. 73 (1993). For Pasto's involvement in the War of Independence, see Sergio Elías Ortiz, *Agustín Agualongo y su tiempo* (Bogotá, 1958).

the province of Pasto, precisely because successive governments had feared that it would provoke a rebellion. The law remained on the books, but unenforced in Pasto, for another 18 years, when it was fished out under the presidency of José Ignacio de Márquez. In June 1839 Congress specifically ordered the closing of the monasteries of San Francisco, San Agustín, Santo Domingo and La Merced in the city of Pasto. The monastery of San Francisco had eight members, San Agustín and Santo Domingo had four each and the last, La Merced, was reduced to two monks. The law thus directly affected a total of 18 people. The suppressed convents were to donate half their property and income to the Christian missions of Mocoa and the remainder was to be used to support state-run education schemes in the Province of Pasto.[7]

Except in Pasto, the measure met with much approval. It seems the suppressed monks had few friends among the powerful. Church officials, including the local bishop, supported the closure, as did Pasto's representatives to Congress. None of them thought that the 18 monks merited any special consideration. On the contrary, the governor of Pasto, Dr Antonio José Chaves, reported that the suppressed priests 'neither lived in the convents, nor even wore ecclesiastical robes, but instead living as they pleased, without order or rules, remained entirely independent of the authorities, even those of their own orders'.[8] Worse, the majority of the suppressed monks were Ecuadorian, not Colombian. Not only were the Ecuadorian clergy regarded as particularly bereft of morals, but their links to a foreign country were considered a 'monstrous irregularity' by Colombian officials.[9] The presence of the monks in Pasto, then, was positively pernicious. Altogether, Colombia's political leaders felt that money raised by closing the monasteries would be better spent, as the historian and politician José Manuel Restrepo put it, in the missions of Mocoa 'converting and civilising those barbarous Indians, than in Pasto maintaining immoral and lazy priests'.[10] In Bogotá, at least, the closure seemed like a very reasonable measure.

---

[7] Restrepo, *Diario político*, vol. 3, (Bogotá, 1954) p. 134; Alejandro Ortiz López, 'Parte que cupo al padre Francisco de la Villota y Barrera en la revolución llamada "de los conventillos"', *Boletín de Estudios Históricos*, vol. 6 (Pasto, 1934); and Joaquín Posada Gutiérrez, *Memorias histórico-políticas*, Biblioteca de la Historia Nacional, vol. 41 (Bogotá, 1929), vol. 3, pp. 229–30. The suppression was discussed calmly in Pasto in 1822 by the interim republican government of Ramón Zambrano. See the letters of Ramón Zambrano to Colonel José Concha, 1822, Archivo Central del Cauca (ACC), signatura 6852, Independencia CII–6g.

[8] Restrepo, *Diario político*, vol. 3, p. 134; and Posada, *Memorias*, vol. 3, p. 241.

[9] Posada, *Memorias*, vol. 3, p. 230. There were long-standing complaints about the behaviour of the Ecuadorian clergy. See the letter from the newly appointed bishop of Quito in Archivo Nacional de Ecuador (ANE), Religiosos, caja 65 (1819–1821), '1800–iv–6'. Also consider the remarks by the same bishop quoted in Carlos Manuel Larrea, *El Barón de Carondelet, XXIX presidente de la Real Audiencia de Quito*, (Quito, n.d.), p. 129: '[The priests] spend long periods of time away from their monasteries, do not wear their habits, say mass in less then ten minutes, [and] don't observe the prescribed ceremonies for funerals, etc.'

[10] Restrepo, *Diario político*, vol. 3, p. 134.

In Pasto, however, the decree took on a very different hue. There had been rumours since 1838 of radical anticlerical measures which were going to be sprung on the city by the government in Bogotá. (Who was spreading these rumours will be considered in a moment.) Distorted reports of the new law circulated through Pasto. By June 1839 popular outrage was running high, the weather was oppressively hot and Governor Chaves became increasingly worried. Eventually a priest, Father Francisco de la Villota, the provost of the congregation of Saint Philip Neri in Pasto and a popular local figure, was railroaded into fronting an armed protest against the closures.[11] Within days an alarmed Governor Chaves signed a treaty overturning the closure.[12] The treaty was signed not only by Father Villota and Governor Chaves, but also by Lieutenant Coronel Mariano Alvarez, who had appointed himself acting military chief of Pasto, the actual chief, Manuel Mutis, having fled in alarm. Lieutenant Colonel Alvarez was a close friend of José María Obando, the region's most powerful caudillo. In the preceding months Alvarez had been one of the principal rumour-mongers, spreading exaggerated reports of the intended closure and now he took charge of the revolt he had carefully orchestrated.

Meanwhile, reports were arriving in Bogotá of the uprising. All supporters of President Márquez were alarmed, worried that the revolt could bring down his fragile government. President Márquez announced that he had no intention of honouring Governor Chaves's capitulation, and despatched the secretary of interior relations, Pedro Alcántara Herrán, to Pasto at the head of a 2,000-strong army to restore order. Herrán reached Pasto in August 1839 and reported that: 'The sedition in Pasto has turned into rebellion. The *cabecillas* have removed their masks ... On August 24 ... they proclaimed a federal system, naming as chief of military operations the Lieutenant Colonel Antonio Mariano Alvarez.'[13]

Alvarez's revolt did not last long. Leading an army of several hundred Indians and, reportedly, a few priests, he was defeated by government forces at the battle of Buesaco on the 30 August 1839. Father Villota was pardoned and the suppression of the small monasteries was carried out without disturbance in early September 1839. Some observers thought the war, such as it was, had ended.[14] They were wrong.

This account of the war thus stresses the importance of both skilled local leadership and also religion in causing the revolt. José María Sam-

---

[11] For several rather different accounts of the riot, see Posada, *Memorias*, vol. 3, pp. 230–4; José María Obando, *Apuntamientos para la historia*, (Bogotá, 1945), vol. 2, p. 43–4; Restrepo, *Diario político*, p. 135; 'Memorial de Don Tomás de Ayerve', *Boletín de Estudios Históricos*, vol. 9, (Pasto, 1939) p. 325; and Ortiz, 'Parte que cupo', p. 82.

[12] Posada, *Memorias*, vol. 3, pp. 234–5.

[13] Pedro Alcántara Herrán, quoted in Restrepo, *Diario político*, vol. 3, p. 139.

[14] See, for example, the letter from the British consul to the Home Office from 13 November 1840 in the Public Record Office, F.O. 135/31; or US Chargé d'Affaires James Semple to US Secretary of State John Forsyth, Bogotá, 25 April 1840, in William Manning (ed.), *Diplomatic Correspondence of the United States. Inter-American Affairs, 1831–1860*, vol. 5: *Chile and Colombia*, (Washington, 1935), p. 567.

per summed up this view when he declared that the revolt was the consequence of 'the fanaticism of a few friars and ... of some ignorant and superstitious Indian villagers'.[15]

Narrative 2: José María Obando

Another reading of the war revolves around the activities of José María Obando. Obando, a veteran of the revolutionary wars, was perhaps the most influential caudillo in southern Colombia. After losing the presidential elections of 1836–37, in which he had stood on a proto-liberal ticket, Obando had retreated to his base outside Popayán, from where he plotted his political comeback and awaited the downfall of the Márquez regime.

Obando watched the unrest in Pasto with keen interest. 'The rebellion in Pasto ... is the knife that will destroy the republic', he opined hopefully in July 1839.[16] Then, in late 1839, Obando's hand was forced. The Márquez government announced its intention of prosecuting Obando for the murder of Antonio José de Sucre.[17] (Sucre, the revolutionary hero, had been assassinated near Pasto in 1830) This announcement, according to José Manuel Restrepo, led to great anxiety, for everyone feared that Obando would cause a rebellion in order to avoid standing trial.[18] This suspicion proved to be well founded. On 26 January 1840 Obando restarted hostilities against the government. Drawing on his well-developed clientelistic links with veterans of the Wars of Independence and his own earlier revolts, Obando amassed a force of some 200 black and Indian followers.[19] Skirmishes between Obando's forces and government troops under Herrán continued on and off until July 1840, when Obando issued the long-expected *pronunciamiento*. Obando declared himself 'supreme director of the war in Pasto, general of the restoring army and protector of the religion of the crucified one'.[20] He explained that he was fighting against the unpopular government of Márquez and promised

---

[15] José María Samper, 'Los partidos en Colombia' (1873), in Jorge Orlando Melo (ed.), *Origenes de los partidos políticos en Colombia (textos de Manuel María Madiedo, José María Samper y Tomás Cipriano de Mosquera)* (Bogotá, 1978), p. 80. Samper further mentioned the persecution of Obando and liberal resentment as factors in the revolt.

[16] José María Obando to Francisco de Paula Santander, Popayán, 8 July 1839, in Luis Martínez Delgado and Sergio Elías Ortiz (eds.), *Epistolario y documentos oficiales del General José María Obando*, Biblioteca de Historia Nacional, vol. 123 (Bogotá, 1973), vol. 1, p. 296.

[17] See, for example, Leopoldo López Alvarez, 'Fuga y rebelión del General José María Obando', in *Boletín de Estudios Históricos*, vol. 3 (Pasto, 1930); and Thomas McGann, 'The Assassination of Sucre and its Significance in Colombian History', *Hispanic American Historical Review*, vol. 30 (1950).

[18] Restrepo, *Diario político*, vol. 3, pp. 140–1. Also see Obando, *Apuntamientos*, for his side of the story.

[19] Restrepo, *Diario político*, vol. 3, p. 140–54. In fact, the connection between Obando and the guerrillas is clear even from Obando's own account. See Obando, *Apuntamientos*. See also Francisco Zuluaga, *José María Obando: de soldado realista a caudillo republicano* (Bogotá, 1985).

[20] The text of the *pronunciamiento*, issued at Chaguarbamba on 16 July 1840, is in Martínez and Ortiz (eds.), *Epistolario*, vol. 3, pp. 216–7.

to restore southern Colombia to its former glory. He continued to lead a rebel force until early 1841, when military defeat forced him to abandon his efforts at unseating Márquez. Indeed, Márquez's ally, General Herrán, was elected president in March 1841 on the basis of his reputation as a war hero, earned largely through his campaign against Obando.

Narrative 3: los Supremos

Although the war began in southern Colombia, it did not remain there. A third narrative focuses on the activities of the 'Supremos', or supreme leaders, who, following Obando's lead, initiated anti-government revolts across Colombia. In late 1840, military leaders in Vélez, Socorro, Antioquia, Cartagena, Santa Marta and Panama pronounced against the government of Márquez and announced the separation of their provinces from Bogotá.[21] These revolts were not united under a single rebel command. They were rather a series of simultaneous regionalist uprisings. Several of these revolts were led by former heroes of the Wars of Independence, and most articulated some variety of federalist programme granting greater autonomy to Colombia's provinces. Many of the leaders, moreover, had specific grudges against the Márquez regime. Victor Uribe-Uran has recently suggested that these complaints often revolved around exclusion from political office and unresolved tensions between provincial lawyers and aristocratic *bogatanos*.[22] The reports of foreign diplomats give some sense of the revolution's confused development:

> On the 19th ultimo, General Juan José Patria raised a force in Sogamoso, marched to Tunja, took possession of that city without opposition, took all the money in the treasury (about $2000) and returned again to Sogamoso. Tunja is about four days ride north of this city. The government immediately sent all the disposable force to put down Patria, but as yet nothing decisive has transpired. On 21 September the people of the province of Socorro declared independence from the government and formed a provisional government of their own, with Colonel Manuel Gonsales at their head which they said shall continue until the abuses of which they complain are remedied. It is daily expected that the province of Antioquia will declare against the government under Colonel Cordova ... By last week's mail the news was received here, of the provinces of Rio Hacha, Santa Martha, Carthegena and Mompox, having declared independence of the government. All following the example of Socorro, say-

---

[21] For details, see Posada, *Memorias*, vol. 4. See also Tomás Herrera to Martin Van Buren, Panama, 5 December 1840, in Manning (ed.), *Diplomatic Correspondence of the United States*, vol. 5, pp. 570–1, in which Herrera attempts to explain Panama's motives for rebelling against the central government.

[22] Victor Uribe –Uran, *Honorable Lives: Lawyers, Family and Politics in Colombia, 1780-1850* (Pittsburgh, 2000), pp. 118–37.

ing that they would not obey the orders of the central government until a convention was called and a general reform made in the constitution.[23]

Few of these revolts stood any real chance of spreading beyond the province where they began, although Colonel Manuel González, leading troops from Socorro, threatened the capital itself in October 1840. None of the Supremos led large armies; González was defeated by fewer than 800 men.[24] This was fortunate for the central government, as Herrán's army, which marched north from Pasto to confront these new threats, contained only about 5,000 men in total.[25] While these revolts did not individually pose a serious threat to the national government, together they were a major drain on government resources. Increased military expenses caused the government deficit to mushroom after 1839.[26]

Not only did leaders in individual provinces attempt to reshape the republic through declarations of federalism. Neighbouring states also got in on the act, attempting to seize chunks of Colombian territory to enlarge their own domain. The break-up of Spain's colonial empire had left somewhat unclear the territorial extent of the new republican states and for this reason the nineteenth century saw a number of border conflicts in Latin America, some serious, some less so. During the *Guerra de los Supremos*, Ecuador tried to use the state of unrest to appropriate part of southern Colombia. This was not the first time Ecuador had made such an attempt. Colombia and Ecuador had already gone to war in 1832 over the precise location of the international boundary, and during the War of Independence itself Quito had sent republican troops to Pasto in an attempt to seize control of the region. The outbreak of the *Guerra de los Supremos* provided a pretext for Ecuador to make a further incursion into Colombia. Following Obando's revolt in 1840, Juan José Flores, the president of Ecuador, began massing an army on his country's northern border. Within the province of Pasto itself agents for Flores tried to drum up support for a transfer to Ecuador.[27] The cabildos of several towns, including the capital of the province of Pasto, agreed to accept union with Ecuador. This elite decision proved unacceptable to the other sectors of Pasto's society, and a guerrilla force consisting largely of Indians forcibly expelled the Ecuadorian troops from

---

[23] US Chargé d'Affaires James Semple to US Secretary of State John Forsyth, Bogotá, 2 October 1840 and 21 November 1840, in Manning (ed.), *Diplomatic Correspondence of the United States*, vol. 5, pp. 568–9.

[24] Posada, *Memorias*, vol. 4, pp. 9–14.

[25] William Paul McGreevey, *An Economic History of Colombia, 1845–1930* (Cambridge, 1971), p. 87. McGreevey gives the figure of 5,000 as the actual (as opposed to the larger legal) size of the army in 1842.

[26] Restrepo, *Diario político*, vol. 3, pp. 161, 166, 238; Luis Ospina Vásquez, *Industria y protección en Colombia, 1810–1930* (Medellín, 1955), chapter 3; Antonio Alvarez Restrepo, 'Las guerras civiles y el desarrollo económico', *Boletín de Historia y Antigüedades*, vol. 69, no. 736 (1982); and José Antonio Ocampo, 'Comerciantes, artesanos y política económica en Colombia, 1830–1880', *Boletín Cultural y Bibliográfico*, vol. 27, no. 22 (1990).

[27] See ANE, Gobierno, tomo 78 (1839–43), 'Gb. 4–ix–1840', military reports from 1840.

Colombian territory and declared the province's restitution to Colombia.[28] In other words, two decades after Independence, there was not complete agreement among Colombia's population about whether they wanted to be Colombian at all. In the end, the war did not result in any alteration to Colombian territory. This account of the *Guerra de los Supremos* thus illustrates not only the fragility of the national government in the face of the regionalist demands articulated by the supremos, but also the instability of the nation state vis-à-vis its neighbours.

Interpreting the *Guerra de los Supremos*

These three accounts offer rather different narratives of the *Guerra de los Supremos*. One stresses the role of religion in causing the conflict. The others highlight the power of regionalism and the importance of political ambitions. Let us now to return to the question posed at the beginning of this chapter: what were the origins of this conflict? As we have noted, the interpretative schema suggested by individuals such as José María Quijano Wallis stressed that these civil wars were caused essentially by the unchecked ambitions of political figures and the collapse of the old structures of the colonial state, which left no reliable route to power other than civil war. This interpretation implies three corollaries:

1. These civil wars would not have occurred were it not for ambitious politicians. In other words, we should seek the origins of Colombia's civil wars, not in social conflict, but in the realm of political history, particularly in the careers of the principal political figures and in the economic structures that drove men into politics.

2. The civil wars had little ideological content. This view suggests that the programmatic or ideological differences between the contending parties were usually slight.

3. The wars were not 'popular'. They were the consequence of clever manoeuvring by a few elite politicians.

Let us now assess the usefulness of this interpretation by considering the accuracy of these three corollaries in the case of the *Guerra de los Supremos*. Consider first the suggestion that the *Guerra de los Supremos* was essentially the consequence of the personal ambitions of a few elite politicians. More specifically, can one argue that the sole cause of the war was José María Obando and his insatiable appetite for intrigue? The suggestion is not preposterous. Obando had clearly been plotting against the Márquez government since the election of 1836–37. His intention was either to overthrow the government or, at the very least, to

---

[28] ANE, *ibid.*, 'Gb. 31–viii–1840', military reports from 1840; and also Restrepo, *Diario político*, pp. 197, 266.

engineer its downfall. 1838 and 1839 thus saw Obando engaged in feverish manipulation of the press, composing favourable articles, subscribing to new journals, and leaning on editors.[29] Few observers doubted that Obando had his eye on the presidency. 'I'm told that in Pasto a "hidden hand" is directing everything, and even though it hasn't been said in so many words, I suppose it must be Obando', wrote General Joaquín Acosta to Herrán in July 1838.[30] Moreover, it seems that the actual outbreak of rebellion in Pasto in June 1839 was largely orchestrated by Mariano Alvarez, a close ally of Obando ('*nuestro célebre amigo*', Obando called him on one occasion).[31]

Obando was thus heavily implicated in the outbreak of the rebellion. His motives in wishing to overthrow the Márquez government were twofold. Firstly, he still hankered after the presidency, despite his defeat in the elections of 1837. Secondly, he had a more immediate motive for wishing to unseat Márquez once he was officially charged with the murder of Antonio José de Sucre, the revolutionary hero found dead in southern Pasto in 1830. Obando, always denying his guilt, fled house arrest in June 1840 and issued a classic *pronunciamiento* the next month. Observers at the time did not fail to notice the contemporaneous nature of the impending trial and Obando's official entry into the war.

Altogether, this might seem to add up to a ringing indictment of Obando as the intellectual author of the *Guerra de los Supremos*. Indeed, even if one does not accept that Obando was solely responsible for the outbreak of war, one might argue that the war was largely the consequence of high-level political manoeuvrings among a small number of ambitious politicians struggling for positions in the emerging party system.[32] Does this, then, suggest that the origins of the war indeed lie in the manoeuvrings of ambitious politicians? Were there no social origins to this conflict? Was the *Guerra de los Supremos* essentially an elite-level conflict with little 'popular' content? A number of historians certainly take this view, as we noted earlier. Various authors have described Colombia's civil wars, including the *Guerra de los Supremos*, as ritual blood-baths between elite figures, into which the popular classes were dragged unwillingly to act as cannon fodder.[33] The situation is of course somewhat more complex.

---

[29] See Obando's 1838 correspondence with Francisco de Paula Santander, cited in Martínez and Ortíz (eds.), *Epistolario*.

[30] Joaquín Acosta to Pedro Alcántara Herrán, Quito, 24 July 1838, in Julio Humberto Ovalle, 'Archivo Epistolar del General Pedro Alcántara Herrán', *Boletín de Historia y Antigüedades*, vol. 70, no. 741 (1983), pp. 470–1. Or see Posada, *Memorias*, vol. 3, pp. 236, 248.

[31] José María Obando to Francisco de Paula Santander, Popayán, 11 December 1838, Martínez and Ortiz, *Epistolario*, vol. 1, p. 288.

[32] Uribe suggests that *empleomanía*, or unrestrained competition over government posts, in fact reflects the *social* importance of government employment in maintaining personal honour. His interpretation of the *Guerra de los Supremos* nonetheless presents the war as prompted essentially by such competition. See Uribe, *Honorable Lives*, pp. 133–7.

[33] See, for example, Tirado, *Aspectos sociales*; and Antonio Alvarez Restrepo, 'Las guerras civiles y el desarrollo económico'.

To begin with, it is problematic to suggest that political factionalism itself precludes popular involvement. While I do not intend to rehash the substantial historiography on the origins of political parties in Colombia, it is worth recalling that an interest in politics was not confined to the elite.[34] Evidence of this comes from a number of different areas. One of the more interesting concerns the growth of the political press. During the colonial and independence periods, journalistic activity of any sort had been extremely limited. At the outbreak of the War of Independence, New Granada as a whole had contained a total of five printing presses, and the number of printing workshops (an obvious prerequisite for an active political press) did not increase substantially until after 1820. From 1820 onwards, however, the number of printing presses, and, more significantly, the number of newspapers published in Colombia increased dramatically.[35] Already in the first ten years after Independence, the rate at which new newspapers appeared more than doubled compared to the period before 1821.[36] These new newspapers concerned themselves particularly with the developing political system. As Eduardo Posada-Carbó has shown, they were often published in conjunction with electoral campaigns, and work by historians such as both Posada and David Bushnell indicates that the editors of these journals believed, or at least hoped, that they were able to influence public opinion.[37] Politicians, who were often themselves also journal editors, seemed to have shared these views. Political figures opined about the accuracy of the press's coverage of events and debated whether freedom of the press had gone to far. Were newspapers serving to educate the public, or merely to spread discord and political strife? All this suggests that an interest in politics was not confined to a tiny minority. Evidence from the *Guerra de los Supremos* further supports the view that newspapers were believed to play a significant role in shaping political opinion and, more importantly, that politicians hoped to garner support from a broad public. Obando, for example, followed the political press with close attention. He frequently

---

[34] For the formation of political parties, see Frank Safford, 'Social Aspects of Politics in Nineteenth Century Spanish America: New Granada, 1825–1850', *Journal of Social History*, vol. 5, no. 3 (1972) pp. 344–5; David Bushnell, 'Política y partidos en el siglo XIX; algunos antecedentes históricos' in Gonzalo Sánchez and Ricardo Peñaranda (eds.), *Pasado y presente de la violencia en Colombia* (Bogotá, 1986), pp. 31–9; and J. Leon Helguera, 'The Problem of Liberalism versus Conservatism in Colombia, 1849–1885', *Latin American History: Select Problems* (New York, 1969), p. 226.

[35] For the colonial and independence periods, see Rebecca Earle, 'Information and Disinformation in Late Colonial New Granada,' *The Americas*, vol. 54, no. 2 (1997).

[36] From 1785, when the first Colombian journal was published, to 1820, approximately 30 different newspapers appeared, at an average rate of 0.8 new titles per year. From 1821 to 1830, at least 20 new titles appeared, at an average rate of two new titles per year.

[37] Eduardo Posada-Carbó, 'The Role of Newspapers and Leaflets in Electoral Campaigns in Colombia, 1830–1930', Latin American Studies Association (1995); and David Bushnell, 'The Development of the Press in Great Colombia', *Hispanic American Historical Review*, vol. 30 (1950), pp. 432–52. Eduardo Posada also discusses the political importance of newspapers in 'Elections and Civil Wars in Nineteenth-century Colombia: The 1875 Presidential Campaign', *Journal of Latin American Studies*, vol. 26 (1994).

composed articles for insertion in friendly newspapers and rejoiced when new periodicals supported him. Indeed, in 1850 he was to use his own savings to purchase a printing press for supporters of the Liberal Party in Cali.[38] José Manuel Restrepo, on the other hand, deplored the impunity with which the liberal press attacked the Márquez regime:

> Over this last year the so-called opposition has made great efforts to render unpopular the president and his administration through the medium of *La Bandera*, *La Calavera* and other newspapers ... The *Bandera Nacional*, *La Calavera* and *El Diablo Cojuelo* continue their furious attack on the president and his secretaries and friends, with a scandalous violence ... The acrimony with which the opposition attacks makes one suspicious of their intentions, which seem to be none other than the destruction of the government's popularity.[39]

Politicians, in other words, regarded the press as an important tool in the battle for political support, because it helped them shape public opinion, and because public opinion was considered to be important.

Moreover, it is not only the vibrant political press that suggests that Colombia's population were not uncomprehending pawns uninterested in politics. Consider, for example, the large number of rumours that circulated in southern Colombia prior to the outbreak of war. Rumours of revolution in Bogotá circulated as far as Quito, and individuals spread fears that Colombia planned to invade Ecuador, that all rebels would be taken as prisoners to Cartagena, that a massive uprising was being planned. Indeed, the spread of political gossip in southern Colombia was such that in 1839 Herrán felt it necessary to outlaw explicitly the dissemination of 'false or alarming rumours'.[40] Individuals were clearly talking about the political situation, which suggests at least some level of interest. Information about the national political situation thus spread

---

[38] Obando's correspondence with Francisco de Paula Santander in 1838 makes very frequent reference to the use of newspapers to stir public opinion. Virtually every letter from that year cited in Martínez and Ortiz (eds.), *Epistolario* discusses the appearance of new periodicals or the need to plant favourable articles in a particular newspaper. Obando purchased the 900 *peso* printing press in Lima. See J. Leon Helguera, 'Antecedentes sociales de la revolución de 1851 en el sur de Colombia (1848–1849)', *Anuario Colombiano de Historia Social y de la Cultura*, no. 5 (1970), p. 60. Malcolm Deas similarly reports that 'there is an extensive pamphlet literature from the Guerra de los Supremos, in which for the first time in republican history — with the exception of the Patria Boba — there are concentrated efforts to mobilise provincial opinion in favour of a new definition of the national structure, efforts that have left many surprising printer's marks'. See 'La presencia de la política nacional en la vida provinciana, pueblerina y rural de Colombia en el prímer siglo de la república', in Malcolm Deas, *Del poder y la grámatica y otros ensayos sobre historia, política y literatura colombianas* (Santafé de Bogotá, 1993) pp. 179–80.

[39] Restrepo, *Diario político*, vol. 3, pp. 122–4.

[40] Pedro Alcántara Herrán to the parish priest of Funes, Pasto, 27 September 1839, printed in *Boletín de Estudios Históricos*, vol. 2 (Pasto, 1929), pp. 163–4. For just a few examples of such gossip, see the correspondence from Joaquín Acosta to General Herrán in Ovalle, 'Archivo Espitolar', pp. 459–87. Posada, *Memorias*, vol. 4, also discusses the many rumours that circulated throughout Colombia during these years, some spread by newspapers; as does Restrepo, *Diario político*, vol. 3.

by a number of means, as Malcolm Deas has noted in his study of the dissemination of national politics in nineteenth-century Colombia. Referring to the period of the *Guerra de los Supremos*, Deas notes that:

> Not all [the news] that arrives is correct. But a great deal does arrive, with detail and drama, and by many different routes. The diary [of María Martínez de Nisser] mentions proclamations, personal letters (which are quickly passed on to political allies, and probably also to political enemies, in the case of public letters), bulletins, papers, the Bogotá press, the arrival of refugees, of troops, of volunteers, the rebel press, *El Cometa*, 'four letters from my husband', etc.[41]

As Deas argues, an interest in national politics was not confined to the economic or social elite. The growth of the political media, and the rich world of political rumour, are good evidence for the popular dimension of party politics.

Moreover, it is not merely that the political dimension of the *Guerra de los Supremos* was to some extent popular. The war also contained other dimensions as well. This civil war, while unfolding underneath an umbrella of high politics, also fed off pre-existing social conflicts with little direct connection to the emergent politics of liberalism and conservatism. Joanne Rappaport, in her study of the Nasa Indians' historical traditions, argues that during the *Guerra de los Supremos* 'indigenous caudillos used the battleground to acquire ascendancy within their own communities'. The Nasa of southern Colombia, according to Rappaport, participated in the generalised conflict, but for their own, local motives:

> We are witness to independent actions, led and fought by the Nasa for their own unstated reasons, probably related to the acquisition of political power, the protection and reclamation of aboriginal lands and the infliction of punishment on local non-Indians. This is the hearth in which nineteenth-century caciques without *cacicazgos* were forged, enabling them to move across a territory as though it were a single, broad *cacicazgo*.[42]

Rappaport is vague about the precise reasons that propelled the Nasa into the war, although she is clear about the consequences of Indian participation. In other cases, the motivation for popular mobilisation was stated explicitly by local leaders, but this does not always illuminate the event as much as one might hope. One of the more striking features of the *Guerra de los Supremos* is the appearance during the war of royalist guerrillas in southern Colombia. During the War of Independence, southern Colombia had been a stronghold of popular royalism. These sentiments had not vanished with the creation of the republic. Memories

---

[41] Deas, 'La presencia de la política', pp. 185–6. Popular politics in nineteenth century Colombia is further discussed in Malcolm Deas, 'La política en la vida cotidiana republicana', in Beatríz Castro Carvajal (ed.), *Historia de la vida cotidiana en Colombia* (Santafé de Bogotá, 1996).
[42] Joanne Rappaport, *The Politics of Memory. Native Historical Interpretation in the Colombian Andes*, (Durham, NC, 1998) pp. 99–100.

of Spanish rule still exerted a powerful force on the imagination of the province's indigenous population. Thus, the *Guerra de los Supremos* saw the reappearance of royalist guerrillas, fighting in the name of the Spanish king Ferdinand VII, who was in fact dead. The most significant of these was the mestizo guerrilla leader Andrés Noguera, at one point loosely allied with Obando's forces, who enjoyed tremendous popularity with the region's slave and Indian population. Leading a force of perhaps 800 Indians and escaped slaves (one diarist referred to Noguera's troops as an '*indiada*', or Indian horde), Noguera began intercepting the mail and ambushing government troops in the name of the Spanish monarch, allegedly with the support of the province's priests. Noguera issued proclamations in support of the Catholic religion, his career ending when he was shot by his erstwhile ally Obando. Contemporary observers offered a variety of uncomplementary explanations as to why Catholicism and the deceased Spanish king proved so compelling to the region's slaves and Indians, and the scare writings of the guerrillas themselves throw very little additional light on their activities.[43]

The activities of individuals such as Noguera do, however, draw attention to another well-known feature of Colombian history. This is the popular nature of regionalism. Not only in the south, but also in Cartagena, Socorro and elsewhere, the rebellion's leaders, or *Supremos*, declared the independence of their province from Bogotá and called for an urgent revaluation of the structure of the nation. What are we to make of these outbreaks of federalism? David Bushnell has noted that federalism seems to exert its strongest appeal on factions out of power, warning that we should not accord it undue importance.[44] It is nonetheless significant that the regions where federalist proclamations were made had histories of opposition to rule from Bogotá. The Province of Pasto is a notable example, as is Cartagena. Both had rivalries with the capital dating back to at least the eighteenth century.[45] This suggests that, at the very least, greater independence from Bogotá was perceived as an appealing rallying-cry by the rebellion's various leaders.

I want to draw attention to a final popular feature of the war. This concerns the role of religion. Particularly in the south of Colombia, the defence of religion was a genuinely popular cause. During the *Guerra de los Supremos*, indigenous and mestizo guerrillas under the leadership of Gregorio Sarría or Andrés Noguera, for example, fought in the name of the Catholic faith against troops from Bogotá. What did this mean? Some observers were cynical; José Manuel Restrepo sneered that while the leaders

---

[43] Restrepo, *Diario político*, vol. 3, p. 141–53; and Posada, *Memorias*, vol. 3, pp. 251–9. See Posada, *Memorias*, vol. 4, p. 3 for '*indiada*'.

[44] David Bushnell, *The Making of Modern Colombia: A Nation in Spite of Itself*, (Berkeley, 1993), p. 91.

[45] For Pasto, see Rebecca Earle, *Spain and the Independence of Colombia* (Exeter, 2000); for Cartagena, see Anthony McFarlane, *Colombia before Independence: Economy, Society, and Politics under Bourbon Rule* (Cambridge, 1993).

claimed to be defending the faith, their Indian followers had not the slightest idea what this meant.[46] Others, however, acknowledged that religion exerted a powerful hold on the minds of the indigenous population. Disappointed that the auxiliary bishop of Pasto had declined to accompany his troops, Herrán urged his allies to find another bishop: 'this measure is more important than you can imagine ... With priests and money you can do what you like in this province', he commented.[47] One does not have to argue, as so many historians have, that southern Colombia is the preserve of religious fanatics to accept that defending the autonomy of the Catholic church can be a genuinely popular cause.

The *Guerra de los Supremos* was certainly about more than elite infighting. The issues around which it revolved (political leadership, regional autonomy, defence of religion) were of interest to a wider section of the population than the political elite alone. Of course, the motives for individual participation in the war varied. Perhaps very particular issues drove María Martínez de Nisser to cut her hair, dress as a soldier and join the national army in the battle of Salamina. On the other hand, perhaps her own explanation that she was simply defending the integrity of the nation illustrates the extent to which the rhetoric of party politics had penetrated Colombia's female population.[48] Nor is it realistic to claim that all individuals participated in the war voluntarily. Nonetheless, I hope I have indicated that the origins of this war do not lie solely in the egotistical struggles of a few ambitious politicians.

The aftermath of the war

The *Guerra de los Supremos* played an important role in the consolidation of the liberal and conservative parties in Colombia. Indeed, this is seen by many historians as its primary significance. I would like here, however, to consider by way of conclusion the impact of the war on another area: slavery.

---

[46] Restrepo, *Diario político*, p. 166; or see Posada, *Memorias*, vol. 3, p. 251.

[47] Pedro Alcántara Herrán, quoted in Tirado, *Aspectos sociales*, p. 58. See also José María Samper, quoted in Tirado, *Aspectos sociales*, p. 83.

[48] In her 1843 memoir of the war, Martínez de Nisser described her decision to join the national army after the arrest of her husband: 'What sad ideas surround me! ... My tender feelings advise me to go to Rionegro to accompany [my husband] to prison ... but the public good tells me otherwise; what use can I be [in Rionegro] to either my fatherland or my spouse? Tomorrow I will present myself to [General] Braulio [Henao]; I will ask him for a lance; I will march in the company of my two brothers and the other patriots of this town; and I will contribute in this way to the liberation of my soil.' María Martínez de Nisser, *Diario de los sucesos de la revolución en la Provincia de Antioquia en los años de 1840 y 41* (Bogotá, 1843), cited in Nestor Botero Goldworthy, 'Los esposos Pedro Nisser y María Martínez de Nisser,' *Boletín de Historia y Antigüedades*, vol. 76, no. 766 (1989), p. 605. Martínez de Nisser was subsequently awarded a medal for her participation in the Battle of Salamina. See Botero Goldsworthy, 'Los esposos'; and Jorge Orlando Melo (ed.), *Reportaje de la Historia de Colombia* (Bogotá, 1989), pp. 413ff.

After the end of the war, the victorious conservatives imposed a series of restrictive laws, aimed at tightening the slave owner's grip on his human property. Measures effectively reintroduced the slave trade, and also limited the impact of previous pro-abolition legislation.[49] The motives for these laws may be found in the activities of slaves during the war itself. Rebel leaders such as Obando and José María Vezga, in Antioquia, had offered freedom to slaves joining their armies and escaped slaves also fought with guerrillas such as Gregorio Sarría, Andrés Noguera and José Antonio Tascón.[50] The behaviour of these individuals had challenged the authority of the slave-owning elite in southern Colombia. The new conservative government, closely linked to slave-owners in the Cauca, now retaliated with restrictive legislation.

The *Guerra de los Supremos* thus increased tension between slave-owners and those sectors of Colombian society inclined towards abolition (a sector which included slaves themselves). After the election of the radical liberal José Hilario López to the presidency in 1849, hostility between the slave-owning elite and the reforming branch of the liberals reached a new high.[51] Armed bands had begun attacking landowners in the Cauca Valley and elsewhere. Slave-owners complained that the government encouraged these attacks, complaints that were given greater force when the president, after a visit to the south, stated that the unrest was the result of the feudal conditions imposed on the population by wealthy landowners.[52] Then, on 21 May 1851 the López government abolished slavery. This reform was accompanied by a series of other laws that limited the authority of the Catholic Church.

In response, armed groups opposed to the new measures appeared in various parts of the country, in a desperate attempt to prevent the application of these laws.[53] The revolt dragged on until 1852, and a complete pardon for those involved was not issued until February 1853. The Guerra de los Supremos thus contributed both to the abolition of

---

[49] Jorge Castellanos, 'The Failure of the Manumission Juntas in the Colombian Province of Popayán, 1821–1851', *Michigan Academician*, vol. 14, no. 4 (1982).

[50] Tirado, *Aspectos sociales*, pp. 94–112, 407–8.

[51] The slave-owning elite was not the only sector of Colombian society to oppose the López administration. See Frank Safford's chapter in this volume for further comment on the origins of the 1851 war.

[52] José Manuel Restrepo, *Historia de la Nueva Granada*, vol. 2, (Bogotá, 1963) p. 214. See also Richard P. Hyland, 'A Fragile Prosperity: Credit and Agrarian Structure in the Cauca Valley, Colombia, 1851–87', *Hispanic American Historical Review*, vol. 62, no. 3 (1982), especially p. 380.

[53] See Restrepo, *Historia*, vol. 2, pp. 191–247 and *passim*; letters to Tomás Cipriano de Mosquera in ACC, Sala Mosquera, carpeta A–1, año de 1851; and Archivo Histórico Nacional de Colombia, (Bogotá), Secretaria de Guerra y Marina, tomo 101, 450–792 ff., for a description of the war. Helguera discusses the revolution's social roots in 'Antecedentes sociales de la revolución de 1851', pp. 53–63; and the US chargé d'affaires offered his view that the revolt was provoked largely by the expulsion of the Jesuits in Yelverton P. King to US Secretary of State Daniel Webster, Bogotá, 30 August 1851, in Manning (ed.), *Diplomatic Correspondence of the United States*, vol. 5, pp. 668–9.

slavery and also to the prolongation of civil unrest. In 1853 José María Obando succeeded his friend López to the presidency, following an acrimonious election. The events of 1851–53 were soon overshadowed by the unrest of 1854, when another civil war broke out. The succeeding decades saw a series of civil wars and regional revolts, culminating in the monumental *Guerra de los Mil Días* at the turn of the century.

CHAPTER 7

God and Federation: The Uses and Abuses of the Idea of 'Federation' during the Federal Wars in Venezuela, 1859–63

Elena Plaza*

The so-called Federal War or Long War was the second civil war that Venezuela experienced during the nineteenth century. It began at the start of 1859 and culminated formally with the signing of the Treaty of Coche in the Hacienda Coche on the outskirts of Caracas on 22 May 1863. Studying the Federal War has prompted me to ask the following question: what was the relationship between the two most widely used political slogans of the war? These were, on the one hand, 'God and Federation', and on the other, 'Oligarchies tremble', or, in a more violent version, 'To Caracas to kill the whites, and everyone who can read and write'. Trying to answer this question has led me to analyse the meaning attributed to the term 'Federation' by two of the sectors involved in the conflict: the civil elite and the caudillos who embarked upon guerrilla warfare. I explore this analysis in the following chapter.

I. The civilian elite and the centralisation-federation debate of 1858

The March Revolution

In 1857 General José Tadeo Monagas, who was occupying the position of President of the Republic for the second time in the period 1855–59, instigated a constitutional reform which allowed him to make preparations for his immediate re-election to another presidential term, a move which was prohibited by the 1830 Constitution in force at the time. In this we witness a typical characteristic of Monagas' political personalism: the manipulation of the existing constitutional-legal order to meet the President's own personal ends. The new Constitution, tailored to General Monagas' aspirations to remain in power, provoked the alliance between the liberal and conservative parties, both in opposition at the time, and one sector of the army, which effected a coup d'état on 5 March 1858. On learning of the impending revolution, General Monagas took refuge in the French Embassy.

The triumph of the March Revolution initiated a period of provisional government headed by General Julián Castro, the coup's military leader, whose fundamental objective was to create a National Constitutional Assembly, which would define a new constitutional order and allow the resumption of normal political life. General Castro's government initially

---

* Translated by Fiona Mackintosh.

had the political backing of both the liberal and conservative parties. Within a short period, however, the signing of the Urrutia Protocol[1] and the resolution to try members of the Monagas administration for misappropriation and embezzlement of state funds provoked a schism within the Liberal Party. This last measure hit the liberals hard, since important members of this party had collaborated with General José Tadeo Monagas' first administration (1847–51). Fearful of being implicated in the investigation, the most compromised section of the party, led by Antonio Leocadio Guzmán, decided to leave Venezuela and withdraw their political support from General Julián Castro's government. Guzmán withdrew into voluntary exile, together with those liberal caudillos that placed their hopes in revolutionary, rather than institutional, change.

The National Convention of Valencia

The National Constitutional Assembly held its first session in the city of Valencia on 5 July 1858 and closed early in the following year, on 3 February 1859. It was attended by representatives of the institutional wing of the Liberal Party and by Conservative Party representatives. The latter, imbued with anti-militarist ideas, sought to create a new constitutional order that would overcome the defects of the 1830 Constitution, which the conservatives believed had unleashed great evils on Venezuelan political life. These included the unchecked spread of personal political ambition and the manipulation of the existing constitutional-legal order to suit the personal ends of those in power, militarism — through the prominent role played by former officers from the War of Independence in the political running of the country, who thereby blocked the way for the civilian elite — corruption and nepotism. As was typical of nineteenth century Venezuelan political culture, the vision of an ideal social order crystallised around the constitution.

The internal division of the Liberal Party provided the conservatives with a majority in the Constitutional Assembly. The conservatives' anti-militarism and their support for the political reorganisation of the state clashed violently with the views held by the liberal delegates. The debate centred on issues of constitutional law, but for the purpose of this chapter we shall concentrate solely on the polemic over centralism versus federation: should Venezuela employ a central or a federal system of government?

The delegates of the Liberal Party maintained that the new state organisation should be of a federal nature. They based their position on the following arguments:[2]

---

[1] The Urrutia Protocol was an agreement reached between the Venezuelan minister for foreign affairs, the liberal politician Wenceslao Urrutia, and the French chargé d'affaires, to allow General Monagas' departure from the French Legation, in which he had taken refuge. The terms of the Protocol so favoured General Monagas that the state could take no measures against him save that of decreeing his expulsion from the country.

[2] Here I summarise the contributions of delegates Francisco Mejía, Estanislao Rendón and Enrique Pérez de Velasco to the sessions of 30 July 1858 and 28 September 1858. See

a) A federal state is more democratic than a centralist one, because it decentralises the administration. The citizen is consequently closer to the centres of power in which decisions that affect his daily life are taken. At the same time, decentralisation ensures a more equitable regional distribution in the administration of the *res publica*. Finally, by decentralising and widening participation in the electoral process to include all citizens, individuals will be able to choose their local political representatives.

b) A centralist state, by restricting its organisation to the national level, facilitates the proliferation of those vices that have blighted Venezuelan political life, namely the abuse of power on the part of governors, corruption and nepotism. In a federal state, on the other hand, these vices could not prosper, since federalism permits less concentration of power and greater control over the administration of the *res publica*.

c) The North American parallel: a federal state stimulates national development, whereas a centralist state hinders it. To verify this one need look no further than the United States. The liberal representatives asked themselves the following question: why had the United States, which was, like Spanish America, a former colony, enjoyed such progress while the Spanish American nations had not? For the liberals, the answer lay in the form of political organisation. A federal state permitted greater freedom than a centralist state, and greater liberty necessarily brought greater progress. North American federalism was, therefore, an example worthy of imitation.

d) Federalism is superior to centralism because, under federalism, localities select their own regional governments from among their local leaders. Thus, with a federal system the national government does not intervene in regional problems.

For these reasons, the creation of a federal state was, for the liberal representatives, the solution to all the political problems facing Venezuela. For the conservative representatives, the federation was simply a form of political organisation of the state that they did not favour, and which would not necessarily bring with it all the benefits ascribed to it by the liberals. Their responses to the liberal arguments can be summarised as follows:[3]

a) A federal state was not synonymous with greater democracy. The liberal vision was distorted by the false belief that closer ties between

---

Presidencia de la República, *Pensamiento político venezolano del siglo XIX* (Caracas, 1961), vol. 12, pp. 601ff.

[3] Here I summarise the contributions of delegates Pedro Gual and Fermín Toro to the sessions of 4 August 1858 and 25 September 1858. See Presidencia de la República, *Pensamiento político venezolano*, vol. 12, pp. 610–8; and vol. 1, pp. 294–301 respectively.

the citizen and the centres of power necessarily implied a more democratic way of life. A centralist constitution could be just as democratic, or just as undemocratic, as a federal constitution. The important thing was that the new constitution should broaden the political participation of the people and, to this end, the conservatives proposed abandoning the census-like character of elections, adopting instead universal suffrage for all citizens and election of the highest authorities, both national and provincial. With respect to the benefits of decentralisation, the conservatives agreed fully with the liberals and proposed the adoption of a decentralised unitary state with direct election of governors and delegates to provincial assemblies. This system was perfectly compatible with a unitary state, which the conservatives believed was necessary in order to prevent the political disintegration of the state, the proliferation of local caudillos, political instability and anarchy, all of which they insisted would follow the introduction of federalism.

b)   The Conservative representatives maintained that vices such as corruption and nepotism were not the inevitable consequence of a centralist constitution. On the contrary, they were the product of the Independence process and of the dominant role which the military had played in it and in political life immediately after Independence. This is not to say that the conservatives defended those aspects of Venezuelan political life; on the contrary, they proposed that measures be taken to weaken the role of the military and of presidents in national political life. In accordance with this they proposed to weaken executive power, making it more dependent on legislative power, to limit the powers of the government in the imposition of states of emergency, and to include in the new constitution articles that would prevent nepotism. Conservatives insisted that all of these measures could be included in the structure of executive power, without the need for a federal-style constitution.

c)   Conservatives did not agree with the proposal to imitate the North American model. They considered North American federalism to be somewhat experimental and it seemed to them premature to propose it as a model for Venezuela. North American progress was not due to its federal constitution, but to its culture, its industrious habits and its social customs, all of which were very different from Spanish-American customs, which the conservatives in turn attributed to the Spanish inheritance and to racial mixing. Two different colonisation processes, two distinct societies: therein lay the difference, and not in the constitution. To think that a simple imitation of the North American constitutional experiment would guarantee a solution to Venezuela's problems was highly naïve. Rather than imitating North Americans' constitution, the Venezuelans should imitate their industrious habits.

d) With regard to the selection of local officials, Conservatives maintained that this should not be a prerogative of the federal state, since by adopting direct election of provincial authorities, as they proposed, this problem would not arise in the first place.

The 1858 Constitution

The 1858 Constitution has been considered by subsequent Venezuelan historiography to be one of the most advanced of its time.[4] It established a decentralised unitary state, and reflected the civilian ideals of the Conservative Party which imposed it in the 1858 Convention. Contemporaries held widely differing views on its merits. The Liberal Party, defeated at the Convention, and the caudillos who launched the Federal War considered it unacceptable, and from the moment it first appeared it became the target of their criticisms, since it did not organise the nation from a federal point of view. As a result, the caudillos ignored the 1858 Constitution from the start and the Liberal Party, for their part, devoted themselves to discrediting it. For the Conservative Party, it was the most advanced document of its kind which had ever existed in the republican history of Venezuela, sanctioning as it did political rights such as universal suffrage for all citizens, the elimination of the census-like character of elections (with the exception of the elections for senators), the direct election of the president, governors, national and provincial representatives and members of the judiciary, the elimination of the death penalty for political crimes and the inclusion of decrees aimed at strengthening civil society and at weakening militarism and nepotism in high-ranking public posts.

However, once the federal guerrilla war had begun in early 1859, some sectors of the Conservative Party came to view the 1858 Constitution as an inadequate instrument with which to tackle the new situation. It was very complicated in terms of its electoral method. Moreover, in response to the desire to limit the personal political ambition so characteristic of previous decades, the 1858 Constitution had greatly weakened the figure of the president of the republic by making him more dependent on Congress than had the 1830 Constitution. At the same time, in limiting the funds on which the executive power could rely in an emergency, in the articles corresponding to the imposition of states of emergency, the 1858 Constitution tied the hands of the president of the republic, leaving him very few alternative courses of action when faced with exceptional circumstances. The measure, which had been introduced in order to avoid the constant use and abuse of this resource typical in previous presidential terms, would have a high political cost for the presidents of the nation. Ironically, this power had been weakened just when it was most needed.

---

[4] See, for example, José Gil Fortoul, *Historia constitucional de Venezuela* (Caracas, 1930), second edition, vol. 2, pp. 115–9.

In short, the 1858 Constitution, although certainly the most advanced in Venezuela's history, enjoyed very little credibility. It was criticised and attacked constantly by the elite and was ignored altogether by the guerrillas.

II. 'God and Federation'

This, then, was the significance of the term 'Federation' for the conservative and liberal civilian elites present at the National Convention of Valencia in 1858. We shall now describe the meaning it had for the caudillos who became involved in the Federal War in the first months of 1859.

Venezuelan federalism in the proclamations of the Federal War

The idea of federation present in the *pronunciamientos, manifiestos* and *proclamas* of the Federal War may be reduced to two features: provincial autonomy (the oldest and most Spanish political tradition in Venezuela) and social equality. Indeed, in these guerrilla documents we find a moralistic discourse of protest, in which the idea of federalism had become diluted in a philosophy of a distinctly social and moral bent on the one hand, and in the aspiration to establish regional autonomy on the other. In addition to their proclamations, manifestos and pronouncements, the federal guerrillas published a newspaper entitled *El Eco del Ejército*, in which they reported the development of the guerrilla war.[5] There appear in these texts the typical social demands of nineteenth-century Venezuela — land distribution, the attainment of equality for all Venezuelans, the broadening of democracy to allow higher degrees of civilian participation, the elimination of the death penalty for political crimes, the complete abolition of slavery, the improvement of the country's moral well-being, etc. — which were possible, according to them, only in a federal state. Although many, if not all, of these demands had already been conceded by the 1858 Constitution, the guerrilla claimed these causes as theirs alone. As regards the idea of federation, it was reduced solely to the call for regional autonomy, one of the oldest political traditions in Spanish America, based on the argument that regional administrations are more safely and reliably left in the hands of locals than in the hands of outsiders. According to these caudillos, the creation of true regional autonomy would be possible only with the triumph of the federation. General Juan Antonio Sotillo illustrates this point well. Sotillo, a caudillo, a leader of the revolution in eastern Venezuela and a persistent fighter for federation even after the war had come to an end, maintained even in 1867 that federalism was an important issue:

> I have struggled all my life for the holy cause of federation, so that each person may govern his own territory without the interference of others; I want the Barceloneses to rule in Barcelona; the Cumaneses in Cumaná;

---

[5] Frequent citations from this periodical may be found in Francisco González Guinán, *Historia contemporánea de Venezuela* (Caracas, 1910), vols 6–10.

the Apureños in Apure; the Barineses in Barinas ... This idea of sacrificing oneself so that strangers can come to govern is a tyranny and makes a mockery of principles.[6]

In this example, Sotillo invokes virtually every region in eastern Venezuela, reducing the idea of federation exclusively to the principle of regional autonomy.

The development of the Federal War (1859–63)

In order to follow the development of the war as a whole, it is necessary to negotiate two parallel scenarios which we cannot describe here in any detail. The first consists of the successive political crises that occurred in the heart of the national government as a consequence of its failure to defeat the guerrillas. It is necessary to describe two attempts at solving this political crisis that were put forward by different sectors (the civilian and the militarist) of the Conservative Party, which had recently regained power. The second scenario consists of the development and vicissitudes of the guerrilla movement proper until its triumph in 1863. We will first give a very schematic description of both aspects.

At the beginning of 1859, General Julián Castro, leader of the March Revolution, was elected president of Venezuela under the electoral system of the recently enforced 1858 Constitution. However, in July 1859 General Castro secretly converted to the cause of the federation. This provoked an immediate reaction from Congress: he was placed under house arrest by his personal guards and was stripped of the office of president. On 28 September 1859 Vice-president Manuel Felipe Tovar assumed the presidency. Since Castro's term in office had only just begun it was decided to call new elections, which took place at the beginning of 1860. Manuel Felipe Tovar was elected president and Dr Pedro Gual vice-president, according to the official count of votes that was performed in the Legislative Chamber on 10 April 1860 in accordance with the rules laid down by the 1858 Constitution. Both Tovar and Gual were civilians.

Between May and December 1860, the three major political groupings engaged in intense activity, in a deliberate effort to resolve the most pressing problems through the existing legal-institutional channels. The following examples in themselves illustrate the complexity of the existing political situation at that time. On 15 May 1860 President Tovar requested extraordinary powers from Congress in accordance with Articles 95 and 96 of the Constitution to combat the guerrilla war. These powers were immediately granted to him. In the period between 11 and 15 June 1860, Congress disputed whether or not there were grounds for bringing legal proceedings against General Castro. It concluded that there were and initiated Castro's trial in the Supreme Court of Justice.

---

[6] General Juan Antonio Sotillo to a friend from Caracas, 1867, cited in Laureano Vallenilla Lanz, 'Argentina y Venezuela. Afinidades sociales y políticas', *Hispanía* (London, 1912).

On 19 June 1860 Congress reformed the 1849 law on the political crime of conspiracy, leaving in force the abolition of the death penalty for political crimes. On 20 July 1860 Congress set the budget for the financial year 1860–61. On 28 July 1860 the Supreme Court of Justice pronounced its verdict on the trial of ex-President Castro. On 28 September 1860, the Legislature being in recess, President Tovar convoked an Extraordinary Council of State to request an extension to the extraordinary powers granted to him by Congress.

On 20 January 1861 the preparatory commissions of the legislative chambers began operating. As a consequence, the conservative press became completely divided. One faction, which termed itself 'legalist', saw in the actions of President Tovar's government the only possible route towards the conservative civilian ideals of the March Revolution. Another faction, which called itself 'dictatorial', maintained that the new constitutional order put excessive limitations on the president's authority and thus impeded his ability to achieve national peace. This faction therefore backed an unusual proposal: Congress should grant special powers for peacemaking to someone with sufficient authority and prestige to dominate the federal guerrilla war. For them, the only person who met these requirements was General José Antonio Páez. President Tovar, for his part, thought that the benefits which the introduction of General Páez into the peace process would bring were greater than the risks. Páez represented a new element, a highly prestigious political player who was not worn down by the conflicts of recent years and a person to whom several federal leaders had stated their willingness to submit. President Tovar therefore invited Páez to return to Venezuela. On Páez's arrival from the United States in March 1861, he was named chief of the national army in order to lead the peace process. 'Peace without bloodshed' was the phrase which summed up President Tovar's policy: the search for a consensus with the federal guerrillas and the different political tendencies, and the wish to give the new constitutional order a chance, as the 1858 Constitution met practically all the social and political demands made by the guerrillas, with the exception of the federal organisation of the state. Yet these views notwithstanding, neither President Tovar nor the 'legalists' trusted General Páez. The conduct of the latter in the months between March and May 1861 was plagued with misunderstandings between him and the government, and by the actions and reactions of the legalist and dictatorial tendencies of the Conservative Party in favour of one or the other. As a consequence of these confrontations, General Páez resigned from the post of general in chief of the national army for leading the peace process on two occasions (May and August 1861). Both resignations were greeted by immediate expressions in his favour from the national army.

After the arrival of General Páez in Venezuela, the Conservative Party began to face serious internal problems that made it practically impossible for the work of government to be carried out. These included the all-out war between the legalists and the dictatorialists, the lack of authority of successive presidents (Manuel Felipe Tovar and Pedro Gual) each of whom came to power without their predecessor having completing his respective constitutional term, the mutual suspicion between the presidents Tovar and Gual and General Páez and the futility of the actions carried out by the two presidents to shore up the new constitutional order against two enemies who were themselves enemies: the federal guerrillas and the dictatorialists. The clashes between the different political factions gradually undermined the authority of President Tovar, who resigned as president on 20 May 1861, stating that the abuses committed by the pro-Páez military and the dictatorial wing within his own party made it impossible for him to continue governing. The same day, Vice-president Pedro Gual took office as president. General Páez was restored to the post of general in chief of the armies of the republic on the following day and began exercising his duties immediately.

On 29 May 1861 Congress conferred exceptional powers on President Gual in order that he should bring peace to the country in accordance with articles 95 and 96 of the 1858 Constitution. Moreover, they gave a vote of support and confidence to the executive so that he might pursue national peace by whatever methods he considered effective and which Congress could concede in view of its constitutional authority. May 1861 ended in the collapse of General Páez's peace initiative in the Province of Aragua. His proposals, entitled 'Peace and Union', were not accepted by the federal leaders with whom he had negotiated.

On 19 July 1861, in view of the failure of General Páez's steps towards peace, the government, using that extra authority with which it was endowed, issued two decrees in which it defined the new policy to be followed in the face of the federal guerrilla war. In the first of these decrees, all the provinces were deemed to form part of the assembly, with the exception of Margarita, Trujillo, Mérida and Maracaibo (these exceptions were to last as long as these provinces were not invaded by guerrilla forces). Any individual who threatened society would be subject to trial by a military tribunal and to whatever penalties were determined by army ordinances. Thus, in this first decree the president laid down the legal basis for justifying a repressive policy — as opposed to the conciliatory policy in existence until then — for combating the guerrillas. In the second decree, the president defined several specific measures that the government would take once the new policy of repression had been established.[7]

The reaction of the Conservative Party to these decrees was twofold: the dictatorialists maintained that the president had overstepped the mark in his use of the extraordinary powers given to him by Congress, flouting both the rule of law and the constitution. The legalists believed the opposite: the constitutional dictator had done nothing more than define the state of war and the legal basis for its repression. General Páez, for his part, applauded

---

[7] See González, *Historia contemporánea*, vol. 7, pp. 349 ff; and José Santiago Rodríguez, *Contribucción al estudio de la Guerra Federal* (Caracas, 1910), vol. 2, pp. 265 ff.

the decrees, and instead of abandoning his own efforts at pacification, continued to develop his policy of 'peace and union' independently of the government. Hence, from July 1861, there were two separate and contradictory quasi-governmental policies for ending the federal guerrilla war. The Liberal Party in turn asserted that the government had fallen into a grave contradiction. According to the liberal historian Francisco González Guinán, '... with the decrees of 19 July was established the dictatorship of Doctor Gual, who was older and less respected than the General [Páez]. The government had thus become revolutionary. It had a constitution, and by its own will it has destroyed it ...'[8]

On 15 August 1861 Dr Angel Quintero, the home secretary and recently elected designate,[9] arrived in the city of Valencia with the object of asking General Páez, in the name of the government, to resign his post of commander of the national army. The following day General Páez tendered his resignation. While Dr Gual's government was determining to rid itself definitively of General Páez, several uprisings occurred simultaneously in the provinces of Aragua and Carabobo, whose only common factor was the aim of toppling Dr Gual from the presidency and restoring General Páez as head of the national army. But another uprising preceded all of these in Caracas on 29 August 1861, which, according to historian Francisco González Guinán, reflected the wishes of the dictatorial wing of the Conservative Party. This barracks coup immediately declared the dictatorship of General José Antonio Páez. It is apparent that, although the federal guerrillas failed to overthrow the government, there was no shortage of conservative efforts to do so. Unlike the guerrillas, the conservatives succeeded.

On 31 August 1861 a commission went to meet General Páez in order to present him with the *Pronunciamiento de Caracas*, which declared him supreme chief of the republic.[10] Meanwhile General Páez himself had moved to the city of La Victoria, in the province of Aragua. From there he replied to the commission, refusing to accept the powers they were offering him. Not until 9 September 1861 did he formally accept command, thereby putting an end to the new constitutional order and to the attempts at conservative civilian rule, initiating the regime most driven by pure personal ambition in the entire history of nineteenth-century Venezuela.

General José Antonio Páez's regime lasted from September 1861 to June 1863. It was a regime based exclusively on the military, political and moral prestige of General Páez. Its objective was to defeat the federal guerrillas and pacify the country. As it was impossible for General Páez to govern within the existing constitutional order, the dictatorial wing of the Conser-

---

[8] González, *Historia contemporánea*, vol. 7, p. 351.
[9] The *designatura*, or acting president, was a post created by the 1858 Constitution whose purpose was to stand in for the absent president and vice-president of the republic. See Luis Mariñas Otero, *Las constituciones de Venezuela* (Madrid, 1910), p. 290.
[10] 'Al General José Antonio Páez'; *El Independiente*, Caracas, year II, month V, no. 414 (31 August 1861).

vative Party, which had aided the coup d'état, disowned the Constitution and set about eliminating it. The country was thus without a constitution until 1864. The regime attempted to legitimate itself through the charisma of General Páez's military, political and moral reputation, and through his alleged 'popular mandate'. The elimination of the constitutional order was justified through the legal confusion that had arisen from the decrees issued by President Gual in July 1861.

This final regime of General Páez, which departed from its original objective of pacifying the country, can be divided into two periods. The first period, from September to December 1861, saw a halt to the war and the initiation of a policy of vigorous negotiation with the federal guerrillas, with the aim of reaching a peace agreement and thereby quickly and expediently fulfilling the general's 'mandate'. This first stratagem failed because the federal guerrillas rejected all of the conditions proposed by the regime. Negotiations were thus abandoned in December 1861. The policies employed in the second stage of Páez's dictatorship, from January 1862 to May 1863, were entirely to contrary those of the previous one. Páez realised that his regime would last longer than he had initially thought; as a consequence, he endowed it with a somewhat greater administrative structure through a series of measures derived from the *Decreto Orgánico de la República* issued in January 1862.[11] He simultaneously declared all-out war on the federal guerrillas, in a new strategy based on the use of military force rather than negotiation. This second attempt failed in early 1863, when the federal guerrillas gained control of most of Venezuela's territory. Faced with military defeat, Páez once again initiated negotiations. These negotiations resulted in the Treaty of Coche.

This attempt at conservative militarism thus failed to achieve its objectives, despite having at its disposal the greatest concentration of power that has been given to any head of state in the political history of Venezuela.

The federal guerrillas

Guerrilla activity began at the start of 1859 in the city of Coro, in what is now the state of Falcón.[12] The guerrillas used a modus operandi which was to be repeated, with slight variations, in various cities in the province. They captured the city, overpowered local authorities, declared the 'independence' of the capital and proceeded to install a provisional federal government which would last until their cause triumphed in the rest of the country. In general, the political objectives of the guerrilla war were expounded in each city's *pronunciamiento* for the federation.

---

[11] See *Registro Oficial*, year I, no. 8, Caracas (4 January 1862) pp. 57–8; *Registro Oficial*, year I, no. 11, Caracas (15 January 1862) p. 82; *Registro Oficial*, year I, no. 13, Caracas (22 January 1862) p. 99; *Registro Oficial*, year I, no. 21, Caracas (1 March 1862) p. 161.
[12] In developing this point I am closely following Nikita Harwich Vallenilla, 'Guerra Federal', in Fundación Polar, *Diccionario de Historia de Venezuela* (Caracas, 1988), vol. 2, pp. 381–5.

The Federal War did not involve all of Venezuela's territory. The zones most affected were the east, the central plains and the present-day state of Falcón. The Andes, the capital and the south did not experience the guerrilla onslaught. The Andean zone was at this time undergoing a great expansion in coffee production, a veritable boom, which brought great prosperity to the region. The south-eastern region of Guayana was experiencing the cotton boom stimulated by the worldwide drop in supply caused by the American Civil War. England strongly supported the cultivation of cotton in the region, following the recommendations made by the British consul in Guayana, Mr Mathison.[13] In the capital, General Páez's regime initiated large scale improvements in infrastructure and services which modernised Caracas through the introduction of gas street lighting and the construction of railways, new highways, an aqueduct, a theatre, etc. These public works were all undertaken with foreign capital, which made important investments in Venezuela in spite of the guerrilla activity.

From the military point of view only two important battles took place during the war. These were the battles of Santa Inés, on 10–11 December 1859, and Coplé, on 17 December 1860. The federal guerrillas won the former, while government forces won the latter. The remainder of the conflict was fought essentially as a guerrilla war that exposed successive Venezuelan governments to a constant drain of resources, both military and political. Government forces had to respond to actions such as the capture of cities, towns and villages, disruption to the country's main commercial highways, and the destruction of property owned either by individuals considered to be enemies or by resident foreigners.

By the beginning of 1863 the federal guerrillas dominated the east, the central plains and the north-west. This hegemony was extended through a phenomenon which had been relatively common since late 1862, and which gave rise to the conjugation of a new verb: '*federarse*' ('to federate'). To federate meant to join the revolution. The governor of the province in question would abandon his support for Páez's regime and reach a political agreement with the guerrillas. Faced with this situation, General Páez decided to negotiate. This was quite embarrassing for the regime, given the violent, aggressive and inflexible nature of the official discourse on the guerrilla war, particularly after the failure of negotiations in December 1861.[14] The uncomfortable position in which his regime found itself from the end of 1862, combined with his wish not to appear to have been publicly overthrown at the age of 73, convinced

---

[13] 'Report on the whole import and export trade of the river Orinoko [sic], Province of Guayana, with general information during the year ending 31st December, 1862'; Public Record Office, F.O. 80, 162, ff.103–12.

[14] See the articles by Pedro José Rojas, the regime's chief ideologist, in *El Independiente* from 1861 to 1863: Pedro José Rojas, 'Revelaciones y reflexiones', *El Independiente*, año II, mes X, no. 521 (11 April 1862); Pedro José Rojas, 'Rumores y alarmas', *El Independiente*, año III, mes V, no. 691 (9 August 1862); and Pedro José Rojas, 'Frutos de la dicatadura', *El Independiente*, año III, mes XII, no. 871 (19 March 1863).

General Páez to seek the assistance of the three most important chargés d'affaires in the country: the British, French and Brazilian. He entrusted them with the delicate and difficult task of building a political bridge to the guerrilla leaders. They did so; the British chargé d'affaires, Mr Frederick Doventon Orme, directed the initial stages of this process, which culminated in the signing of the Treaty of Coche on 22 May 1863.

The Treaty of Coche stipulated the cessation of hostilities on both sides and the convocation to a National Constitutional Assembly of 80 representatives (40 for each side). General Páez was to remain in charge of the country until the installation of the Assembly, at which point he had to relinquish his 'special powers' which 'had been conferred upon him' by the Venezuelan people; once this was done, the assembly would decide the political future of the nation and would elect its new provisional authorities. The assembly was installed on' 15 June 1863. There, General Páez relinquished control and abandoned forever his public life in Venezuela. He remained in the country until August 1863, when he went abroad. He lived for a further ten years, travelling through different Spanish American countries and finally settled in the United States, where he died in 1873.

Epilogue: 'Vivan los Amarillos, Mueran los Rojos'

The establishment of a federal state in Venezuela proved to be a longer and more difficult process than the federal guerrillas had initially imagined.[15] A unitary state had existed since 1830, and since 1861 political power had been highly concentrated in the hands of General Páez. Moreover, although Venezuelan law had been derived from the constitution, the country had no constitution after 1861. The creation of a federal structure thus took the following steps:

1. Installation of the National Constitutional Assembly and the election of a provisional government.

2. Drafting of the Federal Constitution, which transformed the twenty existing provinces into 20 independent states, which federated to form the United States of Venezuela.

3. Election of federal authorities in accordance with the electoral rules of the new Federal Constitution.

4. Convocation to a Constitutional Assembly in each of the member states created by the Federal Constitution.

5. Election of a provisional government in each of the 20 states.

---

[15] See González, *Historia contemporánea*, vol. 8, pp. 149–518, vol. 9, pp. 9–162.

6. Drafting of the State Constitution and the definition of boundaries in each of the 20 states.

7. Election of an official state government in each of the 20 states.

In addition to being complicated, the process encountered many problems which slowed it down and made it even more difficult. The election of representatives to the state constitutional assemblies was plagued by all sorts of difficulties. Rivalries emerged between regional caudillos each of whom wanted to occupy positions of power in their state, which in turn led to civil unrest, invasions, coups, etc. Border disputes broke out between neighbouring states. Regional authorities either misunderstood or wilfully ignored the legislation on the role of the national government, particularly in relation to the division of authority between the national government and the member states and the interpretation of the concept of state sovereignty. The combined effect was enormous disorganisation, disintegration and political instability in the years immediately following the end of the war.

In terms of politics, the triumph of the federation signified the death of the Conservative Party and the end of two-party politics in nineteenth century Venezuela. From 1863 until the end of the century, the men who led Venezuelan political life were individuals who had participated in the Federal War. Venezuelan historiography refers to this period as '*Venezuela liberal-amarilla*' ('liberal-yellow Venezuela'), since the Liberal Party (whose official colour was yellow) ostensibly dominated the national political scene. The Conservative Party was in ruins after the military and political defeat at the hands of the federation and the loss of support suffered as a consequence of the internal divisions between legalists and dictatorialists. The most prominent conservative politicians of the time — General Páez, Pedro José Rojas, Angel Quintero, Manuel Felipe Tovar and Pedro Gual — died in exile. The remainder disappeared from Venezuelan political life.

The Liberal Party also underwent an important transformation. Its elite no longer consisted a group of talented civilian intellectuals. Rather, it was in the hands of a new generation of caudillos and young people who did not feel bound to the party's original ideals. The Liberal Party grew so much during the 'yellow era' that it encompassed many distinct tendencies based on the personal authority of regional caudillos. Thus we find different tendencies in the east, the west or the central region, each revolving around the local politician who led them. This structure gradually adapted to the federative organisation of the state which was implemented from 1864 onwards and which was successively reformed by General Antonio Guzmán Blanco, in line with personal and/or regional political interests, after he came to power in 1870.

In conclusion, the concept of 'federation' in mid-nineteenth century Venezuela was understood by a few limited sectors of the national elite belonging to the two main political parties of the time. For the caudillos who directed the guerrilla war, federation was reduced to the principle of autonomy for the '*patria chica*' and a collection of social and moral demands. For the people who identified with the federal guerrillas, it was an abstract term that signified only the continuing failure to fulfil the promises of social equality made at the time of political independence from Spain. It is perhaps thus that we can understand how this strange term, combined with great faith and hope, brought forth a cause which for some, like General Juan Antonio Sotillo, was holy and above everything except God himself.

CHAPTER 8

On the Origins of the Bolivian Civil War of 1898–99

Marie-Danielle Demélas-Bohy[*]

The civil war of 1898, which shattered a period of stability that had been exceptionally long in the agitated history of Bolivia,[1] invites enquiry into the causes of the conflict. Political, regional or ethnic, the reasons for this confrontation continue to divide historians,[2] given that, from the first days of the rebellion, the three interpretations seemed to be equally justified. The Liberal Party heading the rebellion contested the monopoly on power exercised for nearly 20 years by the conservatives; but in addition, forces from the department of the north, led by a coalition formed in La Paz, confronted those of the south, led from Sucre. Moreover, after several months the Indians, mobilised at first behind one of the belligerents, declared war on all whites. The conflict, officially unleashed by regional antagonism (La Paz rebelled against Sucre, the capital of the north laid claim to the preponderance of the south), ended in the Conservative Party's loss of power to the Liberal Party, which in turn set about putting an end to the Indian insurrection with which it had been allied, and indeed had its leaders executed.

Might it be possible to reconcile the different aspects of the civil war, by superimposing multiple levels of analysis, or else perhaps by evoking three successive points of view? It seems not, as the different causalities do not coincide. The political division does not align with the regional antagonism. In December 1898 the entirety of La Paz's political class, including the conservatives, rose up against the mining oligarchy of Sucre. On the other hand, once the conflict was over the federalist programme in whose name the war had been conducted was immediately put into cold storage. In short, the victorious Liberal Party rapidly crumbled into multiple rival tendencies.

---

[*] Translated by Rebecca Earle.

[1] C. Mesa, *Presidentes de Bolivia: entre urnas y fusiles* (La Paz, 1984) p. 177. For an analytical overview of this period of stability, see Marie-Danielle Demélas, *L'invention politique. Bolivie, Équateur, Pérou au XIXe siècle* (Paris, 1992) pp. 506–14. For an excellent study of Bolivian political instability, see J.-P. Lavaud, *L'instabilité politique de l'Amérique Latine. Le cas de la Bolivie* (Paris, 1991).

[2] S. Almaraz Paz, *El poder y la caída. El estaño en la historia de Bolivia* (La Paz, 1987); James Dunkerley, *Orígenes del poder militar en Bolivia* (La Paz, 1987); E. Grieshaber, 'Resistencia indígena a la venta de tierras comunales indígenas del sur de Bolivia en el siglo XIX', *Data*, no. 1 (La Paz, 1991); M. Irurozqui Victoriano, 'La guerra de razas en Bolivia: la (re)invención de una tradición', *Revista Andina*, no. 1 (Cuzco, 1993) pp. 163–200; Herbert Klein, *Bolivia: The Evolution of a Multi-ethnic Society* (Oxford, 1982); and Tristan Platt, 'La experiencia andina del liberalismo boliviano entre 1825 y 1900: raíces de la rebellión de Chayanta (Potosí) durante el siglo XIX', in Steve Stern (ed.), *Resistencia, rebelión y conciencia campesina en los Andes, siglos XVIII–XIX* (Lima, 1990).

To this political confrontation we can add another factor to which the pioneering work of R. Condarco Morales attracted attention more than 30 years ago: the participation of (Aymara speaking) Indian communities from the *altiplano*, mobilised to assist the Liberal Party.[3] The affirmations of identity asserted by the actors themselves highlight this dimension of the war: in reaction against the inhabitants of La Paz who were considered to be Aymara speakers, the battalions of well-born young people from Sucre went to war singing *yaravis* in Quechua; whereas the moment the war was won by the Liberal Party, the 'indiennerie du palais' (in the words of the French chargé d'affaires), composed of Creole politicians[4] who defended an alliance between the new government and the Indian communities, became active at Pando's side.[5]

The development of events suggests that the civil war of 1899 synthesised all the tensions that had accumulated in Bolivian society over a long period. Is it thus necessary to analyse these tensions in order to understand the conflict? I find the question of the war's *origins* suggested in this chapter's title rather puzzling, as is the seductive confusion between 'origins', 'beginnings', 'causes' and 'genesis'. Is choosing to explore only *origins* simply a sort of timidity (historians, now more prudent, would no longer dream of entitling their work 'The causes of ... '), or does this formulation instead suggest an important nuance?

Given this uncertainty, I have chosen to hold to two possible meanings of this term: one which grounds the *origin* of a conflict in its recurrent practices and another which regards the 'hot points' of rebellious periods as a *site of origin*. Thus certain modalities of Bolivian political life put into place in the course of the nineteenth century facilitated recourse to civil war, whatever the latter's causes might be. On the other hand, there existed in Bolivia a point of origin, a peculiar geography, which determined that the civil wars brought together forces from the *altiplano* and from the more temperate valleys (again, whatever the causes of the conflict in question might be). These are the prepositions that I will advance and which the remainder of this chapter will attempt to make explicit.

Parties and regions: a dead end

As is known, in contrast with the French Revolution, the Hispanic Revolution did not attempt to erase the past, but rather claimed inspiration, whenever possible, from a continuous tradition, a respected past.[6] Thus, in

---

[3] R. Condarco Morales, *Zárate, El 'temible' Wilka. Historia de la rebelión indígena de 1899* (La Paz [1966] 1983 (new edition)).

[4] That is, those who were neither Indians nor mestizos.

[5] Archives du Ministère des Affaires Étrangères (AMAE), Paris, *Bolivie, politique intérieure, dossier général*, tome I (1894–99), dispatch of 19 May 1899, fols 192v–193.

[6] Marie-Danielle Demélas-Bohy and François-Xavier Guerra, 'The Hispanic Revolutions: the Adoption of Modern Forms of Representation in Spain and America (1808–1814)', in Eduardo Posada-Carbó (ed.), *Elections Before Democracy. The History of Elections in Europe and Latin America* (London, 1996), pp. 33–60.

nineteenth-century Bolivia, political life merely cloaked factions, lineages and clientelistic networks in modern garb. It is thus an abuse of language to imagine that the groupings that the actors in the 1899 civil war referred to as 'parties' correspond to political parties as defined by modern political science. Until 1880, the country was ignorant of the rules of parliamentary life, of the alternation in power of groups structured around a programme or solidly rooted in a social base. Regular elections did not exist, nor did respect for the rules of constitutional succession. What was a party, if not a grouping gathered around a caudillo, a faction or a lineage, seeking the conquest of power that would permit a redistribution of benefits to those quick enough in joining the victorious 'party'?

In any event, the changing conjuncture that manifested itself in 1880 permitted a break with caudillismo's more debatable practices. The defeat by Chile was the pretext for relegating the army (reduced to 2,000 men) to a subaltern level and military dictatorship disappeared for more than half a century. The laws of October 1880 brought a definitive blow to communal property, the power base of the Indian communities that had blocked all liberal projects. Finally, prosperity from mining made it possible to base government income on abundant customs revenues. Thus, for nearly a century, the development of the state was tied to that of mining.

In this new arrangement, the exercise of power by the conservatives adopted only the outward appearance of normalised parliamentary life. Their practice of power was anything but democratic: the preventative state of siege became banal, the decrees of a state of exception remained constantly in force and presidential succession was regulated by the departing president who designated his successor. Moreover, the democracy established by the constitution was highly exclusive: in a country of nearly two million inhabitants, only 70,000 citizens possessed the right to vote and only half of these exercised their right. Electoral fraud was the norm, as was violence, since the conservatives took their cue from the Argentine *mazorcas* in establishing troupes of paid thugs.

Thus, the period of Conservative Party dominance did not coincide with a decisive rupture with past practices and one is moreover entitled to challenge the very idea of the unshared domination of a single party. The rivalries between parties were overlaid by internal conflicts within the ruling group; thus the president of the republic and his two vice-presidents got on badly, and early post-electoral alliances seeking to merge voters and join together different groupings so as to seize power swiftly fell apart under pressure from associates concerned to affirm their own right to the presidency.

Moreover, stability at the national level did not prevent great local instability. In the departments, prefect followed prefect at a farcical rate — often two or three in a single year — without there being any trace of any sort of spoils system in these handovers, while at the same time, in the provinces, competition between the notables, entirely independent of any partisan affiliation, was lively enough to rouse conflicts that were as deadly as they were numerous.[7]

In return, the exclusive and highly cunning ruling group constituted a force capable of mastering strong tensions. There were about 50 parliamentarians and a half a dozen ministers; the totality of the group with access to power — conservatives, democrats and liberals combined — did not exceed a few hundred individuals. They all knew each other and might well all have been related to each other. This didn't prevent conflict, but it sometimes brought together adversaries who shared the same vision of the country's development. They all assumed that progress was attainable if civil peace could be maintained and that the country would overcome its backwardness were it to become an exporter of primary materials, appeal to foreign capital, open up communications and 'civilise' and homogenise the country. On this last point, there was some divergent opinion: the social Darwinists envisioned the elimination of the Indian majority through massive European immigration and through genocide; others favoured assimilation. All were optimistic.

In this consensual framework, the clientelistic structure of Bolivian society tended to act in favour of stability. A minimal agreement between the leaders checked against the confrontation of vertical networks. The manipulation of traditional ties thus constituted one of the operating rules of political life. Each group and each man employed his family connections, his alliances and his clientele to support his career, on condition he could get some benefits in return. These networks extended far beyond the circle of a few notable families, and through this means those excluded from politics were more often involved in its intrigues than the number of electors alone would lead one to believe.

In addition, although rivalries and violence did not cease between 1880 and 1899, despite the consensus of the ruling groups, the field of political conflict was always fairly circumscribed due to the recourse to negotiation by the differing factions. The latter took up arms only after having exhausted all possibilities for compromise. Before the outbreak of open conflict, the different ministerial cabinets were nearly always a consequence of compromises between the enemy parties.

What then differentiated conservatives from liberals, and what created the circumstances that in December 1898 could be resolved only through force of arms? If one trusts their own writings, the divergence between the two groups seems to have been more cultural and religious than political or economic.[8] The conservatives upheld the prerogatives

---

[7] For a fuller development of the subject of village politics, see Marie-Danielle Demélas and J. Piel, 'Jeux et enjeux du pouvoir dans les Andes. Les cas des départements du Cuzco et de La Paz (1880-1920)', in Asociación Francesa de Ciencias Sociales sobre América Latina (ed.), *Les frontières du pouvoir en Amérique Latine* (Toulouse, 1983) pp. 53–64.

[8] M. Renaud and Marie-Danielle Demélas-Bohy, 'Instability, Networks and Political Parties. A Political History Expert System Prototype', in E. Nissen and K. Schmidt (eds.), *From Information to Knowledge*. vol. 1: *Concepts — Content — Meaning* (Oxford, 1995), pp. 278–315.

of the Church and a tradition challenged by the liberals, enticed by free thinking and social Darwinism. But, in contrast to Mexico, in Bolivia the religious question did not generate civil war.[9]

In the absence of structured parties, regional divergences could have taken the place of significant political divisions. One Bolivian author has thus ventured to argue that the history of the country could be summarised as confrontations between regions.[10] He maintained that the difficulties in communication strengthened local identities, and that the discovery and development of new resources (principally in mining) created new forces or reinforced old powers, but is this sufficient to make the dominant groups in regions with differing interests decide to declare war? This is far from certain. Bolivia did not experience the tensions that marked the history of Ecuador, which culminated in the project of constructing a railway linking Quito with Guayaquil, in order to avert the risks of upheaval in a small country torn since its foundation between the coast and the sierra.[11] In addition, the most substantial studies available to us on this subject reveal the diversity of these regional leadership groups, their capacity for alliance and the flexibility of their strategies.[12] This fits very poorly with schemas of bipolar regional confrontation.

In the absence of significant regional and partisan tensions, we need to look closely, not at structures, but rather at practices favourable to civil war, a direction of research which appears to me to be more productive than the vain pursuit of political and regional divergences. I have thus sought the origins of the 1899 civil war in practices such as the *pronunciamiento* and in the creation of links between the political classes and their Indian clientele.

The *pronunciamiento* as the beginnings of the civil war

The civil war, which began with a declaration rejecting the government party's proposals, continued with a rapid campaign of petitions and manifestos and concluded with several months of violent confrontations, is closely related to a *pronunciamiento*, that invention of nineteenth-century Spain.[13]

From the *pronunciamiento* of Riego and Quiroga in January 1820 onwards, each subsequent *pronunciamiento* replayed the dissolution and reformation of social bonds through the declamation of a rupture and the

---

[9] For a recent re-evaluation of the religious question in Latin America in this period, see Austen Ivereigh (ed.) *The Politics of Religion in an Age of Revival* (London, 2000).

[10] J.L. Roca, *Fisionomía del regionalismo boliviano* (La Paz, 1979) p. 9.

[11] As J.P. Deler shows in *La formation de l'espace national équatorien* (Paris, 1982).

[12] See for example E. Langer, *Economic Change and Rural Resistance in Southern Bolivia, 1880–1930* (Stanford, 1989).

[13] Marie-Danielle Demélas-Bohy, 'Le pronunciamiento, genèse d'une pratique', in M. Bertrand, N. Laurent and M. Taillefer (eds.), *Violences et pouvoirs politiques* (Toulouse, 1996) pp. 73–92. With regard to Mexico, Professor Josefina Vásquez seems to have arrived at conclusions very similar to my own.

threat of a resort to force that might or might not take the form of a civil war. More than a programme, it was a statement enunciated publicly that determined the course of events. José Ortega y Gasset was correct and only highlighted the trait when he mocked the authors of *pronunciamientos* and their 'blind faith in the magical effect of "pronouncing" a phrase'.[14] The *pronunciamiento* was a word-act to which its authors sought to impart the virtue of transmuting the tyrannical state into one of liberty.

In order to understand the *pronunciamiento* of December 1898, let us leave Spain to return to a local example, that of a banal *pronunciamiento* — one selected from hundreds of a similar type which can be found in the Bolivian archives — which the inhabitants of Tapacarí, a prosperous town in the valley of Cochabamba, enunciated on 12 January 1889. The text was read in the *plaza de armas*, and the manuscript was accompanied by several dozen signatures:

> Art. 1: Considering that only the *vecinos* of a province are able to judge the capacity of the citizens called to carry out public duties.
>
> Art. 2: That the town of Tapacarí, aware of the incapacity of the minister Don Enrique Borda, cannot accept any imposition stemming from the minister at the instigation of the criminal who currently exercises the post of *corregidor*, Teófilo Gutiérrez.
>
> Art. 3: ... That, with the intention of defending their rights, the citizens are called to guarantee their liberties through force of arms ... and declare that they do not recognise the authority of Teófilo Gutiérrez ... [15]

Addressed by the people to the authority whose power it contests, the *pronunciamiento* takes the form of a written proclamation, read in the presence of the People from whom it emanated, who are supposed to have written and, in endorsing, adhered to it. The general assembly of inhabitants composed in this way, which is representative not through the process of election, becomes the originary people. Under the pretext of exercising the rights enunciated by the new regime, a fraction of the villagers resorted to the *pronunciamiento* as a meaningful summons by the *pueblo* to the authority over it, and as a warning that sketches an embryonic theory of local power whose ultimate consequences lead to insurrection.

Such a model can be fairly easily applied to the processes by which the civil war of 1898 started. These were immediately characterised by a territorial dimension, only the scale of the *pueblo* having grown so as to be conflated first with a large city, later with a department. In opposition to a vote in the chamber attributing to the town of Sucre the title of capital of the country, the deputies from La Paz pronounced in favour of their own city. Manifestations that were soon baptised as 'popular' occurred at just the right moment to add weight to the declaration of these representatives. On 12 December 1898, at the announcement that the

---

[14] José Ortega y Gasset, *España invertebrada* (Madrid, 1969) p. 80.
[15] Archivo Nacional de Bolivia (ANB), MI, t. 250, no. 92.

government was mobilising troops to restore order in La Paz, the pro-
testors formed a revolutionary junta to organise the uprising.

Through the aid of its representatives, which included all parties, a
decisive subset of the *vecinos* of La Paz thus claimed to constitute the
pueblo, which was rising up against a power that they no longer recognised and affirmed their own legitimacy which they declared to be will-
ing to defend by force of arms. The actors in this event sought in this
way to prevent the imminent conflict from being designated a civil war:
it was not a case of the partition of the political body into two opposing
camps, but of a matter between the people and a government which the
pronunciamiento had deprived of legitimacy.

Indian clienteles

This practice was soon accompanied by the mobilisation of a group of
Indian communities from the department of La Paz in the service of the
Liberal uprising. From the end of December 1898, a network of barricades was constructed in La Paz; 'this was done in a methodical way',
wrote the French chargé d'affaires, 'and in an orderly fashion, as the
Indian element ... had for several months been organised into corps of
sappers'.[16] General Pando paraded about, accompanied by Aymara
scouts: 'Viva Pando! Viva the Federation! Viva communal property!'[17]

This sort of mobilisation, most often structured by personal ties established between a political (or military) leader and the Indian authorities, has
been documented from well before the war of 1899. From the time of its invention, during the War of Independence, guerrilla war had involved recourse to Indian communities which were given the role of scouting and
food supply and were charged with harassing the enemy, providing intelligence on his movements and simultaneously acting as cannon-fodder during combat and also responsible for summary executions of captives with
which the guerrillas did not wish to be encumbered.

During the course of the nineteenth century, they were mobilised on
various occasions, and the recurrent attacks led by the groups in power
against communal property shaped their participation in national conflicts,
in the service of a party, but in defence of their own interests. This was the
case with the mobilisation of communities of the *altiplano* in December
1870–January 1871, which occurred in alliance with the opponents of the
dictator Mariano Melgarejo, an alliance authorised by the communities with

---

[16] AMAE, *Bolivie, politique intérieure, dossier général*, tome 1 (1894–99), dispatch of 28
December 1898, fol. 123v.

[17] AMAE, *Bolivie, politique intérieure, dossier général*, tome 1 (1894–99), dispatch of 1 February
1899, fol. 155v. For more details on the participation of *altiplano* communities in the war, I refer the reader to the previously-cited works of R. Condarco Morales, as well as to the
prosographical enquiry which I reviewed in a much earlier article. Marie-Danielle Demélas-
Bohy, 'Jacqueries indiennes, politique créole. La guerre civile de 1899', *Caravelle: Cahiers du
monde hispanique et luso-brésilien*, no. 44 (Toulouse, 1985), pp. 91–111.

the aim of recovering their lands that had been put up for sale by the administration. Through the initiative of a politician, Casimiro Corral, old stager of coups d'état during the 1850s–60s, a network of clientelistic links led to the leaders of Indian communities. This is a process comparable to that which occurred in 1898, Indian communities being unable to advance their project of recovering their lands except in times of civil war, which in turn was able to blossom only with their participation.

Certain features of this process remain unclear, notably the form (patronage, *compadrazgo*, or other) and the rationale behind the personal ties that the principal directors of the parties leading the uprising were able to establish with the Indian communities. Drawing on the personal archives of General Pando (the head of the Liberal Party) to which he had access, R. Condarco Morales has provided a valuable suggestion: General Pando and Zárate, leader of the communities of the canton of Mohoza, which was one of the most active during the course of the war, were *compadres*. But had they been *compadres* for a long time, in a strictly private context, or was the sole function of this spiritual relationship the reinforcement of a political alliance? The question remains open.

It remains the case that the intervention of certain Indian communities in the national political life, in the service of an opposition party, is a recurrent fact in republican Bolivia. It seems worthwhile to push back this regressive approach, from the civil war of 1898–99 back to the War of Independence; then from the latter to the Great Rebellion at the end of the eighteenth century. My investigation will stop there, but it would be desirable to take it even further, as certain indications suggest that such research would not be fruitless.[18]

Los valles as a cradle of rebellion

This final section of this chapter owes much to chance, which presides over the conservation of archives. It is in effect a series of findings[19] which mark the zone designated by the name of *los valles*, in which the canton of Mohoza is located, as a cradle of recurrent rebellions, of which I will summon three moments.

1) 1898–99: Mohoza turns against its liberal allies

The participation of the communities of Mohoza in the civil war of 1899 is well-known thanks to a massacre that they committed on encountering a

---

[18] Thus Gunnar Mendoza, director of the National Archive, indicated that in the seventeenth century the *valles* had served as a refuge for some of the principal protagonists of the war of the '*vicuñas contra vascongados*'.

[19] Findings by three recently deceased historians: María Eugenia del Valle de Siles, Gunnar Mendoza and Thierry Saignes.

battalion of the liberal army.[20] The affair, which was briskly repressed, gave rise to a famous court case in the course of which the liberals were able to settle some scores with the Church, through accusing the village priest of complicity with the butchers. This *cause célèbre* was also an issue which nicely illustrated theories of social Darwinism thanks to the confident defence of the lawyer Bautista Saavedra, who later became president of the republic. A French scientific expedition, the Créqui Montfort-Sénéchal de la Grange mission, which had the opportunity to study these actors, provides extensive information not found in the Bolivian sources.[21]

2) 1813–25: *los valles* consolidates the guerrilla

The second period in this research is marked by the discovery in the Sucre archives of two manuscripts of the journal kept during the War of Independence by the guerrilla José Santos Vargas.[22] This exceptional document concerns the only guerrilla force that existed in Upper Peru from the departure of the expeditionary Argentine corps in 1815 to the victory of Ayacucho in 1824.

Its first leader, Commander Eusebio Lira, native of Mohoza, which he had made the epicentre of his *republiqueta*, had based his troops and his power on the support of the Indian communities of a region that extended across the whole of the *valles*, as far as the *Yungas* of La Paz. Although it reveals nothing about the bases of this support, Vargas's *Diario* nonetheless highlights that these communities did not content themselves with the role of auxiliary, and that at the death of their commander Lira, their privileged ally, they demanded to participate in the leadership of the guerrilla war and the *republiqueta* of *los valles*.[23]

On 16 December 1817, Commander Lira was assassinated. 25 December 1817 saw a protest by the communities representing some 20 villages that had elected a junta charged with negotiating a redistribution of power in their favour. The representatives of the villages loyal to Lira addressed themselves in these terms to their new commander:

---

[20] The balance sheet of the slaughter at Mohoza reached 16 *vecinos* and 130 soldiers (AHLP, *Proceso de Mohoza, cuerpo* no. 8, p. 24, debate of 24 July 1901).

[21] I have explored this moment extensively in Marie-Danielle Demélas-Bohy, 'Darwinismo a la criolla: el darwinismo social en Bolivia, 1880–1910', *Historia Boliviana*, vol. 1, no. 1 (Cochabamba, 1981) pp. 55–82.

[22] There are two manuscripts of José Santos Vargas's diary, both published: Tambour Major Vargas, *Diario de un soldado de la independencia altoperuana en los valles de Sicasica y Hayopaya, 1816–1821*, edited by Gunnar Mendoza L. (Sucre, 1952); and José Santos Vargas, *Diario de un comandante de la independencia americana, 1814–1825*, edited by Gunnar Mendoza L. (Mexico, 1982). For the problems posed by the existence and publication of these two manuscripts, consult Marie-Danielle Demélas-Bohy, 'Les deux journaux de José Santos Vargas (1814–1825). 1: Problèmes d'édition', *Bulletin de l'Institut Français d'Études Andines*, vol. 24, no. 1 (Lima, 1995), pp. 107–26; and Marie-Danielle Demélas-Bohy, 'Les deux journaux de José Santos Vargas (1814–1825). 2: Deux manuscrits', *Bulletin de l'Institut Français d'Études Andines*, vol. 26, no. 2 (Lima, 1997), pp. 247–68.

[23] Vargas, *Diario de un comandante*, pp. 202–3.

These five said ... that the towns were those that should name the chief who would govern them; that for this purpose 20 towns had gathered; that if they were not permitted to do so then everyone would see the consequences; that they [the Indians] were doing nothing more than fulfilling their obligations and that they held them [the commanders of the guerrillas] responsible for any events that might take place in the sight of God, the Patria and the officials in Buenos Aires.

This demand was at first short-lived, but, four months later, the guerrillas, surrounded by two thousand *comuneros*, saw imposed on them as commander a former lieutenant of Lira, head of the indigenous troops, who was designated by acclamation by the Indians (and not chosen by the *oficialidad*, as had been the custom).[24]

3) 1780–82: Mohoza, last sanctuary of the Great Rebellion

In the course of her research into the Great Rebellion in the Audiencia of Charcas, María Eugenia del Valle de Siles dedicated a chapter in her book to a hitherto unknown expedition:[25] an enterprise by the Spanish official don José Reseguín, who sought to reduce the last pocket of indigenous resistance that remained, in 1782, in the province of Sicasica, after the execution of Túpac Amaru and Túpac Catari. The study of del Valle de Siles is based principally on the journal of the military expedition, a journal whose interpretation was made even more difficult by the loss of the map that had accompanied it. Discovered by Thierry Saignes in the *Archivo General de la Nación* in Buenos Aires, and identified with the help of the author, the map for the time being allows us to close the enquiry by demonstrating that these three zones of resistance were identical over the *longue durée*.

Mohoza occupies a central position on the map, and was treated by the royal expedition as one of the bastions of resistance to be eradicated.[26] On 4 June 1782, militia captain Blas Mariano Vargas[27] left with two companies to punish the rebel village of Mohoza, which he had burned, sparing only the church, on whose doors was placed the following sign: 'That the lands of these communities would be sold by the king to those individuals who wanted to purchase them as the extinction of these obstinate people was deemed appropriate'.[28]

---

[24] *Ibid.*, p. 225.
[25] María Eugenia del Valle de Siles, *Historia de la rebelión de Túpac Catari, 1781–1782* (La Paz, 1990). One chapter is devoted to José de Reseguín's expedition ('Una pacificación desconocida. Campañas de Reseguín en los valles nor-orientales de Sicasica', pp. 389–412).
[26] 'Two Companies posted to the Altos de Mohoza to protect and sustain Velazco's march, directed to punish the town of this name, and to facilitate the climb.'
[27] The father of the guerrilla José Santos Vargas.
[28] AGI, Charcas 595, cited by Valle de Siles, *Historia de la rebelión*, p. 399.

Conclusions

The notion of civil war is somewhat difficult to employ when it is applied to societies that scarcely correspond to criteria defining membership of the nation in terms similar to our democracies. In the case of Bolivia in the nineteenth century, prudence is essential. We agree to designate as civil war that type of confrontation which represents the last resort of adversaries who have exhausted attempts at negotiation and which makes manifest, less divisions, than alliances and continuities which hitherto had not been clear.

In the complex case of the civil war of 1899, I have tried to go beyond the intricacies of the possible causes of the confrontation in proposing to concentrate on the continuities, rather than the ruptures: continuities in social practice, which made Bolivian society into a fabric woven out of personal ties of all sorts. This study takes into consideration those that bound the leaders of Indian communities to those of the Creole parties. But the study also highlights geographical continuities in the great waves of rebellion; in the war of 1899, in the War of Independence (which was a civil war) and in the course of the Great Rebellion, on at least three occasions the town of Mohoza, and, more broadly, the Indian communities of the provinces of Sicasica and Hayopaya, were at the centre of a rebel project directed against the state and its representatives.

If this work of reconstructing continuities (which should be extended to other regions, as Tristan Platt has proposed for the province of Chayanta) does not in any way allow us to choose between the many possible causalities, it does permit us to underline how much more a civil war owes to the density and the structure of the social fabric over the *longue durée* than to the outcome of unsuccessful negotiations between politicians.

Bibliography

Unpublished Sources
Archival Material
Argentina
Archivo General de la Nación, Buenos Aires
Mapoteca

Bolivia
Archivo Histórico de La Paz, La Paz
Proceso de Mohoza
Correspondencia oficial de la prefectura y subprefecturas del departa-
    mento de La Paz
Serie Z: Intendencia de La Paz
Archivo Nacional de Bolivia, Sucre
Manuscript of the Diario de José Santos Vargas
Fondo del Ministerio del Interior
Fondo del Cuerpo Legislativo
Expedientes Coloniales

Brazil
Arquivo Público do Pará, Belém
Códice 972
Instituto Histórico e Geográfico Brasileiro, Rio de Janeiro
Coleção Alencar Araripe.
Coleção Instituto Histórico
Coleção Manuel Barata

Colombia
Archivo Central del Cauca, Popayán
Sala Mosquera
Signatura 6852, Independencia CII–6g
Archivo Histórico Nacional de Colombia, Santafé de Bogotá
Secretaria de Guerra y Marina.

Ecuador
Archivo del Banco Central del Ecuador, Quito
Fondo Jijón y Caamaño: papeles del Presidente don Ignacio Flores
Archivo Nacional de Ecuador, Quito
Gobierno, tomo 78 (1839–1843).
Religiosos, caja 65 (1819–1821).

France
Archives du Ministère des Affaires Étrangères, Paris
Correspondence Consulaire et Commerciale

Bolivie, politique intérieure, dossier général, tome I (1894–1899).
Musée de l'Homme, Paris
Mission Créqui Montfort-Sénéchal de Lagrange

Great Britain
Public Record Office, London
Foreign Office: FO 80: 146, 150, 151, 152, 153, 154, 156, 157, 161, 162, 165, 166; FO 135/31.

Spain
Archivo General de Indias, Seville
Audiencia de Charcas
Archivo General de Simancas, Simancas
Secretaría de Guerra

United States of America
United States National Archives, Washington D.C.
Record Group 59, 815.00/4188

Venezuela
Archivo General de la Nación, Caracas
Secretaría del Interior y de Justicia, 1861–1863
Secretaría de Guerra y Marina, 1861–1863

Theses and Unpublished Conference Papers

Barahona G., José, et al (1989) 'La evolución de la propiedad privada terrateniente en el municipio de Choluteca, 1864–1891', unpublished *Licenciatura* Thesis, Universidad Nacional Autónoma de Honduras.

Bonilla, A. (1996) 'The Central American Enlightenment, 1770–1838', unpublished D.Phil. dissertation, University of Manchester.

Brand, Charles (1972) 'The Background of Capitalist Underdevelopment: Honduras to 1913', unpublished D.Phil. dissertation, University of Pittsburgh.

Euraque, Darío A. (1996) 'La historiografía hondureña y el caudillismo indígena: entre Lempira y Gregoria Ferrera', paper presented to the Tercer Congreso Centroamericano de Historia, San José, Costa Rica, 15–18 July.

Fowler, Will (1994) 'José María Tornel y Mendívil, Mexican General/Politician (1794–1853)', unpublished D.Phil. dissertation, University of Bristol.

Guevara-Escudero, Francisco (1983) 'Nineteenth-Century Honduras: A Regional Approach to the Economic History of Central America,

1839–1914', unpublished D.Phil. dissertation, New York University.

Holden, Robert H. (1996) 'Caudillos, partidos, elecciones y guerras: hacia un entendimiento de la violencia en la historia política centroamericana', paper presented at the Tercer Congreso Centroamericano de Historia, San José, Costa Rica, 15–18 July.

Mahoney, J.L. (1997) 'Radical, Reformist, and Aborted Liberalism: Origins of National Regimes in Central America', unpublished D.Phil. dissertation, University of California.

Muller, Gene (1982) 'The Church in Poverty: Bishops, Bourbons, and Tithes in Spanish Honduras, 1700–1821', unpublished D.Phil. dissertation, University of Kansas.

Pérez Chávez, Porfirio (1996) 'Estructura económica de Honduras: gobierno del General Francisco Ferrera (1833–34, 1841–45, 1847)', unpublished *Licenciatura* thesis, Universidad Nacional Autónoma de Honduras.

Posada-Carbó, Eduardo (1995) 'The Role of Newspapers and Leaflets in Electoral Campaigns in Colombia, 1830–1930', paper presented at the Annual Conference of the Latin American Studies Association.

Samuels, Jeff (1990) 'Another Tale of Two Cities: Political Rivalry and Economic Change during the Decline of Comayagua and Rise of Tegucigalpa, 1821–1876', dissertation prospectus, Tulane University.

Samuels, Jeff (1992) 'Zonas regionales en la historia de la formación del estado de Honduras: 1830s–1930s: la Zona Central', paper presented at the Conference of the Latin American Studies Association, Los Angeles, California, 25 Sept..

Sierra Fonseca, Rolando (1996) 'Manuel Subirana y el movimiento mesianico en Honduras, 1857–1864', paper presented at the Museo de la República, Instituto Hondureño de Antropología e Historia, Tegucigalpa, Honduras, 20 Sept.

Taracena Arriola, Luis (1993) 'Minas, sociedad y política: la Alcaldía Mayor de Tegucigalpa', unpublished MA thesis, Universidad Nacional de Costa Rica (1993).

Velez O., Ammarella and Herrera, Ivan (1982) 'Historia de la Municipalidad de Tegucigalpa, años 1870–1903', unpublished Licenciatura thesis, Universidad Nacional Autónoma de Honduras (1982).

Zelaya, Oscar (1992) 'Tipificación del grupo social dominante en el Antiguo Departamento de Tegucigalpa, 1839–1875', unpublished Licenciatura thesis, Universidad Nacional Autónoma de Honduras.

Published Sources

Alamán, Lucas (1969) *Historia de Méjico*, 5 vols (Mexico City: Editorial Jus).

Almaraz Paz, S. (1987) *El poder y la caída. El estaño en la historia de Bolivia* (La Paz: Los Amigos del Libro).

Altamirano, Ignacio M. (1984) *El Zarco, La navidad en las montañas* (Mexico City: Porrúa).

Alvarez Restrepo, Antonio (1982) 'Las guerras civiles y el desarrollo económico,' *Boletín de Historia y Antigüedades*, vol. 69, no. 736 (1982).

Alvarez, Juan (1936) *Las guerras civiles argentinas y el problema de Buenos Aires en la República* (Buenos Aires, 1936).

Alvarez, Juan (1941) *Estudio sobre las guerras civiles argentinas* (Buenos Aires: Círculo Militar, Biblioteca del Oficial).

Alzugarat, Alfredo (ed.) (1996) *Desde la otra orilla (documentos inéditos y olvidados de la revolución de 1897)* (Montevideo: Ediciones de la Banda Oriental).

Anderson, Benedict (1983) *Imagined Communities: Reflections on the Origin and Spread of Nationalism* (London: Verso).

Anna, Timothy E. (1993) 'Demystifying Early Nineteenth–Century Mexico', *Mexican Studies/Estudios Mexicanos*, vol. 9, no. 1 (1993), pp. 119–37.

Anna, Timothy E. (1998) *Forging Mexico 1821–1835* (Lincoln: University of Nebraska Press).

Argueta, Mario R. (1982) *Cronología de la reforma liberal hondureña*, (Tegucigalpa: Colección Cuadernos Universitarios no. 23, Editorial Universitaria).

Arnold, Linda (1996) *Política y justicia. La suprema corte mexicana (1824–1855)* (Mexico City: UNAM).

Arrangoiz, F. de P. (1872) *México desde 1808 hasta 1867*, 2 vols (Madrid).

Arrom, Silvia M. (1988) 'Popular Politics in Mexico City: The Parián Riot, 1828', *Hispanic American Historical Review*, vol. 68, no. 2, pp. 245–68.

Avalos, Kevin (1995) 'Fiestas y diversiones urbanas: una ventana a las mentalidades colectivas de la época colonial', *Paraninfo*, no. 8 (Tegucigalpa) pp. 57–74.

Avendaño Rojas, Xiomara (1998) 'La evolución histórica de la ciudadanía: un punto de partida para el estudio del Estado y la nación', in Luis Jáuregui and José Antonio Serrano Ortega (eds.), *Historia y nación. vol 2: Política y diplomacia en el siglo XIX mexicano* (Mexico City: El Colegio de México), pp. 171–82.

Ayerve, Tomás de (1939) 'Memorial de Don Tomás de Ayerve', *Boletín de Estudios Históricos*, vol. 9 (Pasto).

Barahona, Marvin A. (1991) *La evolución de la identidad nacional* (Tegucigalpa: Editorial Guaymuras).

Barahona, Marvin A. (1995) 'Honduras: el estado fragmentado (1839–1876)', *Paraninfo*, no. 7 (Tegucigalpa), pp. 1–33.

Barahona, Marvin A. (1996a) 'Caudillismo y política en Honduras (1894–1913)', *Paraninfo*, no. 9 (Tegucigalpa, 1996), pp. 1–25.

Barahona, Marvin A. (1996b) 'La Alcaldía Mayor de Tegucigalpa bajo el régimen de intendencias (1788–1812)', *Estudios Antropológicos e Históricos*, no. 11 (Tegucigalpa), pp. 1–38.

Barman, Roderick J. (1988) *Brazil: The Forging of a Nation, 1798–1852* (Stanford: Stanford University Press).

Bazant, Jan (1985) *Antonio Haro y Tamariz y sus aventuras políticas, 1811–1869* (Mexico City: El Colegio de México).

Bazant, Jan (1992) 'From Independence to the Liberal Republic, 1821–1867', in Leslie Bethell (ed.), *Mexico since Independence* (Cambridge: Cambridge University Press), pp. 1–48.

Bergquist, Charles (1978) *Coffee and Conflict in Colombia, 1886–1910*, (Durham: Duke University Press).

Bethell, Leslie (ed.) (1989) *Brazil: Empire and Republic, 1822–1930* (Cambridge: Cambridge University Press).

Bethell, Leslie (ed.) (1991) *Central America since Independence* (Cambridge: Cambridge University Press).

Bocanegra, José María (1987) *Memorias para la historia de México independiente, 1822–1846*, 3 vols (Mexico City: Fondo de Cultura Económica).

Botana, Natalio (1977) *El orden conservador. La política argentina entre 1880 y 1916*, (Buenos Aires: Editorial Sudamericana, 1995 (4th edition with 'Estudio Preliminar')).

Botero Goldworthy, Néstor (1989) 'Los esposos Pedro Nisser y María Martínez de Nisser,' *Boletín de Historia y Antigüedades*, vol. 76, no. 766.

Bricker, Victoria Reifler (1981) *The Indian Christ, The Indian King: The Historical Substrate of Maya Myth and Ritual* (Austin: University of Texas Press).

Bruno, Ernani Silva (1966) *Amazônia (Acre – Amazônas – Pará – Territórios)*, vol. 1 of *História do Brasil – Geral e regional* (São Paulo: Editôra Cultrix).

Buarque de Holanda, Sergio (ed.) (1967) *História geral da civilização brasileira*, tomo II: *O Brasil monárquico*, vol. 2: *Dispersão e unidade*, second edition (São Paulo: Difusão Européia do Livro).

Burgin, Miron (1946) *The Economic Aspects of Argentine Federalism, 1820–1852* (Cambridge: Harvard University Press).

Burns, E. Bradford (1975) 'The Intellectuals as Agents of Change and the Independence of Brazil, 1724–1822', in A.J.R. Russel-Wood (ed.), *From Colony to Nation: Essays on the Independence of Brazil*

(Baltimore: Johns Hopkins University Press).

Bushnell, David (1950) 'The Development of the Press in Great Colombia,' *Hispanic American Historical Review*, vol. 30, pp. 432–52.

Bushnell, David (1986) 'Política y partidos en el siglo XIX; algunas antecedentes históricos', in Gonzalo Sánchez and Ricardo Peñaranda (eds.), *Pasado y presente de la violencia en Colombia* (Bogotá: Fondo Editorial EREC), pp. 31–9.

Bushnell, David (1993) *The Making of Modern Colombia: A Nation in Spite of Itself,* (Berkeley: University of California Press).

Bustillo, José María (1959) 'Estudio preliminar', in Carlos Pellegrini, *Discursos y escritos*, (Buenos Aires: Editorial Estrada).

Calderón de la Barca, Fanny [1843] (1987) *Life in Mexico* (London: Century).

Calogeras, João Pandia (1963) *A History of Brazil* (New York: Russel and Russel).

Cardoso, Ciro F.S. (1991) 'The Liberal Era, c. 1870–1930', in Leslie Bethell (ed.), *Central America since Independence* (Cambridge: Cambridge University Press), pp. 37–67.

Caro, José Eusebio (1953) *Epistolario* (Bogotá: Ministerio de Educación Nacional).

Castellanos, Jorge (1980) *La abolición de la esclavitud en Popayán, 1832–1852* (Cali: Universidad del Valle).

Castellanos, Jorge (1982) 'The Failure of the Manumission Juntas in the Colombian Province of Popayán, 1821–1851', *Michigan Academician*, vol. 14, no. 4 (1982).

Catama, Carlos (1987) *Genio y figura de Ernesto Sábato* (Buenos Aires: Editorial Universitaria de Buenos Aires).

Chaverri, Marielos (1996) 'La protesta social en Honduras colonial', *Paraninfo*, no. 10 (Tegucigalpa), pp. 15–34.

Chiaramonte, José Carlos (1993) 'El federalismo argentino en la primera mitad del siglo XIX', in Marcello Carmagnani (ed.), *Federalismos latinoamericanos, México/Brasil/Argentina* (México: Fondo de Cultura Económica).

Chiaramonte, José Carlos (1995) '¿Provincias o Estados? Los orígenes del federalismo rioplatense', in François-Xavier Guerra (ed.), *Revoluciones hispánicas. Independencias americanas y liberalismo español* (Madrid: Ediciones Complutense).

Cleary, David (1998) '"Lost Altogether to the Civilized World": Race and the Cabanagem in Northern Brazil, 1750 to 1850', *Comparative Studies in Society and History*, vol. 40.

Condarco Morales, R. [1966] (1983) *Zárate, El 'temible' Wilka. Historia de la Rebelión Indígena de 1899* (La Paz: Talleres gráficos bolivianos, new edition).

Connaughton, Brian (1992) *Ideología y sociedad en Guadalajara (1788–1853)* (Mexico City: UNAM).

Connaughton, Brian, and Lira, Andrés (eds.) (1996) *Las fuentes eclesiásticas para la historia social de México* (Mexico City: UAM/Mora).

Costeloe, Michael P. (1966) 'The Mexican Church and the Rebellion of the Polkos', *Hispanic American Historical Review*, vol. 46, no. 2, pp. 170–78.

Costeloe, Michael P. (1983) *La primera república federal de México (1824–1835)* (Mexico City: Fondo de Cultura Económica).

Costeloe, Michael P. (1988) 'A *Pronunciamiento* in Nineteenth Century Mexico: '15 de julio de 1840', *Mexican Studies/Estudios Mexicanos*, vol. 4, no. 2, pp. 245–64.

Costeloe, Michael P. (1988) 'The Triangular Revolt in Mexico and the Fall of Anastasio Bustamante, August-October 1841', *Journal of Latin American Studies*, vol. 20, pp. 337–60.

Costeloe, Michael P. (1993) *The Central Republic in Mexico, 1835–1846. Hombres de Bien in the Age of Santa Anna* (Cambridge: Cambridge University Press).

Costeloe, Michael P. (1996) 'Mariano Arizcorreta and Peasant Unrest in the State of Mexico, 1849', *Bulletin of Latin American Research*, vol. 15, no. 1, pp. 63–79.

Cruz, Ernesto (1960) *Temas da história do Pará* (Belém: SPVEA).

Davis, Shelton H. (1988) 'Agrarian Structure and Ethnic Resistance: The Indian in Guatemalan and Salvadoran National Politics', in Remo Guidieri et al. (eds.), *Ethnicities and Nations* (Austin: University of Texas Press), pp. 78–106.

Deas, Malcolm (1993) *Del poder y la gramática y otros ensayos sobre historia, política y literatura colombianas* (Bogotá: Tercer Mundo).

Deas, Malcolm (1996) 'La política en la vida cotidiana republicana', in Beatríz Castro Carvajal (ed.), *Historia de la vida cotidiana en Colombia* (Santafé de Bogotá: Grupo Editorial Norma).

Deler, J.-P. (1982) *La formation de l'espace national équatorien* (Paris: ERC).

Demélas-Bohy, Marie-Danielle (1981) 'Darwinismo a la criolla: el darwinismo social en Bolivia, 1880–1910', *Historia Boliviana*, vol. 1, no. 1 (Cochabamba), pp. 55–82.

Demélas-Bohy, Marie-Danielle (1985) 'Jacqueries indiennes, politique créole. La guerre civile de 1899', *Caravelle: Cahiers du monde hispanique et luso-brésilien*, no. 44 (1985), pp. 91–111.

Demélas, Marie-Danielle (1992) *L'invention politique. Bolivie, Équateur, Pérou au XIXe siècle* (Paris: ERC).

Demélas-Bohy, Marie-Danielle (1995) 'Les deux journaux de José Santos Vargas (1814-1825). 1: Problèmes d'édition', *Bulletin de l'Institut Français d'Études Andines*, vol. 24, no. 1 (Lima), pp. 107–26.

Demélas-Bohy, Marie-Danielle (1996) 'Le pronunciamiento, genèse d'une pratique', in M. Bertrand, N. Laurant and M. Taillerer (eds.), *Violences et pouvoirs politiques* (Toulouse).

Demélas-Bohy, Marie-Danielle (1997) 'Les deux journaux de José Santos Vargas (1814–1825). 2: Deux manuscrits', *Bulletin de l'Institut Français d'Études Andines*, vol. 26, no. 2 (Lima), pp. 247–68.

Demélas-Bohy, Marie-Danielle and Guerra, François-Xavier (1996) 'The Hispanic Revolutions: the Adoption of Modern Forms of Representation in Spain and America (1808–1814)', in Eduardo Posada-Carbó (ed.), *Elections Before Democracy. The History of Elections in Europe and Latin America* (London: Institute of Latin American Studies), pp. 33–60.

Demélas-Bohy, Marie-Danielle and Piel, J. (1983) 'Jeux et enjeux du pouvoir dans les Andes. Les cas des départements du Cuzco et de La Paz (1880–1920)', in Asociación Francesa de Ciencias Sociales sobre América Latina (ed.), *Les frontières du pouvoir en Amérique Latine*, (Toulouse: Publications de l'Université de Toulouse), pp. 53–64.

Desahogo de D. José M. Tornel bajo la firma de José López de Santa Anna (Mérida, n.p., 1843).

Di Tella, Torcuato S. (1996) *National Popular Politics in Early Independent Mexico, 1820–1847* (Albuquerque: University of New Mexico Press).

Díaz Chávez, F. (1972) *Sociología de la desintegración regional* (Tegucigalpa: Litografica Calderón).

Díaz Díaz, Fernando (1972) *Caudillos y caciques. Antonio López de Santa Anna y Juan Álvarez* (Mexico City: El Colegio de México).

Doblado, General (1909) *La Revolución de Ayutla* (Mexico City: Librería de Bouret).

Dudley, William S. (1975) 'Institutional Sources of Officer Discontent in the Brazilian Army, 1870–1889', *Hispanic American Historical Review*, vol. 55, no. 1, pp. 44–65.

Dunkerley, James (1987) *Orígenes del poder militar en Bolivia* (La Paz: Quipus).

Earle, Rebecca (1993) 'Indian Rebellion and Bourbon Reform in New Granada: Riots in Pasto, 1780–1800', *Hispanic American Historical Review*, vol. 73.

Earle, Rebecca (1997) 'Information and Disinformation in Late Colonial New Granada', *The Americas*, vol. 54, no. 2.

Earle, Rebecca (2000) *Spain and the Independence of Colombia*, (Exeter: University of Exeter Press).

Escobar Rodríguez, Carmen (1990) *La revolución liberal y la protesta del artesanado* (Bogotá: Fundación Universitaria Autónoma de

Colombia).

Escorcia, José (1983) *Sociedad y economía en el Valle del Cauca*, vol. 3: *Desarrollo político, social y económico, 1800–1854* (Bogotá: Biblioteca Banco Popular).

Etchepareborda, Roberto (1959) *Homenaje al Dr. Lisandro de la Torre. Las revoluciones de 1893 en la provincia de Santa Fe y Lisandro de la Torre* (Buenos Aires).

Euraque, Darío A. (1996) *Estado, Poder, Nacionalidad y Raza en la Historia de Honduras: Ensayos* (Tegucigalpa: Centro de Publicaciones, Obispado de Choluteca).

Euraque, Darío A. (1996) *Reinterpreting the 'Banana Republic': Region and State in Honduras, 1870s–1972* (Chapel Hill: University of North Carolina Press).

Finney, Kenneth V. (1979) 'Rosario and the Election of 1887: The Political Economy of Mining in Honduras', *Hispanic American Historical Review*, vol. 59, no. 1, pp. 81–107.

Flory, Richard Thomas (1981) *Judge and Jury in Imperial Brazil, 1808–1871: Social Control and Political Stability in the New State* (Austin: University of Texas Press).

Foster, David William (1975) *Currents in the Contemporary Argentine Novel: Arlt, Mallea, Sábato and Cortázar* (Columbia: University of Missouri Press).

Fowler, Will (1995) 'Dreams of Stability: Mexican Political Thought During the 'Forgotten Years'. An Analysis of the Beliefs of the Creole Intelligentsia (1821–1853)', *Bulletin of Latin American Research*, vol. 14, no. 3 (1995), pp. 287–312.

Fowler, Will (1996) 'Introduction: The Forgotten Century, 1810–1910', *Bulletin of Latin American Research*, vol. 15, no. 1 (1996), pp. 1–6.

Fowler, Will (1996) 'The Repeated Rise of General Antonio López de Santa Anna in the So-Called Age of Chaos', in Will Fowler (ed.), *Authoritarianism in Latin America Since Independence* (Westport, CT: Greenwood), pp. 1–30.

Fowler, Will (1996) *Military Political Identity and Reformism in Independent Mexico. An Analysis of the* Memorias de Guerra *(1821–1855)* (London: Institute of Latin American Studies).

Fowler, Will (1997) *The Liberal Origins of Mexican Conservatism, 1821–1832* (Glasgow: Institute of Latin American Studies).

Fowler, Will (1998) *Mexico in the Age of Proposals, 1821–1853* (Westport, CT: Greenwood Press).

Fowler, Will (1999) 'Goatsuckers, Guerrillas and Democracy: Mexico in the 1990s', *Vida Hispánica*, no. 19 (March 1999), pp. 12–16.

Fowler, Will (2000) *Tornel and Santa Anna. The Writer and the*

Caudillo, Mexico 1795–1853 (Westport, CT: Greenwood Press).

Fraga, Rosendo (1993) *El general Justo* (Buenos Aires: Editorial Emecé).

Fundación Polar (1988) *Diccionario de Historia de Venezuela*, 3 vols (Caracas: Polar Foundation).

Gallo, Ezequiel (1984) *La pampa gringa. La colonización agrícola en Santa Fe (1870–1895)*, (Buenos Aires: Editorial Sudamericana).

García Márquez, Gabriel (1970) *One Hundred Years of Solitude* (London: Picador).

Gil Fortoul, José (1930) *Historia Constitucional de Venezuela*, 3 vols (Caracas: Hermanos Parra León).

Gilmore, Robert L. (1964) *Caudillism and Militarism in Venezuela, 1810–1910* (Athens, OH: Ohio University Press).

Goldman, Noemí and Salvatore, Ricardo (eds.) (1998) *Caudillos rioplatenses. Nuevas miradas a un viejo problema* (Buenos Aires: Eudeba).

González de Oliva, Alexis Argentina (1996) *Gobernantes hondureños: siglos XIX y XX* (Tegucigalpa: Universidad Nacional Autónoma de Honduras).

González Guinán, Francisco (1910) *Historia contemporánea de Venezuela*, 15 vols (Caracas: Tipografia Empresa El Cojo).

González Navarro, Moisés (1970) *Raza y tierra: la guerra de casta y el henequén* (Mexico City: El Colegio de México).

González, Joaquín V. (1935) *Obras Completas*, vol. 6 (Buenos Aires: Universidad Nacional de la Plata).

Gootenberg, Paul (1989) *Between Silver and Guano: Commercial Policy and the State in Post-Independence Peru* (Princeton: Princeton University Press).

Gou-Gilbert, Cecile (1985) *Una resistencia india. Los yaquis* (Mexico City: INI/Centro de Estudios Mexicanos y Centroamericanos).

Graham, Richard (1990) *Patronage and Politics in Nineteenth-Century Brazil* (Stanford: Stanford University Press).

Grieshaber, E. (1991) 'Resistencia indígena a la venta de tierras comunales indígenas del sur de Bolivia en el siglo XIX', *Data*, no. 1 (La Paz).

Guardino, Peter (1996) *Peasants, Politics and the Formation of Mexico's National State. Guerrero, 1800–1857* (Stanford: Stanford University Press).

Gudmundson, Lowell and Lindo-Fuentes, Héctor (1995) *Central America, 1821–1871: Liberalism before Liberal Reform* (Tuscaloosa, AL: University of Alabama Press).

Guerra, François-Xavier (1995) 'Lógicas y ritmos de las revoluciones hispánicas', in François-Xavier Guerra (ed.), *Revoluciones hispánicas. Independencias americanas y liberalismo español* (Madrid: Ediciones Complutense).

Haigh, Roger M. (1964) 'The Creation and Control of a Caudillo', *Hispanic American Historical Review*, vol. 44, no. 4, pp. 481–90.

Haigh, Roger M. (1968) *Martín Güemes: Tyrant or Tool? A Study of the Sources of Power of an Argentine Caudillo* (Fort Worth: Texas Christian University).

Halperín Donghi, Tulio (1995) 'The Buenos Aires Landed Class and the Shape of Argentine Politics (1820–1930)', in Evelyne Huber and Frank Safford (eds.), *Agrarian Structure and Political Power* (Pittsburgh: Pittsburgh University Press), pp. 39–66.

Hamnett, Brian (1987) 'Partidos políticos mexicanos e intervención militar, 1823–1855', in Antonio Annino et al (eds.), *America Latina dallo stato coloniale allo stato nazione*, vol. 2 (Milan: Franco Angeli), pp. 573–91.

Hamnett, Brian (1995) 'Las rebeliones y revoluciones iberoamericanas en la época de la Independencia. Una tentativa de tipología', in François-Xavier Guerra (ed.), *Revoluciones hispánicas. Independencias americanas y liberalismo español* (Madrid: Ediciones Complutense).

Helguera, J. Leon (1969) 'The Problem of Liberalism versus Conservatism in Colombia, 1849–1885', In Frederick Pike (ed.), *Latin American History: Select Problems: Identity, Integration, and Nationhood* (New York: Harcourt, Brace and World).

Helguera, J. Leon (1970) 'Antecedentes sociales de la revolución de 1851 en el sur de Colombia (1848–1849)', *Anuario Colombiano de Historia Social y de la Cultura*, no. 5.

Hemming, John (1987) *Amazon Frontier: The Defeat of the Brazilian Indians* (London: MacMillan).

Herrera Alarcón, Dante (1961) *Rebeliones que intentaron desembrar en el sur del Perú* (Lima: Imprenta Colegio Militar Leoncio Prado).

Holden, Robert H. (1997) 'El carácter del ejército de Honduras en los finales del siglo XIX: Bandos Armados o Institución Nacional', *Revista de Historia*, no. 9 (Nicaragua, 1997).

Hu-DeHart, Evelyn (1984) *Yaqui Resistance and Survival. The Struggle for Land and Autonomy, 1821–1910* (Madison: University of Wisconsin Press).

Hyland, Richard P. (1982) 'A Fragile Prosperity: Credit and Agrarian Structure in the Cauca Valley, Colombia, 1851–87', *Hispanic American Historical Review*, vol. 62, no. 3.

El Independiente (1861) Caracas, year II, month V, no. 414 (31 August 1861).

Irurozqui Victoriano M. (1993) 'La guerra de razas en Bolivia: la (re)invención de una tradición', *Revista Andina*, no.1 (Cuzco, 1993), pp. 163–200.

Ivereigh, Austen (ed.) (2000) *The Politics of Religion in an Age of Re-*

vival: Studies in Nineteenth-Century Europe and America (London: Institute of Latin American Studies).

Joseph, Gilbert and Nugent, D. (eds.) (1994) *Everyday Forms of State Formation: Revolution and the Negotiation of Rule in Modern Mexico* (Durham: Duke University Press).

Katz, Friedrich (1974) 'Labor Conditions on Haciendas in Porfirian Mexico: Some Trends and Tendencies', *Hispanic American Historical Review*, vol. 54, no. 1 (1974), pp. 1–47.

Katz, Friedrich (ed.) (1988) *Riot, Rebellion and Revolution: Rural Social Conflict in Mexico* (Princeton: Princeton University Press).

Katz, Friedrich (ed.) (1990) *Revuelta, rebelión y revolución: La lucha rural en México del siglo xvi al siglo xx*, 2 vols (Mexico City: Era).

Katz, Friedrich (1998) *The Life and Times of Pancho Villa* (Stanford: Stanford University Press).

Klein, Herbert (1982) *Bolivia: The Evolution of a Multi-ethnic Society* (Oxford: Oxford University Press).

Kraay, Hendrik (1992) '"As Terrifying as Unexpected": The Bahian Sabinada, 1837–1838', *Hispanic American Historical Review*, vol. 72:4 (1992), pp. 501–27.

Krauze, Enrique (1994) *Siglo de caudillos* (Barcelona: Tusquets Editores).

Langer, E. (1989) *Economic Change and Rural Resistance in Southern Bolivia, 1880–1930* (Stanford: Stanford University Press).

Lapointe, Marie (1983) *Los mayas rebeldes de Yucatán* (Mexico City: El Colegio de Michoacán).

Larrea, Carlos Manuel (n.d.) *El Barón de Carondelet, XXIX presidente de la Real Audiencia de Quito* (Quito: Editorial Fray Jodoco Ricke).

Lavaud, J.-P. (1991) *L'instabilité politique de l'Amérique latine. Le cas de la Bolivie* (Paris: L'Harmattan-IHEAL).

López Alvarez, Leopoldo (1930) 'Fuga y rebelión del General José María Obando', in *Boletín de Estudios Históricos*, vol. 3, (Pasto).

López-Alves, Fernando (1995) 'Wars and the Formation of Political Parties in Uruguay, 1810–1851', in Eduardo Posada-Carbó (ed.), *Wars, Parties and Nationalism. Essays on the Politics and Society of Nineteenth-Century Latin America* (London: Macmillan), pp. 5–26.

Loveman, Brian (1999) *Por la Patria: Politics and Armed Forces in Latin America* (Wilmington: SR Books).

Lynch, John (1981) *Argentine Dictator: Juan Manuel de Rosas, 1829–1852* (Oxford: Clarendon Press).

Lynch, John (1992) *Caudillos in Spanish America, 1800–1850* (Oxford: Clarendon Press).

Maingot, Anthony P. (1969) 'Social Structures, Social Status and Civil-

Military Conflict in Urban Colombia, 1810–1858', in Stephan Thernstrom and Richard Sennett (eds.), *Nineteenth-Century Cities: Essays in the New Urban History* (New Haven: Yale University Press), pp. 297–355.

Malamud, Carlos (ed.) (1995) *Partidos políticos y elecciones en América Latina y la Península Ibérica, 1830–1930*, 2 vols (Madrid: Ortega y Gassett).

Malamud, Carlos (1998) 'La restauración del orden, represión y amnistía en las revoluciones argentinas de 1890 y 1893', in Eduardo Posada-Carbó (ed.), *In Search of a New Order, Essays on the Politics and Society of Nineteenth-Century Latin America* (London: Institute of Latin American Studies).

Mallon, Florencia E. (1995) *Peasant and Nation: The Making of Post-Colonial Mexico and Peru* (Berkeley: University of California Press).

Manin, Bernard (1997) *The Principles of Representative Government* (Cambridge: Cambridge University Press).

Manning, William (ed.) (1935) *Diplomatic Correspondence of the United States. Inter-American Affairs, 1831–1860*, vol. 5: *Chile and Colombia*, (Washington).

Mariñas Otero, Luis (1910) *Las constituciones de Venezuela* (Madrid: Cultura Hispánica).

Martin, Gerald (1989) *Journeys through the Labyrinth: Latin American Fiction in the Twentieth Century* (London: Verso).

Martínez de Nisser, María [1843] (1983) *Diario de los sucesos de la revolución en la Provincia de Antioquia en los años de 1840–1841* (Bogotá: Editorial Incunables).

Martínez Delgado, Luis and Ortíz, Sergio Elías (eds.) (1973) *Epistolario y documentos oficiales del General José María Obando*, Biblioteca de Historia Nacional, vol. 123 (Bogotá: Editorial Kelly), vol. 1.

Marure, A. (1895) *Efemérides de los hechos notables acaecidos en la República de Centro América* (Guatemala: Tipografía Nacional).

Matienzo, José Nicolás [1910] (1994) *El régimen republicano-federal* (Buenos Aires: Editorial Marymar).

Matthews, Robert Paul (1977) *Violencia rural en Venezuela, 1840–1858: antecedentes socio-económicos de la Guerra Federal* (Caracas: Monte Avila Editores).

Matute, Álvaro, Trejo, Evelia and Connaughton, Brian (eds.) (1995) *Estado, iglesia y sociedad en México, siglo XIX* (Mexico City: UNAM/Porrúa).

Mayer, Jorge M. (1963) *Alberdi y su Tiempo* (Buenos Aires: Eudeba).

McFarlane, Anthony (1993) *Colombia before Independence: Economy, Society, and Politics under Bourbon Rule* (Cambridge: Cambridge University Press).

McGann, Thomas (1950) 'The Assassination of Sucre and its Significance in Colombian History', *Hispanic American Historical Review*, vol. 30.

McGreevey, William Paul (1971) *An Economic History of Colombia, 1845–1930* (Cambridge: Cambridge University Press).

Melo, Jorge Orlando (ed.) (1978) *Origenes de los partidos políticos en Colombia (textos de Manuel María Madiedo, José María Samper y Tomás Cipriano de Mosquera)* (Bogotá: Instituto Colombiano de Cultura).

Melo, Jorge Orlando (ed.) (1989) *Reportaje de la Historia de Colombia* (Bogotá: Editorial Planeta).

Mena, Lucila Inés (1979) *La función de la historia en cien años de soledad* (Barcelona: Plaza y Janes).

Mesa, C. (1984) *Presidentes de Bolivia: entre urnas y fusiles* (La Paz: Periodistas Aciociados Televisión, Banco Boliviano American, and Instituto Latinoamericano ed Investigaciones Sociales).

Minaudier, Jean-Pierre (1992) *Histoire de la Colombie de la Conquête à nos jours* (Paris: L'Harmattan).

Molina-Chocano, Guillermo (1980) 'La formación del estado y el origen minero-mercantil de la burguesía hondureña', *Estudios Sociales Centroamericanos*, no. 25, pp. 56–89.

Moreira Neto, Carlos de Araujo (1988) *Indios da Amazônia, de maioria a minoria (1750–1850)* (Petrópolis: Editôra Vozes).

Myers, Jorge (1998) 'Las formas complejas del poder: la problemática del caudillismo a la luz del régimen rosista', in Noemí Goldman and Ricardo Salvatore (eds.), *Caudillos rioplatenses: Nuevas miradas a un viejo problema* (Buenos Aires: Eudeba).

Noriega, Alfonso (1993) *El pensamiento conservador y el conservadurismo mexicano*, 2 vols (Mexico City: UNAM).

Núñez, Rafael ' La ley o la libertad' (1891), in Rafael Núñez (1944–50), *La reforma política en Colombia*, 7 vols. (Bogotá: Editorial ABC).

Obando, José María (1945) *Apuntamientos para la historia*, 2 vols (Bogotá: Editorial ABC).

Ocampo, José Antonio (1990) 'Comerciantes, artesanos y política económica en Colombia, 1830–1880', *Boletín Cultural y Bibliográfico*, vol. 27, no. 22.

Ochoa, Enrique (1987) 'The Rapid Expansion of Voter Participation in Latin America: Presidential Elections, 1845–1986', in Richard Wilkie and David Lorey (eds.), *Statistical Abstracts of Latin America* vol. 25 (Los Angeles: UCLA Publications), pp. 862–910.

Olivera, Ruth, and Crété, Lilian (1991) *Life in Mexico under Santa Anna, 1822–1855* (Norman and London: University of Oklahoma Press).

Ortega y Gasset, J. (1969) *España invertebrada* (Madrid: Revista de Occidente).

Ortiz Escamilla, Juan (1997) *Guerra y gobierno. Los pueblos y la independencia de México* (Seville: Universidad Internacional de Andalucía/Universidad de Sevilla/Colegio de México/Instituto Mora).

Ortiz López, Alejandro (1934) 'Parte que cupo al padre Francisco de la Villota y Barrera en la revolución llamada "de los conventillos"', *Boletín de Estudios Históricos*, vol. 6 (Pasto).

Ortiz Mesa, Luis Javier (1985) *El federalismo en Antioquia, 1850–1880: aspectos políticos* (Medellín: Universidad Nacional de Colombia, Seccional Medellín).

Ortiz, Sergio Elías (1958) *Agustín Agualongo y su tiempo* (Bogotá: Editorial ABC).

Ospina Vázquez, Luis (1955) *Industria y protección en Colombia, 1810–1930* (Medellín: Editorial Santafe).

Ovalle, Julio Humberto (1983) 'Archivo epistolar del General Pedro Alcántara Herrán,' *Boletín de Historia y Antigüedades*, vol. 70, no. 741.

Oyuela, Leticia (1989) *Historia mínima de Tegucigalpa* (Tegucigalpa: Editorial Guaymuras).

Oyuela, Leticia (1994) *Un siglo en la Hacienda: estancias y haciendas en la antigua Alcaldía Mayor de Tegucigalpa (1670–1850)* (Tegucigalpa: Banco Central de Honduras).

Oyuela, Leticia (1995) *Honduras: religiosidad popular, raíz de la identidad* (Choluteca: Centro de Publicaciones, Obispado de Choluteca).

Paige, Jeoffrey M. (1997) *Coffee and Power: Revolution and the Rise of Democracy in Central America* (Cambridge: Harvard University Press).

Palencia-Roth, Michael (1987) *Myth and the Modern Novel: García Márquez, Mann and Joyce* (New York: Garland Publishing).

'Panfletários da Revolução Praieira', *Revista do Arquivo Público* (Recife, Dec. 1976).

Paolo, Pasquale di (1990) *Cabanagem: a revolução popular da Amazônia* (Belém: Edições CEJUP).

Park, James W. (1985) *Rafael Núñez and the Politics of Colombian Regionalism, 1863–1886* (Baton Rouge: Louisiana University Press).

Pastor Fasquelle, Rodolfo (1988) *Historia de Centro América* (Mexico City: Colegio de Mexico).

Payno, Manuel (1996) *Los bandidos de Río Frío* (Mexico City: Porrúa).

Pellegrini, Carlos (1959) 'Discusión [en el Congreso] del proyecto de levantamiento del estado de sitio' (vii/1901), in Carlos Pellegrini, *Discursos y escritos* (Buenos Aires: Editorial Estrada).

Peloso, V. and Tenenbaum, Barbara (eds.) (1996) *Liberals, Politics and Power: State Formation in Nineteenth-Century Latin America* (Athens: University of Georgia Press).

Peralta, Víctor (1995) 'Elecciones, constitucionalismo y revolución en el Cusco, 1809–1815', in Carlos Malamud (ed.), *Partidos políticos y elecciones en América Latina y la Península Ibérica, 1830–1930*, vol. 1 (Madrid: Ortega y Gasset).

Pereira de Alencastre, J.M. (1872) 'Notas diarias sobre a revolta civil que teve lugar nas províncias de Maranhão, Piauhy e Ceará', *Revista Trimensal do Instituto Histórico Geográfico e Etnográfico do Brasil*, vol. 35 (1872).

Pinto Soria, Julio (1993) 'La Independencia y la Federación (1810–1840)', in Edelberto Torres-Rivas (ed.), *Historia General de Centro América*, vol. 3 (Madrid: Quinto Centenario-Facultad Latinoamericana de Ciencias Sociales), pp. 73–140.

Platt, Tristan (1990) 'La experiencia andina del liberalismo boliviano entre 1825 y 1900: raíces de la rebellión de Chayanta (Potosí) durante el siglo XIX', in Steve Stern (ed.), *Resistencia, rebelión y conciencia campesina en los Andes, siglos XVIII–XIX* (Lima: IEP).

Portilla, Anselmo de la (1993) *Historia de la Revolución de México contra la dictadura del General Santa Anna, 1853–1855* (Mexico City: Fondo de Cultura Económica).

Posada Gutiérrez, Joaquín (1929) *Memorias histórico-políticas*, Biblioteca de la Historia Nacional, vol. 41, (Bogotá: Imprenta Nacional), vols. 3–4.

Posada-Carbó, Eduardo (1994) 'Elections and Civil Wars in Nineteenth Century Colombia, The 1875 Presidential Campaign', *Journal of Latin American Studies*, vol. 26, no. 3.

Posada-Carbó, Eduardo (1998), 'Fiction as History: The *bananeras* and Gabriel García Márquez's *One Hundred Years of Solitude*', *Journal of Latin American Studies*, vol. 30, no. 3.

Posada-Carbó, Eduardo (ed.) (1998) *In Search of a New Order: Essays on the Politics and Society of Nineteenth-Century Latin America* (London: Institute of Latin American Studies).

Presidencia de la República (1961) *Pensamiento político venezolano del siglo XIX*, 15 vols (Caracas: Presidencia de la República).

Presidencia de la República (1962) *Documentos que hicieron historia*, 2 vols. (Caracas: Presidencia de la República).

Raiol, Domingos Antônio (1970) *Motins políticos, ou história dos principais acontecimentos políticos da Província do Pará desde o ano de 1821 até 1835*, 3 vols (Belém: Universidade Federal do Pará).

Rappaport, Joanne (1998) *The Politics of Memory. Native Historical Interpretation in the Colombian Andes* (Durham: Duke University Press)

Reed, Nelson (1964) *The Caste War of Yucatán* (Stanford: Stanford University Press).

Registro Oficial (Caracas, 1861–63).

Reina, Leticia (1980) *Las rebeliones campesinas en México (1819–1906)* (Mexico: Siglo XXI).

Renaud, M. and Démelas-Bohy, Marie-Danielle (1995) 'Instability, Networks and Political Parties. A Political History Expert System Prototype', in E. Nissan and K. Schmidt (eds.), *From Information to Knowledge.* vol. 1: *Concepts – Content – Meaning* (Oxford: Publication from the Society of Conceptual and Content Analysis by Computer, Intelligent Books), pp. 278–315.

Restrepo, José Manuel (1954) *Diario político y militar,* vol. 3, (Bogotá: Imprenta Nacional).

Restrepo, José Manuel (1963) *Historia de la Nueva Granada,* vol. 2, (Bogotá: Editorial El Catolicismo).

Roca, J.L. (1979) *Fisionomía del regionalismo boliviano* (La Paz: Los Amigos del Libro).

Rodríguez O., Jaime E. (1992) 'The Origins of the 1832 Rebellion' in Jaime E. Rodríguez O. (ed.), *Patterns of Contention in Mexican History* (Wilmington: Scholarly Resources), pp. 145–62.

Rodríguez O., Jaime E. (1996) *La independencia de la América española* (México: Fondo de Cultura Económica).

Rodríguez, José Santiago (1910) *Contribución al estudio de la Guerra Federal* (Caracas: Elite), vol.2.

Roldán, Darío (1993) *Joaquín V. González y el pensamiento político liberal en la Argentina* (Buenos Aires: Centro Editorial de América Latina).

Rowe, William (1987) 'Gabriel García Márquez', in John King (ed.), *Modern Latin American Fiction: a Survey* (Cambridge: Faber and Faber).

Ruíz Moreno, Isidoro (1998) *La Marina revolucionaria, 1874–1963* (Buenos Aires: Planeta).

Sábato, Ernesto (1990) *On Heroes and Tombs* (London: Jonathan Cape).

Sábato, Hilda (1998) *La política en las calles. Entre el voto y la movilización. Buenos Aires, 1862–1880* (Buenos Aires: Editorial Sudamericana).

Safford, Frank (1972) 'Social Aspects of Politics in Nineteenth Century Spanish America: New Granada, 1825–1850', *Journal of Social History,* vol. 5, no. 3 (1972).

Safford, Frank (1974) 'The Bases for Political Alignment in Early Republican Spanish America', in Richard Graham and Peter Smith (eds.), *New Approaches to Latin American History* (Austin: University of Texas Press), pp. 71–111

Safford, Frank (1992) 'The Problem of Political Order in Early Republican Spanish America', *Journal of Latin American Studies,* vol. 24, special supplement.

Salgado, F. (1928) *Compendio de historia de Honduras* (Comayaguela: Imprenta 'El Sol').

Salgado, María A. (1976) '"Civilización y barbarie" o "imaginación y barbarie"?', in Francisco E. Porrata (ed.), *Explicación de cien años de soledad* (San José: Porrata y Avedaño).

Samper, José María (1978) 'Los Partidos en Colombia' (1873), in Jorge Orlando Melo (ed.), *Origenes de los Partidos Políticos en Colombia (textos de Manuel María Madiedo, José María Samper y Tomás Cipriano de Mosquera)* (Bogotá: Instituto Colombiano de Cultura).

Samponaro, Frank (1981) 'La alianza de Santa Anna y los federalistas, 1832–1834. Su formación y desintegración', *Historia Mexicana*, vol. 30, no. 3, pp. 359–80.

Sánchez de Tagle, Francisco(1835) *Refutación de las especies vertidas en los números 21, 22 y 23 del periódico titulado 'El Anteojo' contra el proyecto de la primera ley constitucional que presentó al Congreso la Comisión de Reorganización* (Mexico City: Imprenta del Aguila).

Santoni, Pedro (1996) *Mexicans at Arms. Puro Federalists and the Politics of War, 1845–1848* (Fort Worth: Texan Christian University Press).

Sarmiento, José (1990) *Historia de Olancho* (Tegucigalpa: Editorial Universitaria).

Slatta, Richard (1983) *Gauchos and the Vanishing Frontier* (Lincoln, NE: University of Nebraska Press).

Sordo Cedeño, Reynaldo (1993) *El congreso en la primera república centralista* (Mexico City: El Colegio de México/ITAM).

Sowell, David (1992) *The Early Colombian Labor Movement: Artisans and Politics in Bogotá, 1832–1919* (Philadelphia: Temple University Press).

Spalding, Walter (1963) *A Epopéia Farroupilha (pequena história da grande revolução, acompanhada de farta documentação da época, 1835–1845)* (São Paulo: Biblioteca do Exército).

Staples, Anne (1976) *La iglesia en la primera república federal mexicana (1824–1835)* (Mexico City: SepSetentas).

Staples, Anne (1994) 'Clerics as Politicians: Church, State, and Political Power in Independent Mexico' in Jaime E. Rodríguez O. (ed.), *Mexico in the Age of Democratic Revolutions, 1750–1850* (Boulder: Lynne Rienner), pp. 223–41.

Staples, Anne (1996) 'Una falsa promesa: La educación indígena después de la independencia', in Pilar Gonzalbo Aizpuru and Gabriela Ossenbach (eds.), *Educación rural e indígena en Iberoamérica* (Mexico City: El Colegio de México/Universidad Nacional de Educación a Distancia), pp. 53–63.

Stern, Steve J. (ed.) (1987) *Resistance, Rebellion and Consciousness in the Andean Peasant World: Eighteenth to Twentieth Centuries*

(Madison: University of Wisconsin Press).

Stevens, Donald F. (1991) *Origins of Instability in Early Republican México* (Durham, NC: Duke University Press).

Stevens, Donald F. (1994) 'Autonomists, Nativists, Republicans, and Monarchists: Conspiracy and Political History in Nineteenth-Century Mexico', *Mexican Studies/Estudios Mexicanos*, vol. 10, no. 1 (1994), pp. 247–66.

Stokes, W. (1950) *Honduras: An Area Study in Government* (Madison: University of Wisconsin Press).

Suazo Rubí, S. (1991) *Auge y crisis ideológica del Partido Liberal* (Tegucigalpa: Alín Editora).

Svampa, Maristella (1998) 'La dialéctica entre lo nuevo y lo viejo: sobre los usos y nociones del caudillismo en la Argentina durante el siglo XIX', in Noemí Goldman and Ricardo Salvatore (eds.), *Caudillos rioplatenses. Nuevas miradas a un viejo problema* (Buenos Aires: Eudeba).

Szuchman, Mark (1988) *Order, Family and Community in Buenos Aires, 1810–1860* (Stanford, Stanford University Press).

Tabora, Rocío (1995) *Masculinidad y violencia en la cultura política hondureña* (Tegucigalpa, Centro de Documentación de Honduras).

Taylor, William B. (1988) 'Banditry and Insurrection: Rural Unrest in Central Jalisco, 1790–1815', in Katz (ed.), *Riot, Rebellion and Revolution: Rural Social Conflict in Mexico* (Princeton: Princeton University Press). pp. 205–46.

Tenenbaum, Barbara A. (1985) *México en la época de los agiotistas, 1821–1857* (Mexico City: Fondo de Cultura Económica).

Tenenbaum, Barbara A. (1995) 'Mexico: So Close to the United States: Unconventional Views of the Nineteenth Century', *Latin American Research Review*, vol. 30, no. 1 (1995), pp. 226–35.

Thompson, Waddy (1847) *Recollections of Mexico* (New York: Wiley & Putnam).

Thomson, Guy P.C. (1987) 'Movilización conservadora, insurrección liberal y rebeliones indígenas, 1854–76', in Antonio Annino et al., *America Latina: dalla stato coloniale allo stato nazione* (Turin: Universitá di Torino), vol. II, pp. 592–614.

Thomson, Guy P.C. (1990) 'Bulwarks of Patriotic Liberalism: the National Guard, Philharmonic Corps and Patriotic Juntas in Mexico, 1847–88', *Journal of Latin American Studies*, vol. 22, no. 1, pp. 31–68.

Thomson, Guy P.C. (1991) 'Popular Aspects of Liberalism in Mexico, 1848–1888', *Bulletin of Latin American Research*, vol. 10, pp. 265–92.

Throlby, Tiago (1987) *A cabanagem ne fala do povo* (São Paulo: Paulista).

Thurner, Mark (1997) *From Two Republics to One Divided: Contradictions of Postcolonial Nation-making in Andean Peru* (Durham:

University of North Carolina Press).

Tirado Mejía, Alvaro (1976) *Aspectos sociales de la guerras civiles en Colombia* (Bogotá: Instituto Colombiano de Cultura).

Tornel y Mendívil, José María (1835) *Memoria del secretario de estado y del despacho de guerra y marina, leída en la cámara de representantes en la sesión del día veinte y tres de marzo y en la de senadores en la del veinte y cuatro del mismo mes y año de 1835* (Mexico City: Imprenta de Ignacio Cumplido).

Tornel y Mendívil, José María (1844) *Memoria del secretariado de estado y del despacho de guerra y marina, leída a las cámaras del congreso nacional de la República Mexicana en enero de 1844* (Mexico City: Imprenta de Ignacio Cumplido).

Tornel y Mendívil, José María (1985) *Breve reseña histórica de los acontecimientos más notables de la nación mexicana* (Mexico City: INEHRM).

Torre Villar et al., Ernesto de la (eds.) (1987) *Planes de la nación mexicana,* 5 vols. (Mexico City: Senado de la República/El Colegio de México).

Torre, Ernesto de la (1992) *La independencia de México* (Madrid: Mapfre).

Torres-Rivas, Edelberto (1971) *Interpretación del desarrollo social centroamericano* (San José: Editorial Universitaria Centroamericana).

Tutino, John (1986) *From Insurrection to Revolution in Mexico: Social Bases of Agrarian Violence, 1750–1940* (Princeton: Princeton University Press).

Uribe de Hincapié, María Teresa and Alvarez, Jesús María (1987) *Poderes y regiones: problemas de la constitución de la nación colombiana, 1810–1850* (Medellín: Universidad de Antioquia).

Uribe-Uran, Victor (2000) *Honorable Lives: Lawyers, Family and Politics in Colombia, 1780-1850* (Pittsburgh: University of Pittsburgh Press)

Valle de Siles, María Eugenia del (1990) *Historia de la rebelión de Túpac Catari, 1781–1782* (La Paz: Editorial Don Bosco).

Vallejo Hernández, Rene (1990) *Crisis histórica del poder político en Honduras* (Tegucigalpa: Ultra-Graph).

Vallejo, A. (1882) *Compendio de la historia social y política de Honduras* (Tegucigalpa: Tipografía Nacional).

Vallenilla Lanz, Laureano (1912) 'Argentina y Venezuela. Afinidades sociales y políticas', *Hispanía* (London).

Vanderwood, Paul J. (1981) *Disorder and Progress: Bandits, Police and Mexican Development* (Lincoln: University of Nebraska Press).

Vargas, José Santos (1952) *Diario de un soldado de la independencia altoperuana en los valles de Sicasica y Hayopaya, 1816–1821,* edited by Gunnar Mendoza L. (Sucre: Universidad de San Francisco Xavier).

Vargas, José Santos (1982) *Diario de un comandante de la independen-*

cia americana, 1814–1825, edited by Gunnar Mendoza L. (Mexico, Siglo XXI).

Vargas Llosa, Mario (1981) *La guerra del fin del mundo* (Barcelona: Seix Barral).

Vázquez Mantecón, María del Carmen (1986) *Santa Anna y la encrucijada del estado. La dictadura (1853–1855)* (Mexico City: Fondo de Cultura Económica).

Vázquez Mantecón, María del Carmen (1990) 'Rebeliones y revueltas. 1820–1910', hojas I y II, in *Atlas Nacional de México* (Mexico City: UNAM/Instituto de Geografía).

Vázquez Mantecón, María del Carmen (1993) 'Espacio social y crisis política: La Sierra Gorda 1850–1855', *Mexican Studies/Estudios Mexicanos,* vol. 9, no. 1, pp. 47–70.

Vázquez Mantecón, María del Carmen (1997) *La palabra del poder. Vida pública de José María Tornel (1795–1853)* (Mexico City: UNAM).

Vázquez, Josefina Zoraida (1989) 'Iglesia, ejército y centralismo', *Historia Mexicana,* vol. 39, no. 1, pp. 205–34.

Vázquez, Josefina Zoraida (1989) 'Los años olvidados', *Mexican Studies/Estudios Mexicanos,* vol. 5, no. 2.

Vázquez, Josefina Zoraida (1992) 'Los pronunciamientos de 1832: aspirantismo político e ideología', in Jaime E. Rodríguez O. (ed.), *Patterns of Contention in Mexican History* (Wilmington: Scholarly Resources), pp. 163–86.

Vázquez, Josefina Zoraida (1994) 'De la difícil constitución de un estado: México, 1821–1854', in Josefina Zoraida Vázquez (ed.), *La fundación del estado mexicano, 1821–1855* (Mexico City: Nueva Imagen), pp. 9–37.

Vázquez, Josefina Zoraida (1996) 'Political Plans and Collaboration Between Civilians and the Military, 1821–1846', *Bulletin of Latin American Research,* vol. 15, no. 1 (1996), pp. 19–38.

Vázquez, Josefina Zoraida (1997) *La intervención norteamericana 1846–1848* (Mexico City: Secretaría de Relaciones Exteriores).

Veríssimo, José (1887) 'As populações indígenas e mestiças da Amazônia, sua linguagem, suas crenças, e seus costumes', *Revista do Instituto histórico-geográfico brasileiro,* vol. 50.

Viana Filho, Luiz (1938) *A Sabinada (A República Bahiana de 1837)* (Rio de Janeiro: Livraria José Olympio Editôra).

Vianna, Hélio (1945) *Contribução a história da imprensa brasileira (1812–1869)* (Rio de Janeiro: Imprensa Nacional).

Viotti da Costa, Emilia (1985) *The Brazilian Empire: Myths and Histories* (Chicago: Dorsey Press).

Walker, Charles (1990) 'Montoneros, bandoleros, malhechores: criminalidad y política en las primeras décadas republicanas', in Carlos Aguirre and Charles Walker (eds.), *Bandoleros, abigeos y montoneros: criminalidad y violencia en el Perú, siglos XVIII y XIX* (Lima: Instituto de Apoyo Agraria).

Webre, S. (1992) 'Central America', in David G. LaFrance and Errol D. Jones (eds.), *Latin American Military History: An Annotated Bibliography* (New York: Garland Publishing Co.), pp. 557–68.

Werneck Sodré, Nelson (1966) *Historia da Imprensa no Brasil* (Rio de Janeiro: Editôra Civilização Brasileira).

Williams, R.G. (1994) *States and Social Evolution: Coffee and the Rise of National Governments in Central America* (Chapel Hill: University of North Carolina Press).

Williamson, Edwin (1987) 'Magical Realism and the Theme of Incest in One Hundred Years of Solitude', in Bernard McGuirk and Richard Cardwell (eds.), *Gabriel García Márquez: New Readings* (Cambridge: Cambridge University Press).

Williamson, Edwin (1992) *The Penguin History of Latin America* (Harmondsworth: Penguin).

Wolf, Eric R., and Hansen, Edward C. (1967) 'Caudillo Politics: A Structural Analysis', *Comparative Studies in Society and History*, vol. 9, no. 2 (1967), pp. 168–79.

Woodward Jr., Ralph Lee (1991) 'The Aftermath of Independence, 1821–c.1870', in Leslie Bethell (ed.), *Central America since Independence* (Cambridge: Cambridge University Press), pp. 1–36.

Woodward Jr., Ralph Lee (1993) *Rafael Carrera and the Emergence of the Republic of Guatemala, 1821–1871* (Athens: University of Georgia).

Woodward Jr., Ralph Lee (1996) 'The Liberal-Conservative Debate in the Central American Federation, 1823–1840', in Vincent Peloso and Barbara Tenenbaum (eds.), *Liberals, Politics and Power: State Formation in Nineteenth-Century Latin America* (Athens: University of Georgia Press), pp. 59–89.

Zavala, Lorenzo de (1969) *Obras* (Mexico City: Porrúa).

Zeitlin, Maurice (1984) *The Civil Wars in Chile (or the bourgeois revolutions that never were)* (Princeton: Princeton University Press).

Zelaya, Oscar (1996) 'La Alcaldía de Tegucigalpa y su Desarrollo Poblacional', *Paraninfo*, no. 10 (Tegucigalpa), pp. 145–56.

Zimmermann, Eduardo (1998) 'El poder judicial, la construcción del estado y el federalismo, Argentina, 1860–1880', in Eduardo Posada-Carbó (ed.), *In Search of a New Order, Essays on the Politics and Society of Nineteenth-Century Latin America* (London: Institute of Latin American Studies).

Zimmermann, Eduardo (ed.) (1999) *Judicial Institutions in Nineteenth-Century Latin America* (London: Institute of Latin American Studies).

Zuluaga, Francisco (1985) *José María Obando: de soldado realista a caudillo republicano* (Bogotá: Biblioteca Banco Popular).

Index

Lightning Source UK Ltd.
Milton Keynes UK
UKOW01f0809110218
317683UK00001B/63/P